Magento Beginner's Guide
Second Edition

Learn how to create a fully featured, attractive online store with the most powerful open source solution for e-commerce.

Robbert Ravensbergen

Sander Schoneville

[PACKT] open source✳
PUBLISHING   community experience distilled

BIRMINGHAM - MUMBAI

Magento Beginner's Guide
Second Edition

Copyright © 2013 Packt Publishing

First published: March 2009

Second edition: June 2013

Production Reference: 1180613

Published by Packt Publishing Ltd.
Livery Place
35 Livery Street
Birmingham B3 2PB, UK.

ISBN 978-1-78216-270-4

www.packtpub.com

Cover Image by Asher Wishkerman (wishkerman@hotmail.com)

Credits

About the Authors

Robbert Ravensbergen is an open source and e-commerce expert from the Netherlands. He started to work with open source solutions in the early days of Joomla!. He started his own company, `joomblocks.com`, from which he has been serving clients with open source solutions since 2009.

His first book about WordPress, *Kickstart WordPress*, *Pearson Education*, was released in the Netherlands in 2010. After that, several open source related books on Joomla!, Magento, and again WordPress followed. The second edition of *Magento Beginner's Guide* is his first international book.

Sander Schoneville is a Technical Director at GroupDeal, a Dutch daily deals site based on Magento. His has his background set in media psychology and business informatics. He combines both fields to create effective websites.

He has worked with Magento since its early releases in 2008 and has written a Dutch book about Magento.

Together with co-writer Robbert Ravensbergen, he's running an e-commerce blog at `http://www.boostingecommerce.com`.

About the Reviewers

Eugene Ivashin was born in Russia and currently resides in Kiev, Ukraine.

He graduated from Dnepr State Academy of Building and Architecture in Dnepropetrovsk, Ukraine and got a diploma with distinction as a Building Industry Automation Engineer in 1997.

He has since worked at South Ukrainian Nuclear Power Plant as a repair engineer (six and half years) and got interested in web development at that time. By the end of 2003, Eugene left SU NPP, headed to Kiev and became a web programmer in a small private web design agency where he spent more than 2 years building websites for various customers and growing into a project manager in the process. At the same time, he continued freelancing for separate customers and participating in a few sole proprietorship companies in the area of web development and services. From April 2008, Eugene worked as a web developer and a technical support at ExpoPromoter, a company leading in the tradeshow industry, providing for a large catalog of tradeshow organizers across the world.

Finally, in January 2010, Eugene entered Varien Inc., which was later on rebranded as Magento Inc., as a software engineer, but lately became a Technical Trainer. When Magento was acquired by X.commerce, an eBay company, in August 2011, Eugene became a training manager responsible for providing technical knowledge for all X.commerce employees.

Eugene speaks Russian, Ukrainian, and English. He likes to read science fiction books, admire fine arts, and loves to draw pictures in particular by himself.

Karen Kilroy is a freelance e-commerce web developer focused on the Magento Community and Enterprise implementations and theming. Karen has worked as a frontend and backend developer on a variety of Magento projects since early 2009. She is an enthusiastic instructor and developer who enjoys experimenting with HTML5, CSS3, and responsive web designs. She is also an instructor and course author for Magento U. Additionally, Karen is the sole inventor of an e-commerce process called Shared Shopping (United States Patent Pending 13/350,321).

Prior to working with Magento, Karen worked with a wide variety of web and other technologies during her more than 25 years' information technology career. In her spare time, Karen volunteers as head coach of the Dragon Dream Team, an all-breast cancer survivor dragon boat racing crew.

www.PacktPub.com

Support files, eBooks, discount offers and more

You might want to visit www.PacktPub.com for support files and downloads related to your book.

Did you know that Packt offers eBook versions of every book published, with PDF and ePub files available? You can upgrade to the eBook version at www.PacktPub.com and as a print book customer, you are entitled to a discount on the eBook copy. Get in touch with us at service@packtpub.com for more details.

At www.PacktPub.com, you can also read a collection of free technical articles, sign up for a range of free newsletters and receive exclusive discounts and offers on Packt books and eBooks.

http://PacktLib.PacktPub.com

Do you need instant solutions to your IT questions? PacktLib is Packt's online digital book library. Here, you can access, read and search across Packt's entire library of books.

Why Subscribe?

- ◆ Fully searchable across every book published by Packt
- ◆ Copy and paste, print and bookmark content
- ◆ On demand and accessible via web browser

Free Access for Packt account holders

If you have an account with Packt at www.PacktPub.com, you can use this to access PacktLib today and view nine entirely free books. Simply use your login credentials for immediate access.

Table of Contents

Preface

It was a few years ago, I think it was somewhere in 2008, when I first heard about Magento as the new "Top open source e-commerce solution". Actually, at that moment it wasn't yet that good, but I could see the potential of the software already. Especially thinking about other open source solutions such as osCommerce at that time, or VirtueMart running on Joomla. No, those were the days when the e-commerce market was still dominated by large-scale companies and expensive solutions, but things have rapidly changed since then.

During 2009, the first edition of this book was published by Packt, written by William Rice. And at that moment it was actually one of the very first books in the market giving readers the opportunity to learn to work with Magento. Also in that area, times have changed and various new versions of Magento have been released since then. So it's time for a completely updated and rewritten version of that first, popular Magento book. And here it is.

Since 2009 we've been working on several Magento projects and learned to get to know Magento the hard way, sometimes just by trying and failing every now and then. Everyone already experienced with Magento will know what I'm talking about. But don't worry, this book will give you a complete overview of what Magento is, how to install it, and how to use it. When you create an online store with Magento, you usually follow a defined series of steps. This book is arranged to support that process. Each chapter shows you how to get the most out of every step.

By the time you finish reading this book you'll have a basic, but complete online store built on Magento that is ready to start selling.

Robbert Ravensbergen
Sander Schoneville

Introducing Magento

Magento is an "open source" software, which basically means that you are allowed to view, edit, and contribute to the source code. A lot of people also think that "open source" means "free". Although it is certainly true that most open source solutions are available for free, it isn't a mandatory part of the open source principle. Looking at Magento we immediately recognize that, because Magento is available freely as well as in a paid for version. We'll cover more on the differences between those versions later on.

As we already mentioned in this Preface, Magento isn't the only open source e-commerce solution in the market. There are other ones as well. We'll name a few alternatives, without being complete:

+ OpenCart
+ PrestaShop
+ osCommerce (more or less obsolete)
+ Joomla with VirtueMart
+ WordPress with e-commerce plugins like WooCommerce
+ Zen Cart

The first two candidates in this list are the more serious options, whereas the other ones are generally used for smaller shops. But don't get me wrong, as I've already seen excellent shops based on something relatively simple, such as WordPress with WooCommerce as well.

Looking at the commercial/paid market, there are really lots of players and it's hard to make a choice if you're new to the business. Also in here, we'd like to name a few solutions, so that you could get an idea of what's available in the market:

+ Shopify
+ X-Cart
+ Interspire
+ Volusion

Moreover, we see solution providers offering an online solution that you can use straight out of the box, without having to do any installation. Magento is doing this as well and we'll tell you more on this possibility in our Magento version overview.

The history of Magento

It was way back in 2001 when Roy Rubin and Yoav Kutner founded a company named Varien. They did many e-commerce implementations during those years, especially using osCommerce. But they were never satisfied with the solution. The lack of stability and flexibility made them think that it could be done better. So they decided to start a new e-commerce project in 2007 and named it Magento. The very first beta version was released in August of that year and it took them until March 2008 to release Magento Version 1.0. From that moment on, things moved fast. The solution became incredibly popular within a couple of years and new versions were released once or twice per year. Starting from that first version in 2008, we've currently reached Version 1.7 at the beginning of 2013.

Meanwhile, a lot has changed in the Varien company. It is now called Magento Inc. and has been acquired completely by eBay during 2011. The Magento community is a bit worried about the plans that eBay has with Magento, especially now that one of the original founders, Yoav Kutner, has left the company. Even keeping possible scenarios in mind, Magento has currently grown to be by far the most popular e-commerce solutions available:

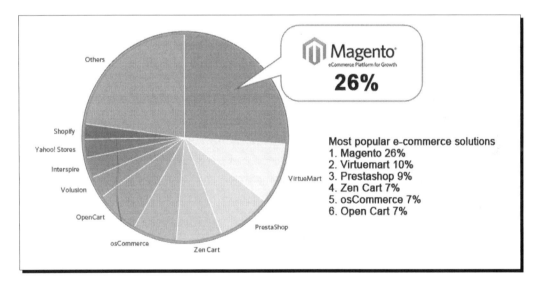

Especially knowing that older solutions such as osCommerce and VirtueMart are losing market shares and Magento is still growing makes this picture even more clear about the major role Magento is playing in the e-commerce market at this moment.

Magento versions

Magento being the number one choice at this moment is great, but what does that mean for the company delivering the solution? How are they making money to continue to support the platform? This is where the various Magento versions come in. During the first few years of Magento, only the free 'Community Edition' was available. Actually, this free Community Edition is the one we'll be covering in this book since most users will start using that version. Magento currently offers two other possibilities:

Enterprise Edition

The Enterprise Edition is Magento's flagship solution, made for large-scale online stores. The Enterprise Edition has functionality on board that the Community Edition is missing and we currently often see that new features are first released in this Enterprise Edition. For companies using this version, the important fact is that Magento offers support on it. The Enterprise Edition has its own version numbers that do not have anything to do with the version number of the Community Edition. Magento Enterprise Edition is currently at Version 1.12 and is currently priced at over $14,000 annually. If you'd like to read more on the Enterprise Edition and its features please browse to:

```
http://www.magentocommerce.com/product/enterprise-edition.
```

Formerly, Magento also offered a "Professional Edition", which was priced in between the Community and Enterprise Editions. It was discontinued, forcing its customers to the more expensive Enterprise Edition.

Magento Go

Seeing more and more competitors like, for instance, Shopify and Volusion offering online e-commerce solutions, Magento has decided to offer such a service as well. Magento Go is an online Magento platform, that you can simply rent by paying a monthly fee. The good thing is that you do not have to worry about hosting, installation, and maintenance. Magento will do it for you. The downside however, is that Magento Go isn't yet suitable for every market and you cannot expand its functionality like you can in running your own installation. If you are interested, please pay special attention to anything that is required for your local market, payment service providers being the most important one. Pricing of Magento Go currently starts at $15 per month for a single store in one language.

More information on Magento Go can be found at:

```
http://go.magento.com.
```

Why choose Magento?

We've already mentioned that Magento is currently the most popular e-commerce solution, but why would you choose Magento? There are plenty of alternatives, so what makes Magento so popular? Since you're reading this book you have probably already made your choice. Still it is good to look at a few pros and cons of Magento, to make sure that you made the right decision for your business.

Magento pros

- ◆ **Multi site**: One of the strongest pros of Magento is that it's relatively easy to set up multiple stores in multiple languages offering different (or the same) products. You are in control.

- ◆ **Product catalog management**: Magento offers extended possibilities to set up and manage your online product catalog. From simple products to complete sets including options and customer variables anything seems to be possible. Magento also supports selling digital (downloadable) products.

◆ **Theming**: If you want to change the look and feel of your store, you have to change your Magento theme or install a completely different one. The number of themes available is huge nowadays, and of course it is also possible to use a custom design for your store. Generally speaking a good Magento theme isn't free. The Marketplace Themeforest (http://themeforest.net) is one of the possibilities to search for and buy a standard Magento theme:

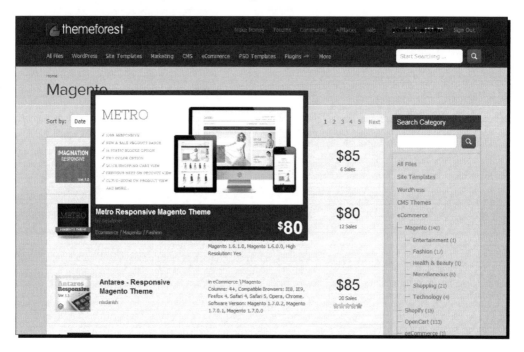

◆ **Extensions**: Magento is already pretty complete out of the box. But there's always room for improvement or maybe you need to change the functionality because of local requirements. The Magento Community offers a lot of extensions that you can install and use to change the behavior of your store. There are free as well as paid for solutions available and there are (commercial) companies that completely focus on delivering one or multiple Magento extensions.

◆ **Scalability**: The Magento solution is not only versatile, it is very scalable as well. You do not need a very large budget to start and once your company is growing, Magento still offers you lots of possibilities. Magento can therefore be a very good choice for small companies with high ambition levels.

◆ **Support**: Although we already mentioned that official Magento support is available for the Enterprise edition, you do not have to worry. There are lots of companies throughout the whole world available to support you and help you achieve your goals. These companies will not work for free, but it's good to know that there's a fallback if you have to go further than this book and information available online have to offer.

Magento cons

A book about Magento describing the downside of the software? Yes, we feel that it is important to tell you the whole story. We are indeed Magento fans, but there are downsides to every solution. And Magento has them as well. Let's take a quick look at them:

◆ **Magento is consumer oriented**: Do you need to run a "Business to business" store? Magento wasn't designed for that originally. Of course it is possible to use Magento that way, but sometimes it doesn't fit so nicely. Recently we've noticed that Magento is adding functionality to better support this customer group.

◆ **Magento is slow**: Haven't you heard this one before? The code of Magento is very well structured but therefore requires more resources than an average website. More on this topic in the next chapter, but remember that if you want to run Magento, you do not go for the cheapest hosting solution.

◆ **Magento is difficult**: Well, it certainly isn't the easiest solution, because of the large number of features and possibilities. But also if you need to do coding yourself, you need a lot of knowledge about the product. This isn't a programmer's book though, and we feel that learning Magento itself isn't too complicated. This book will help you getting the job done.

What this book covers

Chapter 1, *Installation*, explains all you need to know to about setting up your own local installation of Magento, or installing Magento at a hosting provider using Installatron.

Chapter 2, *General Configuration*, talks about Magento as a very versatile but complex product. Before adding your products, you first need to take a closer look at setting up your online store. In this chapter, you'll also learn to set up tax calculations.

Chapter 3, *Categories and Attributes*, explains that one of Magento's strengths is the way it can handle almost every product type. In this chapter you'll learn to work with Product Categories, Product Attributes, and Attribute Sets.

Chapter 4, *Simple Products*, talks about adding your first product in your store. During this chapter, you'll learn how to properly set up your products and which fields are important to pay attention to.

Chapter 5, *Beyond Adding Simple Products*, explains that now that you have added your first product, it's time to explore the other possibilities Magento offers to set up your product catalog. You'll learn to work with downloadable and configurable products.

Chapter 6, *Customer Relationships*, talks about looking at the other areas, starting with the possibilities Magento offers for setting up and maintaining your customer databases.

Chapter 7, Accepting Payments, explains that before being able to start selling, you'll need to set up payment systems, so that you'll be able to receive a payment from your customer. In this chapter we'll show you how to use Magento's common payment methods and how to add your own using a Payment Service Provider.

Chapter 8, Configuring Shipping, will teach you to work with the built-in Shipping Methods of Magento. We also included instructions to work with different kinds of shipping rates.

Chapter 9, Customizing Your Store's Appearance, explains what is often one of the first things you would like to do: changing the look and feel of your online store. However, now that you learned to work with Magento, it's the right time to work in this area and change the way your online store will look.

Chapter 10, Fulfilling Orders. Everything is set up now to start receiving your first orders. But once you do, how do you take control of the order process? In this chapter you will learn you how to work with orders, shipping, invoices, and credit notes.

Chapter 11, Maintaining and Administrating Your Store, explains that once your store has been set up you're not finished yet. Maintaining your online store is an ongoing process and you have just started it. In this chapter you'll learn which areas you should pay attention to. Besides that we added a checklist that you may use before bringing your store live.

What you need for this book

You do not need any specific software to be able to use the instructions in this book. Just use a modern Windows computer or Mac. You'll need the following tools as well, but it's completely up to you to choose the tool you like:

- An FTP client, for instance, Filezilla.

- Photo editing software for your images. Photoshop is often used, but expensive. Actually any editing tool that you know how to use should be able to deliver good results.

- A text editor, such as Notepad++ (Windows) or Coda 2 (Mac).

Who this book is for

If you are a nontechnical person and are discouraged by the complexity of this powerful e-commerce application, this book is ideal for you. This book would also suit someone with e-commerce knowledge, but requires a guide to getting started with Magento.

Conventions

In this book, you will find several headings appearing frequently.

To give clear instructions of how to complete a procedure or task, we use:

Time for action – heading

1. Action 1
2. Action 2
3. Action 3

Instructions often need some extra explanation so that they make sense, so they are followed with:

What just happened?

This heading explains the working of tasks or instructions that you have just completed.

You will also find some other learning aids in the book, including:

Pop quiz – heading

These are short multiple-choice questions intended to help you test your own understanding.

Have a go hero – heading

These practical challenges give you ideas for experimenting with what you have learned.

You will also find a number of styles of text that distinguish between different kinds of information. Here are some examples of these styles, and an explanation of their meaning.

New terms and **important words** are shown in bold. Words that you see on the screen, in menus or dialog boxes for example, appear in the text like this: "On the **Select Destination Location** screen, click on **Next** to accept the default destination."

 Warnings or important notes appear in a box like this.

 Tips and tricks appear like this.

Reader feedback

Feedback from our readers is always welcome. Let us know what you think about this book—what you liked or may have disliked. Reader feedback is important for us to develop titles that you really get the most out of.

To send us general feedback, simply send an e-mail to feedback@packtpub.com, and mention the book title through the subject of your message.

If there is a topic that you have expertise in and you are interested in either writing or contributing to a book, see our author guide on www.packtpub.com/authors.

Customer support

Now that you are the proud owner of a Packt book, we have a number of things to help you to get the most from your purchase.

Downloading the example code

You can download the example code files for all Packt books you have purchased from your account at http://www.packtpub.com. If you purchased this book elsewhere, you can visit http://www.packtpub.com/support and register to have the files e-mailed directly to you.

Errata

Although we have taken every care to ensure the accuracy of our content, mistakes do happen. If you find a mistake in one of our books—maybe a mistake in the text or the code—we would be grateful if you would report this to us. By doing so, you can save other readers from frustration and help us improve subsequent versions of this book. If you find any errata, please report them by visiting http://www.packtpub.com/submit-errata, selecting your book, clicking on the **errata submission form** link, and entering the details of your errata. Once your errata are verified, your submission will be accepted and the errata will be uploaded to our website, or added to any list of existing errata, under the Errata section of that title.

Piracy

Piracy of copyright material on the Internet is an ongoing problem across all media. At Packt, we take the protection of our copyright and licenses very seriously. If you come across any illegal copies of our works, in any form, on the Internet, please provide us with the location address or website name immediately so that we can pursue a remedy.

Please contact us at `copyright@packtpub.com` with a link to the suspected pirated material.

We appreciate your help in protecting our authors, and our ability to bring you valuable content.

Questions

You can contact us at `questions@packtpub.com` if you are having a problem with any aspect of the book, and we will do our best to address it.

1
Installation

OK, so we briefly introduced Magento to you, but actually if all you want to do is to get started? Well, then this chapter is for you. We'll not only discuss how you can set up a local test environment on your machine, but we'll also help you in selecting a good hosting provider for your live store. We'll give an example of installation at a hosting provider, so that you can take all these steps yourself.

This chapter is written especially for you, if you:

◆ Want to set up your own Magento test environment

◆ Want to install Magento using a commonly available hosting service

◆ Are familiar with putting files up on a web server, but that is the limit of your technical knowledge

◆ Are eager to get your store up and running as fast as possible

◆ Already tried installing Magento yourself, but got stuck somewhere

Even if you are an experienced user, this chapter is still worth reading. It can save your time by helping you to avoid problems while installing Magento. Although the installation process in itself isn't a difficult one , there are things that can (and will) go wrong. We know how frustrating it is when you get stuck during the very first steps of using a new piece of software. Therefore, we created an extensive chapter and tried to be as complete as possible.

Installing Magento locally

Whether you're working on a Windows computer, Mac, or Linux machine, you will notice very soon that it comes in handy to have a local Magento test environment available. Magento is a complex system and besides doing regular tasks, such as adding products and other content, you should never apply changes to your store directly in the live environment. When you're working on your own a local test system is easy to set up and it gives you the possibility to test changes without any risk. When you're working in a team it makes sense to have a test environment running on your own server or hosting provider. In here, we'll start by explaining how to set up your local test system.

Requirements

Before we jump into action, it's good to have a closer look at Magento's requirements. What do you need to run it?

Simply put, all up-to-date requirements for Magento can be found here:

`http://www.magentocommerce.com/system-requirements.`

But maybe that's a bit overwhelming if you are just a beginner. So let's break this up into the most essential stuff:

Requirement	Notes
Operating system: Linux	Magento runs best on Linux, as offered by most hosting companies. Don't worry about your local test environment as that will run on Windows or Mac as well. But for your live store you should go in for a Linux solution because if you decide to run it on anything else other than Linux for a live store, it will not be supported.
Web server: Apache	Magento runs on Versions 1.3.x, 2.0.x, and 2.2.x of this very popular web server. As of Version 1.7 of Magento community and Version 1.12 of Magento Enterprise there's a new web server called Nginx that is compatible as well.
Programming language: PHP	Magento has been developed using PHP, a programming language which is very popular. Many major open source solutions such as WordPress and Joomla! for instance, have been built using PHP.
	Use Versions 5.2.13 - 5.3.15. Do not use PHP4 anymore, nor use PHP 5.4 yet!

Requirement	Notes
PHP extensions	Magento requires a number of extensions, which should be available on top of PHP itself. You will need: PDO_MySQL, mcrypt, hash, simplexml, GD, DOM, Iconv, and Curl. Besides that you also need to have the possibility to switch off "safe mode".
	You do not have a clue about all of this? Don't worry. A host offering Magento services already takes care of this. And for your local environment there are only a few additional steps to take. We'll get there in a minute.
Database: MySQL	MySQL is the database, where Magento will store all data for your store. Use Version 4.1.20 or (and preferably) newer.

As you can see, even in a simplified format, there are quite some things that need to be taken care of. Magento hosting is not as simple as hosting for a small WordPress or Joomla! website, currently the most popular open source solutions to create a regular site. The requirements are higher and you just cannot expect to host your store for only a couple of dollars per month. If you do, your online store may still work, but it is likely that you'll run into some performance issues. Be careful with the cheapest hosting solutions. Although Magento may work, you'll be consuming too that need server resources soon. Go for a dedicated server or a managed **VPS (Virtual Private Server)**, but definitely for a host that is advertising support of Magento.

Time for action – installing Magento on a Windows machine

We'll speak more deeply about Magento hosting later on. Let's first download and install the package on a local Windows machine. Are you a Mac user? Don't worry, we'll give instructions for Mac users as well later on. Note that the following instructions are written for Windows users, but will contain valuable information for Mac users as well. Perform the following steps to install Magento on your Windows computer:

1. Download the Magento installation package. Head over to http://www. magentocommerce.com/download and download the package you need. For a Windows user almost always the full ZIP package is the most convenient one. In our situation Version 1.7.0.2 is the latest one, but please be aware that this will certainly change over time when newer versions are released. You will need to create a (free) account to download the software. This account will also be helpful later on. It will give you access to the Magento support forums, so make sure to store your login details somewhere.

The download screen should look something like this:

2. If you're a beginner then it is handy to have some sample data in your store. Magento offers a download package containing sample data on the same page, so download that as well. Note that for a production environment you would never install the sample data, but for a test system like the local installation we're doing here, it might be a good idea to use it. The sample data will create a few items and customers in your store, which will make the learning process easier.

> Did you notice the links to Magento Go at every download link? Magento Go is Magento's online platform, which you can use out of the box, without doing any installation at all. However, in the remaining part of this chapter, we assume that you are going to set up your own environment and want to have full control over your store.

3. Next, you need a web server, so that you can run your website locally, on your own machine. On Windows machines, XAMPP is an easy to use all-in-one solution. Download the installer version via: `http://www.apachefriends.org/en/xampp-windows.html`. XAMPP is also available for Mac and Linux. The download screen is as follows:

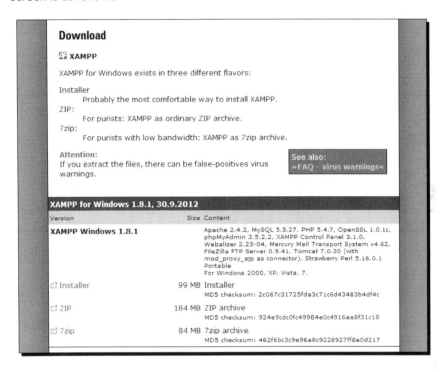

4. Once downloaded, run the executable code to start the installation process. You might receive some security warnings that you have to accept, especially when you're using Windows Vista, 7 or 8, like in the following example:

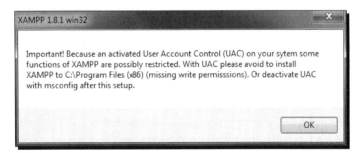

Because of this it's best to install XAMPP directly in the root of your hard drive, c:\xampp in most cases. Once you click on **OK**, you will see the following screen, which shows the progress of installation:

Once the installation has finished, the software asks if you'd like to start the **Control Panel**. If you do so, you'll see a number of services that have not been started yet. The minimum that you should start by clicking the **Start** button are **Apache**, the web server and **MySQL**, the database server.

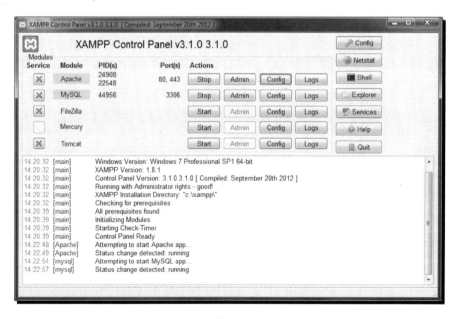

5. Now you're running your own web server on your local computer. Be aware that generally this web server will not be accessible for the outside world. It's running on your local machine, just for testing purposes. Before doing the next step, please verify if your web server is actually running. You can do so by using your browser and going to `http://localhost` or `http://127.0.0.1` If all went well you should see something similar to the following:

No result? If you're on a Windows computer, please first reboot your machine. Next, check using the XAMPP control panel if the Apache service is running. If it isn't, try to start it and pay attention to the error messages that appear. Need more help? Start with the help available on XAMPP's website at: `http://www.apachefriends.org/en/faq-xampp-windows.html`.

Can't start the Apache service? Check if there are any other applications using ports 80 and 443. The XAMPP control panel will give you more information. One of the applications that you should for instance stop before starting XAMPP is Skype. It's also possible to change this setting in Skype by navigating to **Tools | Options | Advanced | Connections**. Change the port number to something else, for instance port 8080. Then close and restart Skype. This prevents the two from interfering with each other in the future.

So, the next thing that needs to be done is installing Magento on top of it. But before we do so, we first have to change a few settings.

6. Change the following Windows file: `C:\Windows\System32\drivers\etc\hosts`.

Make sure to open your editor using administrator rights, otherwise you will not be able to save your changes. Add the following line to the host file:

`127.0.0.1 www.localhost.com.`

This is needed because Magento will not work correctly on a localhost without this setting. You may use a different name, but the general rule is that at least one dot must be used in the local domain name. The following screenshot gives an example of a possible host file. Please note that every host file will look a bit different. Also, your security software or Windows security settings may prevent you from making changes to this file, so please make sure you have the appropriate rights to change and save its contents:

```
 hosts
1   # Copyright (c) 1993-2009 Microsoft Corp.
2   #
3   # This is a sample HOSTS file used by Microsoft TCP/IP for Windows.
4   #
5   # This file contains the mappings of IP addresses to host names. Each
6   # entry should be kept on an individual line. The IP address should
7   # be placed in the first column followed by the corresponding host name.
8   # The IP address and the host name should be separated by at least one
9   # space.
10  #
11  # Additionally, comments (such as these) may be inserted on individual
12  # lines or following the machine name denoted by a '#' symbol.
13  #
14  # For example:
15  #
16  #      102.54.94.97     rhino.acme.com          # source server
17  #       38.25.63.10     x.acme.com              # x client host
18
19  # localhost name resolution is handled within DNS itself.
20  #    127.0.0.1       localhost
21  #    ::1             localhost
22
23  127.0.0.1 www.localhost.com magento.localhost.com
24
```

Do you need a text editor? There are really lots of possibilities when it comes to editing text for the web, as long as you use a "plain text" editor. Something like Microsoft Word isn't suitable because it will add a lot of unwanted code to your files! For very simple things like the one above, even Notepad would work. But soon you'll notice that it is much more convenient to use an editor that will help you in structuring and formatting your files. Personally, I can recommend the free Notepad++ for Windows users, which is even available in lots of different languages: `http://notepad-plus-plus.org`. Mac users can have a look at Coda: `http://panic.com/coda/` or TextWrangler `http://www.barebones.com/products/textwrangler/`.

7. Unzip the downloaded Magento package and put all files in a subfolder of your XAMPP installation. This could for instance be `c:\xampp\htdocs\magento`.

8. Now, go to `www.localhost.com/magento` to check if the installation screen of Magento is visible, as shown in the following screenshot. But do not yet start the installation process!

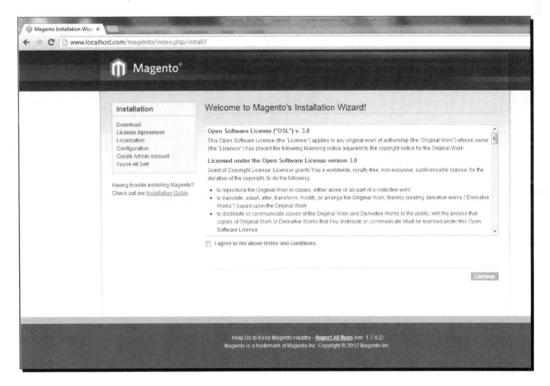

Before you start the installation, first create a MySQL database. To do this, use a second browser tab and navigate to **localhost | phpMyAdmin**. By default the user is root, and so without a password you should be able to continue without logging in. Click on **Databases** and create a database with a name of your choice. Write it down, as you will need it during the Magento installation. After creating the database you may close the browser tab.

9. It's finally time to start the installation process now. Go back to the installation screen of Magento, accept the license agreement and click on **Continue**.

10. Next, set your country, **Time Zone** and **Default Currency**. If you're working with multiple currencies that will be addressed later on:

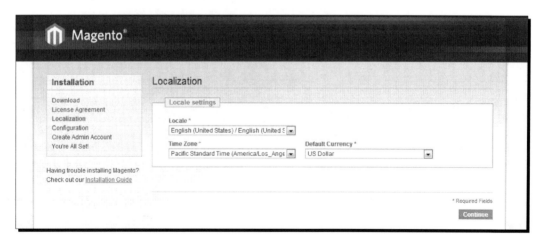

11. The next screen is actually the most important one of the installation process and this is where most beginners go wrong because they do not know what values to use. Using XAMPP this is an easy task, however, fill in your **Database Name**, **User Name (root)** and do not forget to check the **Skip Base URL Validation Before the Next Step** box, otherwise your installation might fail:

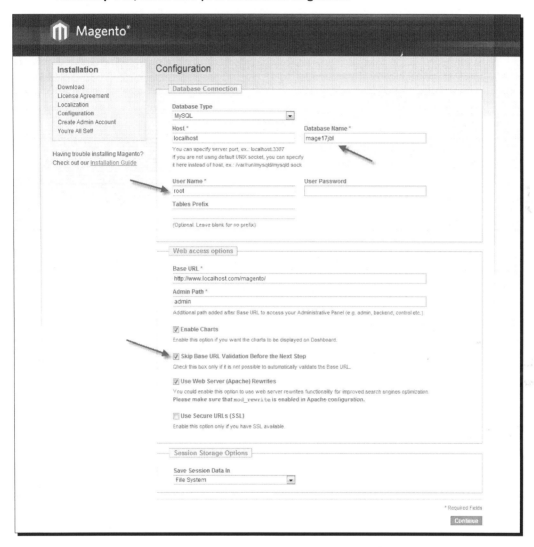

In this same form there are some fields that you can use to immediately improve the security level of your Magento setup. On a local test environment that isn't necessary, so we'll pay attention to those settings later on when we'll discuss installing Magento at a hosting provider. Please note that the **Use Secure URLs** option should remain unchecked for a local installation like we're doing here.

12. In the last step, yes, really! Just fill out your personal data and chose a username and password. Also in here, since you're working locally you do not have to create a complicated, unique password now. But you know what we mean, right? Doing a live installation at a hosting provider requires a good, strong password! You do not have to fill the **Encryption Key** field, Magento will do that for you:

In the final screen please just make a note of the **Encryption Key** value that was generated. You might need it in the future whenever upgrading your Magento store to a newer software version:

What just happened?

Congratulations! You just installed Magento for the very first time! Summarizing it, you just:

◆ Downloaded and installed XAMPP

◆ Changed your Windows host file

◆ Created a MySQL database using PhpMyAdmin

◆ Installed Magento

I'm on Mac; what should I do?

Basically, the steps using XAMPP are a bit different if you're using Mac. We shall be using Mac OS X 10.8 as an example of Mac OS version. According to our experience, as an alternative to XAMPP, MAMP is a bit easier if you are working with Mac. You can find the MAMP software here:

`http://www.mamp.info/en/downloads/index.html.`

And the documentation for MAMP is available here:

`http://documentation.mamp.info/en/mamp/installation.`

The good thing about MAMP is that it is easy to install, with very few configuration changes. It will not conflict with any already running Apache installation on your Mac, in case you have any. And it's easy to delete as well; just removing the `Mamp` folder from your `Applications` folder is already sufficient to delete MAMP and all local websites running on it.

Once you've downloaded the package, it will be in the `Downloads` folder of your Mac. If you are running Mac OS X 10.8, you first need to set the correct security settings to install MAMP. You can find out which version of Mac OS X you have using the menu option in the top-left corner of your screen:

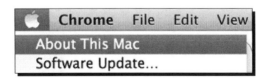

You can find the security settings menu by again going to the Apple menu and then selecting **System Preferences**:

In **System Preferences**, select the **Security & Privacy** icon that can be found in the first row as seen in the following screenshot:

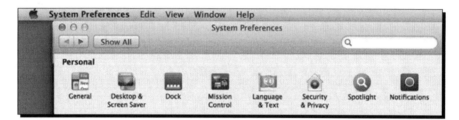

In here, press the padlock and enter your admin password. Next, select the **Anywhere** radio button in the **Allow applications downloaded from:** section. This is necessary because it will not be possible to run the MAMP installation you downloaded without it:

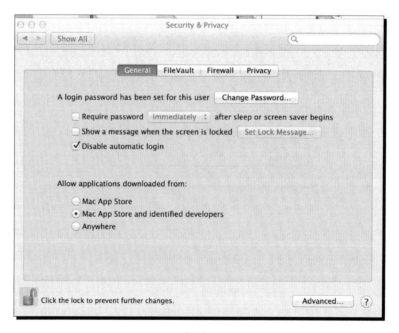

Open the image you've downloaded and simply move the `Mamp` folder to your `Applications` folder. That's all. Now that you've MAMP installed on your system, you may launch `MAMP.app` (located at **Applications | Mamp | Mamp.app**).

While you're editing your MAMP settings, MAMP might prompt you for an administrator password. This is required because it needs to run two processes: `httpd` (Apache) and `mysqld` (MySQL). Depending on the settings you set for those processes, you may or may not need to enter your password.

Once you open MAMP, click on the **Preferences** button. Next, click on **Ports**. The default MAMP ports are 8888 for Apache, and 8889 for MySQL. If you use this configuration, you will not be asked for your password, but you will need to include the port number in the URL when using it (`http://localhost:8888`). You may change this by setting the Apache port to 80, for which you'll probably have to enter your administrator password. If you have placed your Magento installation in the `Shop` folder, it is advised to call your Magento installation through the following URL: `http://127.0.0.1:8888/shop/`, instead of `http://localhost:8888/shop/`. The reason for this is that Magento may require dots in the URL.

The last thing you need to do is visit the Apache tab, where you'll need to set a document root. This is where all of your files are going to be stored for your local web server. An example of a document root is **Users | Username | Sites**.

To start the Apache and MySQL servers, simply click on **Start Servers** from the main MAMP screen. After the MAMP servers start, the MAMP start page should open in your web browser. If it doesn't, click on **Open start page** in the MAMP window. From there please select **phpMyAdmin**. In **PhpMyAdmin**, you can create a database and start the Magento installation procedure, just like we did when installing Magento on a Windows machine. See the *Time for action – installing Magento on a Windows machine* section, point 8 to continue the installation of Magento. Of course you need to put the Magento files in your `Mamp` folder now, instead of the Windows path mentioned in that procedure.

In some cases, it is necessary to change the **Read & Write** permissions of your `Magento` folder before you can use Magento on Mac. To do that, right-click on the `Magento` folder, and select the **Get Info** option. In the bottom of the resulting screen, you will see the folder permissions. Set all of these to **Read & Write**, if you have trouble in running Magento.

Installing Magento at a hosting service

There are thousands of hosting providers with as many different hosting setups. The difficulty of explaining the installation of Magento at a commonly used hosting service is that the procedure differs from hosting provider to hosting provider, depending on the tools they use for their services. There are providers, for instance, who use Plesk, DirectAdmin, or cPanel. Although these user environments differ from each other, the basic steps always remain the same:

◆ Check the requirements of Magento (there's more information on this topic at the beginning of this chapter).

◆ Upload the Magento installation files using an `ftp` tool, for instance, Filezilla (download this free at: `http://filezilla-project.org`).

◆ Create a database. This step differs slightly per hosting provider, but often a tool, such as PhpMyAdmin is used. Ask your hosting provider if you're in doubt about this step. You will need: the database name, database user, password, and the name of the database server.

◆ Browse to your domain and run the Magento installation process, which is the same as we saw earlier in this chapter.

How to choose a Magento hosting provider

One important thing we didn't discuss yet during this chapter is selecting a hosting provider that is capable of running your online store. We already mentioned that you should not expect performance for a couple of dollars per month. Magento will often still run at a cheap hosting service, but the performance is regularly very poor. So, you should pay attention to your choices here and make sure you make the right decision. Of course everything depends on the expectations for your online store. You should not aim for a top performance, if all you expect to do during your first few years is 10,000 dollars of revenue per year. OK, that's difficult sometimes. It's not always possible to create a detailed estimation of the revenue you may expect. So, let's see what you should pay attention to:

◆ Does the hosting provider mention Magento on its website? Or maybe they are even offering special Magento hosting packages? If yes, you are sure that technically Magento will run. There are even hosting providers for which Magento hosting is their speciality.

◆ Are you serious about your future Magento store? Then ask for references! Clients already running on Magento at this hosting provider can tell you more about the performance and customer support levels. Sometimes a hosting provider also offers an optimized demo store, which you can check out to see how it is performing.

- ◆ Ask if the hosting provider has Magento experts working for them and if yes, how many. Especially in case of large, high-traffic stores, it is important to hire the knowledge you need.

- ◆ Do not forget to check online forums and just do some research about this provider. However, we must also admit that you will find negative experiences of customers about almost every hosting provider.

Are you just searching for a hosting provider to play around with Magento? In that case any cheap hosting provider would do, although your Magento store could be very slow. Take for instance, Hostgator (`http://hostgator.com`), which offers small hosting plans for a couple of U.S. dollars per month. Anyway, a lot of hosts are offering a free trial period, which you may use to test the performance.

Installatron

Can't this all be done a bit more easily? Yes, that's possible. If your host offers a service named Installatron and if it also includes Magento within it, your installation process will become a lot easier. We could almost call it a "one-click" installation procedure. Check if your hosting provider is offering the latest Magento version; this may not always be the case!

Of course you may ask your (future) hosting provider if they are offering Installatron on their hosting packages. The example shown is from Simple Helix provider (`http://simplehelix.com`), a well-known provider specialized in Magento hosting solutions.

Time for action – installing Magento using Installatron

The following short procedure shows the steps you need to take to install Magento using Installatron:

1. First, locate the **Installatron Applications Installer** icon in the administration panel of your hosting provider. Normally this is very easy to find, just after logging in:

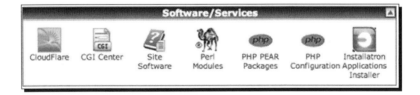

2. Next, within **Installatron Applications Installer**, click on the **Applications Browser** option:

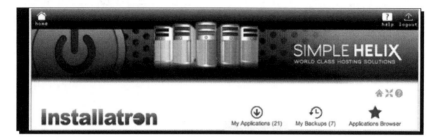

3. Inside **Applications Browser**, you'll see a list of CMS solutions and webshop software that you can install. Generally Magento can be located in the **e-Commerce and Business** group:

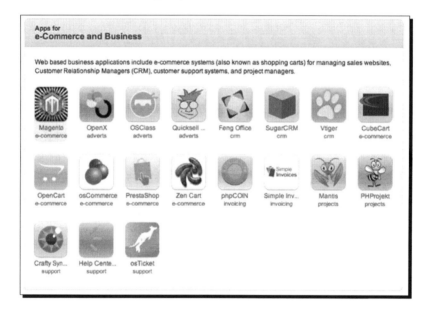

4. Of course, click on **Magento** and after that click on the **Install this application** button. The next screen is the setup wizard for installing Magento. It lists a bunch of default settings, such as admin username, database settings, and the like. We recommend to change as little as possible for your first installation. You should pick the right location to install though! In our example, we will choose the `test` directory on `www.boostingecommerce.com`:

Note that for this installation, we've chosen to install the Magento sample data, which will help us in getting an explanation of the Magento software. It's fine if you're installing for learning purposes, but in a store that is meant to be your live shop, it's better to start off completely empty.

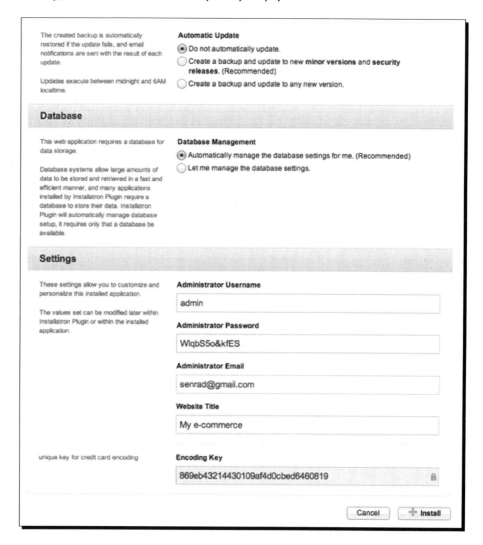

In the second part of the installation form, there are a few fields that you have to pay attention to:

- ❏ Switch off automatic updates
- ❏ Set database management to automatic
- ❏ Choose a secure administrator password

5. Click on the **Install** button when you are done reviewing the form. Installatron will now begin installing Magento. You will receive an e-mail when Installatron is ready. It contains information about the URL you just installed and your login credentials to your newfangled Magento shop. That's all! Our just installed test environment is available at `http://www.boostingecommerce.com/test`. If all is well, yours should look similar to the following screenshot:

How to test the minimum requirements

If your host isn't offering Installatron and you would like to install Magento on it, how will you know if it's possible? In other words, will Magento run? Of course you can simply try to install and run Magento, but it's better to check for the minimum requirements before going that route. You can use the following method to test if your hosting provider meets all requirements needed to run Magento.

First, create a `text` file using your favorite editor and name it as `phpinfo.php`. The contents of the file should be:

```php
<?php
    phpinfo();
?>
```

Save and upload this file to the `root` folder of your hosting environment, using an `ftp` tool such as Filezilla.

Next, open your browser using this address: `http://yourdomain.com/phpinfo.php`; use your own domain name of course. You will see a screen similar to the following:

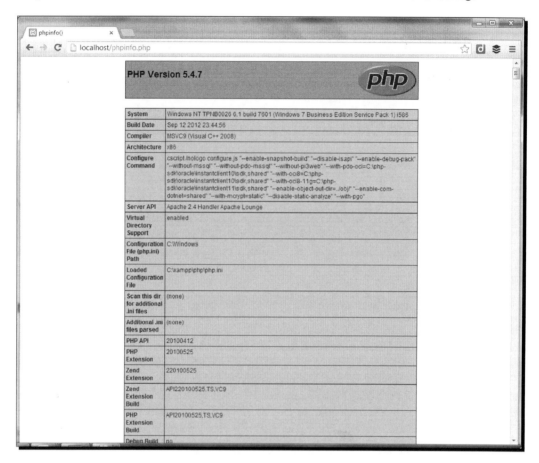

Note that in the preceding screenshot, our XAMPP installation is using PHP 5.4.7. And as we mentioned earlier, Magento isn't compatible with this PHP version yet. So what about that? Well, XAMPP just comes with a recent stable release of PHP. Although it is officially not supported, in most cases your Magento test environment will run fine.

Something similar to the previous screenshot will be shown, depending on your PHP (and XAMPP) version. Using this result, we can check for any PHP module that is missing. Just go through the list at the beginning of this chapter and verify if everything that is needed is available and enabled:

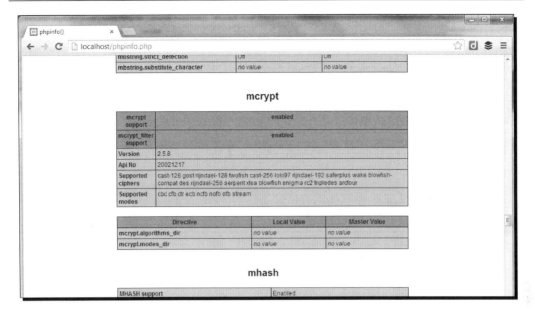

What is SSL and do I need it?

SSL (Secure Sockets Layer) is the standard for secure transactions on the web. You'll recognize it by websites running on `https://` instead of `http://`. To use it, you need to buy an SSL Certificate and add it to your hosting environment. Some hosting providers offer it as a service, whereas others just point to third parties offering SSL Certificates, like for instance, RapidSSL (`https://www.rapidssl.com`) or VeriSign (`http://www.verisign.com`), currently owned by Symantec.

We'll not offer a complete set of instructions on using SSL here, which is beyond the scope of this book. However, it is good to know when you'll need to pay attention to SSL. There can be two reasons to use an SSL certificate:

1. You are accepting payments directly on your website and may even be storing credit card information. In such a case, make sure that you are securing your store by using SSL. On the other hand, if you are only using third parties to accept payments, like for example, Google Checkout or PayPal, you do not have to worry about this part. The transaction is done at the (secure part of the) website of your payment service provider and in such a case you do not need to offer SSL.

2. However, there's another reason that makes using SSL interesting for all shop owners: trust. Regular shoppers know that `https://` connections are secure and might feel just a bit more comfortable in closing the sale with you. It might seem a little thing, but getting a new customer to trust you is an essential step of the online purchase process.

Summary

In this chapter we've gone through several different ways to install Magento. We looked at doing it locally on your own machine using XAMPP or MAMP, or by using a hosting provider to bring your store online. When working with a hosting provider, using the Installatron tool makes the Magento installation very easy. In the next chapter we'll learn to use the huge number of settings that Magento offers, to customize the behavior of your store.

2
General Configuration

The first steps are often the hardest and we've seen lots of users struggling with the installation of their Magento environment. But once done, we're ready to continue and start some sales! Unfortunately, there's more that needs to be done before you can bring your store live to the public. This chapter will help you to learn about the settings that control Magento.

This chapter is written especially for you, if you:

- ◆ Need to take the first steps after installation: what to do next?
- ◆ Want to learn how to set up websites, stores, and storefronts in Magento
- ◆ Need to set up a solid system for calculating tax on your orders
- ◆ Want to learn what you need to do with all those different settings Magento has to offer

The installation is complete; what's next?

Before you can actually start creating products and do the first sales, there's a lot you need to understand about Magento. Flexibility is its strength, but that also means that there's a lot to learn and do before being able to do sales.

In the previous chapter, we did an empty local installation of Magento, as well as an online installation using Installatron. For that second install, we've chosen to install Magento's example data as well. Depending on the steps you've taken, your store might currently be filled or completely empty. In the following screenshot you can see both scenarios:

Don't worry too much if your store looks like the one on the left. Having the sample data available is convenient, but remember that you must find out where everything is located and replace or delete it before you'll be able to bring your store live. An empty store works just as well, because in that case you only have to concentrate on what you need to add. During the next few chapters, we'll be working from our local, empty Magento installation.

The Magento Dashboard

What we didn't do yet, is to take a look at the Magento Admin panel, from which you will configure and maintain your online store. Let's do that first. If you're on a local installation please browse to:

```
http://www.localhost.com/magento/admin
```

Or, when you installed the software at a provider go to:

```
http://www.yourdomain.com/admin
```

Please note that the exact path depends on the settings you used during installation. Our demo store installed using Installatron can for instance be found at:

```
http://www.boostingecommerce.com/test/admin
```

If the URL you used is correct, you should see the Magento login screen as follows:

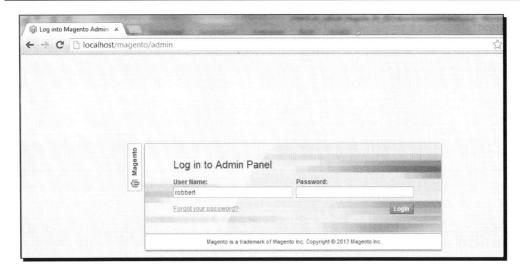

Use the user name and password you created during installation and log in. Next, the Magento Dashboard will appear:

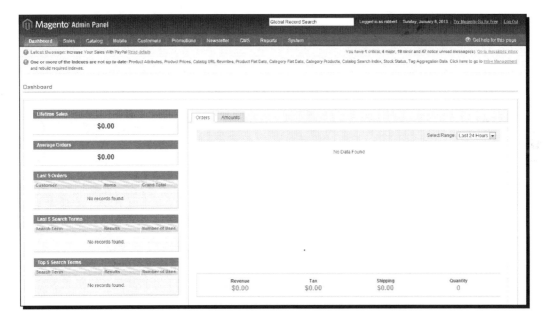

Let's have a quick look at what's available here:

◆ On the top there's a search form, a (commercial) link to Magento Go, and a link to **Log Out**.

◆ Underneath that you'll find the main menu, which we'll soon get to learn more about.

◆ Next, there's space allocated for system messages. In this example, we will immediately see a warning about indexes being out of date. You do not have to worry about this now, since will touch the topics of caching and indexes later on.

◆ Just above that line, there's another commercial link to Paypal and a link to your inbox messages. Just go ahead and click on it to check what's in it. The messages system of Magento will warn you about important (security) updates, so it's wise to pay attention to it. Just after installation, you may assume that you're on the latest version and that all the messages shown here are obsolete already. Especially when you're planning for a production environment, it would be wise to mark the messages "as read", otherwise they'll keep on coming back. After cleaning up, click on the **Dashboard** link in the top left menu to return:

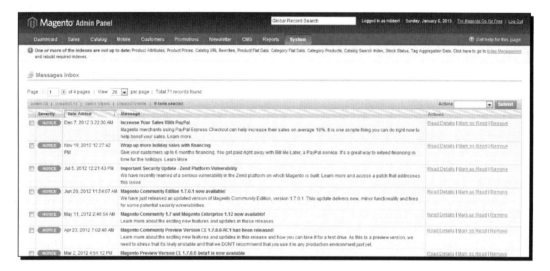

◆ Finally, the largest part of the **Dashboard** screen has been taken by sales statistics. Since we are working on our empty local installation everything is still zero at this moment.

Have a go hero – changing the admin URL

Remember that the Magento admin panel is currently accessible through `http://www.localhost.com/magento/admin` or `http://www.yourdomain.com/admin`, using your own domain name. But there's a downside to this. Having the Magento admin panel reachable in the same way for all Magento stores on the web is a security risk. Hackers will know where to find your admin panel and that's one of the first steps to get access. So, it's better to change this path. Doing so requires some additional, and more difficult steps.

You can find some good instructions using the following link:

`http://blog.chapagain.com.np/magento-how-to-change-admin-url-path/`

Setting up your store

The **System** menu, in the top-right corner, will give you almost everything you need to configure your online store. Almost everything, because some settings, such as taxes for instance, will be set up somewhere else. More about taxes later on in this chapter, but let's first have a look at what the **System** menu has to offer:

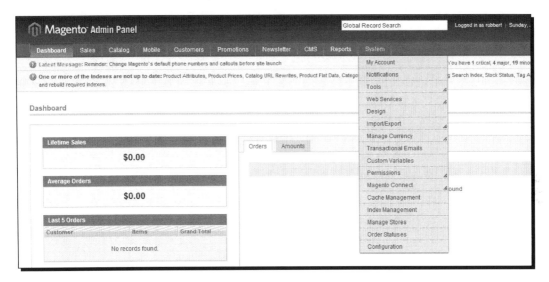

System Menu item	What you will need it for
My Account	A simple screen holding your login details, e-mail address, and password.
Notifications	The messages screen we already visited above.
Tools	Holds a tool to create and manage backups of your store. We will cover more on maintaining your store later in *Chapter 11, Maintaining and Administrating Your Store*. Keep in mind that making backup copies of your store is essential! There's also a tool for compiling Magento, to increase performance, but using it during the set up and development of your store isn't useful.
Web Services	These are tools to let your store interact with other systems. Using these requires a deeper technical knowledge and is beyond the scope of this book.
Design	Holds a tool to add temporary design changes to your store. This could be used to display banners during a certain period, but normally you would handle that kind of things in a different way. We will cover more on using designs for your store in *Chapter 9, Customizing Your Store's Appearance*.

System Menu item	What you will need it for
Import/Export	These are tools to export data from Magento to another solution, or to import data from other sources. This could be used to import a customer- or item-database for instance. This requires some technical knowledge to make use of it.
Manage Currency	This tool can be used to maintain currency rates. It could be important if you want to offer automatic currency calculations. You'll often see that you will prefer manual price changes, even if you're working with multiple currencies. That is caused by the fact that automatic currency changes would result in prices like $14.91 instead of $14.95 or simply $15. But, it is possible to use and maintain this table manually as well as automatically.
Transactional Emails	This is an important area, because in here you'll be able to control the contents of the automatic messages that Magento will send to your customers. More on **Transactional Emails** can be found in *Chapter 9, Customizing Your Store's Appearance.*
Custom Variables	These can be used in your **Transactional Emails**. By defining some custom HTML code here, you'll be able to simply call that piece of code from within your e-mails. This is especially helpful to make sure that you do not have to change every single e-mail template if only one item, (such as a banner for instance) is to be changed. Custom variables can also be used on content pages.
Permissions	This gives you the possibility to define users and their roles in order to make sure that employees can only access the parts they need. This is helpful in larger companies, when you're working with multiple people on the same store.
Magento Connect	In here you'll be able to add extensions to increase the functionality of Magento. Working with extensions through Magento Connect is really great, but you have to be careful as well. We'll cover this part in depth in *Chapter 11, Maintaining and Administrating Your Store.*
Cache Management	Caching is important to keep Magento running at a reasonable speed. In this area, you can refresh your caches. This is often helpful when you're in the process of setting up your store or making changes to it. For now just remember that if you make changes to your store that are not visible to the visitor, please go here to refresh the cache.
Index Management	The same is applicable to (database) indexes, as they make sure that the information being retrieved from your database is found quickly. Every now and then you need to refresh the indexes of your database.
Manage Stores	An important area if you want to run multiple online stores. More on this topic in the next section.

System Menu item	What you will need it for
Order Statuses	A table holding the different statuses an order could have. Normally you do not need to touch it.
Configuration	This is where the action is. In this menu item, there are lots and lots of settings that control your store. The most important ones will be discussed during the remaining part of this chapter.

Managing Stores

Before we jump into the configuration part, it is good to know about the concept of Websites, Stores, and Store Views in Magento.

One of Magento's strong points is the possibility of adding multiple online stores within the same Magento installation. Using this, for example, you have the possibility of running multiple stores in several languages, offering the same (or a similar) set of products. These stores can even use the same settings if you'd like to, or only change those parameters that are important to be different. Magento uses the following naming convention, to set up a structure of online stores:

♦ Website: This is the main level. A Website should contain at least one Store with one Store view underneath it. In the default setup, there is one Website, one Store, and one Store View as shown in the following screenshot:

♦ Store: One level lower you'll find the Store. It's good to know that these three levels are just abstraction levels that you can use to organize your content and settings. The Store level isn't very important, since most settings can be altered on Website or Store View level.

♦ Store View: The Store View is the lowest level in the hierarchy. Store Views are generally used to create exact copies of a store, but using different languages.

When you're maintaining your store's settings or products, you'll notice that every option may be set on one of these levels. This is what we call the scope. If the customer is visiting a certain Store View, the system tries to use options set on that particular level (the Store View scope). If nothing has been set, Magento will fall back to the Store scope and if nothing is set on that level as well, then the Website scope will be used.

Even above the highest level (Website), there are also settings that are "Global", which means that such a setting is the same for your entire Magento installation and there's no possibility to use a different setting on a lower level. This is currently somewhat abstract, but you'll soon see how these levels can be used in practice.

If you'd like to add Websites, Stores, and Store Views, this is the area to do so. Please choose names that make sense as soon as you're going to add anything. The "default" names should only be used if you're sticking with one single setup.

It's important to know that this setup doesn't mean that there's a direct connection with the URL/domain names you're using. You can route URL's to Websites or Stores, as well as Store Views. The different possibilities for your domain are as follows:

- ◆ `myonlinestore.com`: This sets up your store on a new domain.
- ◆ `myonlinestore.com/newstore`: This sets up the new store in a subfolder on your existing domain.
- ◆ `newstore.myonlinestore.com`: This set up your store on a subdomain of your existing domain.

In practice, we often see the first option, where we have a single instance of one Website, one Store and one Store View. This is what we'll be doing throughout this book. The second and third options are often used to offer the same website in a different language, for different Store Views. Using the principles above we can create the following structure:

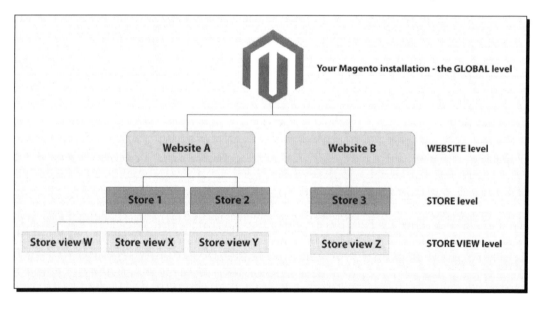

In our example, we're working with the simplest form: one Website, one Store and one Store View. This is the right part of the previous image.

General settings

Once this is clear, it's time to actually go through the settings of Magento and make changes wherever needed.

Navigate to **System | Configuration** using the menu. In there, the first screen you'll see is the **General** section holding data, such as your base country and countries that are allowed. Note that if you're not selling internationally, it would be good to limit the available countries here, so that visitors are not able to select countries that you do not want to do business with.

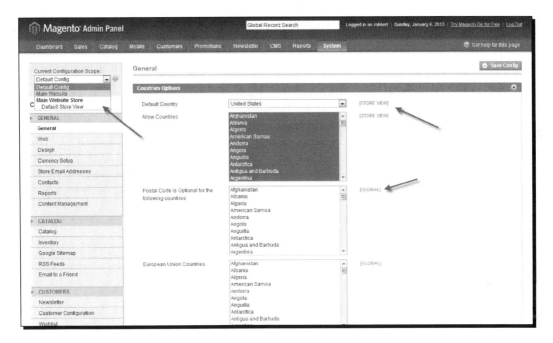

There are two things here that refer back to the topic we learned in the previous section:

1. In the top-left corner you can see that it is possible to select a different Website or Store View, if you have any. This is called the Scope Selector. If you do not change anything, you'll be changing the **Default Config** option which means that the settings being done will also be saved for any Website or Store View that you may add in the future. For our single online store, it's fine to keep this setting as **Default Config**, but pay attention when you are running multiple stores! Keeping an eye on the correct scope is in that case very important! Changing settings in the incorrect scope will almost certainly lead to unexpected behavior.

2. On the right-hand side of every form setting, you will see **[GLOBAL]**, **[WEBSITE]**, or **[STORE VIEW]**. This means that the particular setting can be changed at that level. The **Postal Code is Optional for the following countries** section in the example above for instance is a **[Global]** setting. This means that if you decide to turn off postal (ZIP) codes for Ireland (they do not use such a system), for instance, then all websites and stores within your Magento installation will stop asking for the postal code. On the other hand, the **Allow Countries** section is changeable to **Store View** level, which means that it is possible to run an international and national online store next to each other within the same Magento environment.

Scrolling down a bit shows some other settings that you need to take care of:

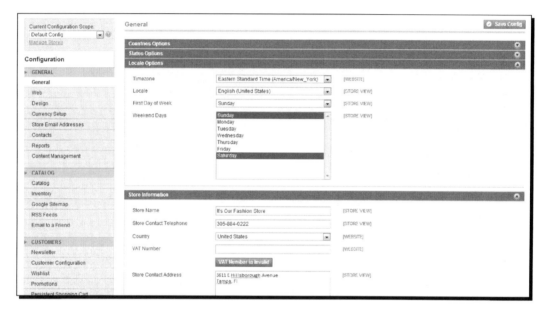

In here, set the **Timezone** you're in and determine your regular working days. Don't worry, as your online store will also be available during weekends. Below that, enter your **Store Name** and contact details. The **VAT Number** field is important for EU businesses, and we will cover more on that topic later on.

> Don't forget to save your changes! If you jump from one section to the other in the **Configuration** screen, you will lose the settings you just made, without any warning. So just save after every change!

Next, we'll have a look at the settings of the **Web** section (click on the **Web** menu on the left):

In this section you'll see the **Base URL** of your store, and in this case our local installation. If you installed Magento at a hosting provider, probably this is already showing your domain name. Although the setting can be changed, please be careful, because changing it without taking the correct steps could break your store!

To explain better what the default content of these fields means, the **{{unsecure_base_url}}** value used in first field, **Base URL**, is used in the fields below. Note that all fields below the **Base URL** field use that variable. Hence, changing the first field, will automatically change the others as well.

Search engine optimization

You might have noticed that we did not mention the first fields of the **Web** section, named, **Url Options** and **Search Engine Optimization**. The default settings are generally fine, but it's still good to know a little bit more on this subject.

When working with Magento, or any other web solution, it's very important to optimize your website for the search engines as much as possible. Although your customers and visitors are the most important, it will lead you nowhere if your store is doing badly in the search engines. There's really a lot you can do in this area. As mentioned, by default, Magento has already enabled Search Engine Friendly URLs. This means that the URL shown in the top of your browser would for instance look like this:

```
http://myonlinestore.com/shoes/womens-boot-brown
```

Whereas a non-optimized URL could look as follows:

```
http://myonlinstore.com/ catalog/product/view/id/1537/category/28
```

The **Use Web Server Rewrites** setting is set to **Yes** by default in Magento. This means that the Search Engine Friendly URLs will be used, which is good, but your webserver has to support it though. When you're working with Apache (or locally Xampp) this generally works fine. You should be able to find a file in the root of your site named `.htaccess`. Note that the file starts with a point and that it cannot have an extension (like `.txt`). Whenever you're editing this file, you need to keep the name as it is.

There's much, much more to discover when we are talking about Magento and Search Engine Optimization. We suggest that you first learn to use all the Magento basics in this book. After that, come back here and find more information on Magento and SEO using the following links:

```
http://www.wamda.com/2012/10/how-to-optimize-seo-on-a-magento-e-
commerce-site
```

```
http://www.boostingecommerce.com/ultimate-magento-seo-tips-and-
tricks-part-1-content
```

```
http://yoast.com/articles/magento-seo/
```

We continue to work in our settings page, in the **Default Pages** area. For example, it can be used to change which page will be the homepage of your store. In a default setup, we can leave it unchanged.

In the European Union (EU) website owners need to ask their visitors if they want to allow the usage of cookies. Cookies are small pieces of information stored on the local computer of your visitor. Magento uses them as well, so as an owner in the EU (or even if you're outside of the EU but targeting EU visitors) you need to ask your visitors for permission. Since Magento CE 1.7 there's a function for this, which you can enable the **Session Cookie Management** area in the current **Web** section. Set the **Cookie Restriction Mode** field to **Yes**, save your settings and look at the results in the frontend of your store:

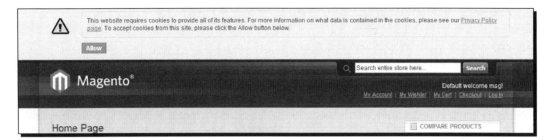

In the next part, we'll look at the **Design** section. So save again and click on **Design** on the left-hand side. The first parts are used to set the design of your store and working with themes. We will cover more on this in *Chapter 9, Customizing Your Store's Appearance*.

We'll look at the settings at **HTML Head**, where you can set your **Favicon icon** (used by browsers) and more important, make some SEO-related settings. Enter your Default meta title and description, just like in the following example. You may also enter a couple of keywords in the **Default Keywords** field, but please be aware that search engines do not really pay attention to it anymore. So don't overdo it.

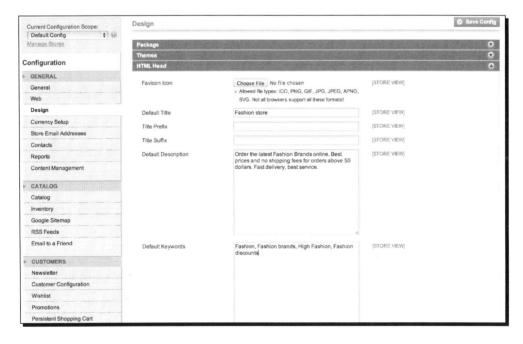

You may also use the **Title Suffix** field if you'd like to see your store name at the end of every meta title, but it's not so common anymore to do so. Also pay attention to the **Default Robots** field. By default it will allow search engines to index your site. If you're on a local test installation, you do not have to worry: Google cannot access and hence will not index it. But if you're using a hosting company, you might want to allow or disallow access to your website.

A bit lower on the same page you'll find settings for **Header** and **Footer** of your store. These fields also contain some default data that you need to overwrite with your own, since these defaults remain visible to your visitors. Note that the logo field can be overwritten, but then there's no possibility to upload it. You need to move your logo image manually by using your FTP client to the correct location, which is `skin/|frontend/|default/|default/| images`. Note that this path is only correct if you are still using the default Magento theme. If you're on a local installation of Magento, you can simply copy and paste your file to the correct location.

> In most cases, you will not be using the default theme of Magento, but will have installed something different. If you plan to do so, it could very well happen that changing the logo of your theme will work differently. Please read *Chapter 8, Configuring Shipping* for further instructions on installing a theme and also read the theme documentation to find out how to configure it.

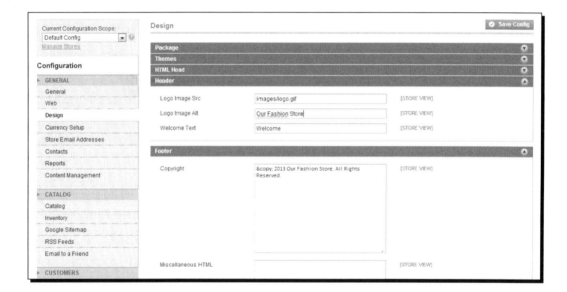

In the next section, **Currency Setup**, you can set how your online store should work with currencies. It's quite common to work with a single currency per Store View, but that isn't mandatory:

Please note the following:

- ◆ The **Default Display Currency** field can only be set on the Website level. This is the currency that is used to display the price of your products. If you want to use multiple stores using different default currencies, this automatically means that you need to create more Magento Websites. A Store View won't work in such a case.

- ◆ If you want to allow other currencies besides the default one, you can enable them by clicking on them in the list. If you want to select multiple currencies, you should press the *Ctrl* key while you click on them.

The last things we are going to do for now is to set up some contact details in the **Store Email Addresses** section:

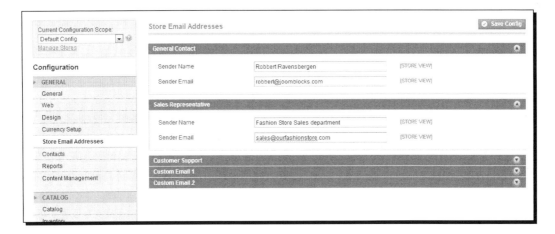

Magento works with various e-mail addresses that will be used as the sender of automatic messages by your store. Please make sure that you fill all of them. If you're a small shop owner, it's fine to use the same e-mail address for all fields, but just don't leave the defaults.

What just happened?

You just started to set up and personalize your online store, and also know about the hundreds of possible settings that Magento offers. There's much more actually, as you may have noticed that we only discussed the first part of the **Configuration** area. The other settings will be discussed during the upcoming chapters, and just at the moment when you need them.

Setting up taxes

Calculating and setting up your tax system isn't maybe the first thing you would think of when starting your online store. But it is a very important step to take and the best time to do it is right now, before you set up your product catalog. Magento offers an extended system of tax calculations, making almost anything possible. On the other hand, there is unfortunately no "one size fits all" approach. Tax laws and calculations simply differ in each country and region.

So, the bad news is, we cannot give you an example for every single country here. So we have to stick with describing what Magento can do in terms of tax calculations. We are neither tax experts, so please always refer to your local tax laws to make sure that you apply to them.

If for instance, you'd like to know more about the United States sales taxes, Wikipedia is a good starting point:

```
http://en.wikipedia.org/wiki/Sales_taxes_in_the_United_States
```

Your taxes setup will contain the following elements. The majority of the needed functions can be found in the **Sales** menu as follows:

- General taxation settings: Navigate to **System | Configuration | Sales | Tax**
- Product Tax classes: Navigate to **Sales | Tax | Product Tax Class**
- Customer Tax classes: Navigate to **Sales | Tax | Customer Tax Class**
- Customer groups: Navigate to **Customers | Customer groups**
- Tax zones and rates: Navigate to **Sales | Tax | Manage Tax zones and rates**
- Tax rules: Navigate to **Sales | Tax | Manage Tax rules**

And finally also your products, where you'll connect your product to a Product Tax Class, followed by customers, who will be part of a specific Customer group. In most cases, you'll need a combination of all of these settings, which can be quite overwhelming.

Since Version 1.7 of the Magento Community edition (and also starting from Version 1.12 of the Enterprise edition), Magento offers some specific tax functions for European Union business to business sales. More on this topic will follow at the end of this chapter.

General taxation settings

At the beginning, let's start by making some general settings that will affect our tax calculations. Navigate to **System | Configuration | Sales** and click on the **Tax** section:

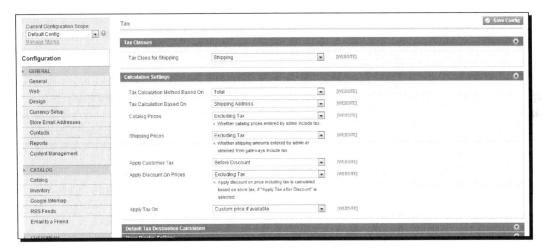

In here you'll find the following settings:

- ◆ **Tax Class for Shipping**: Set the Product Tax Class that is applicable for your shipping cost. By setting a separate (by default for each available) shipping class you have the possibility to use a different rate for shipping if you need to.

Following that, click on the **Calculation Settings** area:

- ◆ In the **Tax Calculation Method Based On** field, select whether the tax is based on the price of each single unit, or on the row total, which is the total for a line item in the order.

- ◆ In the **Tax Calculation Based On** field, select whether the tax is calculated based on the customer's shipping address, billing address, or on your store's shipping origin.

- ◆ For the **Catalog Prices** field, enter whether the catalog prices you'll enter for your products include or exclude tax.

- ◆ At the **Shipping Prices** field, select whether the shipping amount that you'll set later on will include or exclude tax.

- In the **Apply Customer Tax** field, enter whether tax is applicable on the original price or (if available) on the discounted price for a product.

- For the **Apply Discount on Prices** field, set if discounts applied include or exclude the tax.

- In the **Apply Tax On** field, enter if tax is applied to a custom price or to the original price.

If you aren't sure about the effect of a setting, it's fine to come back here once you have entered some products to see the result of applied settings before bringing your store live.

Note that all the mentioned settings can be set on Website level, so everything you set here will have the same behavior for all Stores and Store views within that particular Website.

Scroll down a bit and click on the **Default Tax Destination Calculation**, **Price Display Settings**, and on the **Shopping Cart Display Settings** area:

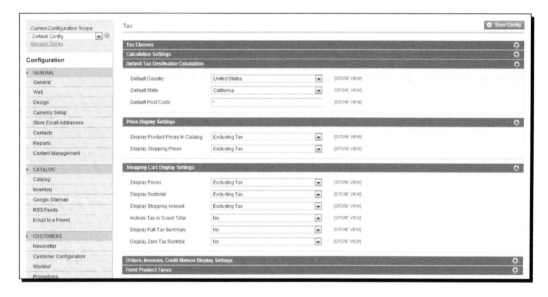

Here, begin with selecting the correct country (and state if applicable). There are only a couple of countries for which a state is available. Otherwise just leave the * mark. Next, you should set how your sales prices are to be displayed. Do you want your products and shipping costs to appear including or excluding tax in the frontend? The same questions appear for the cart display. On top of that you can also specify how to show totals and if a zero tax amount should be visible or hidden.

Underneath this section, exactly the same questions need to be answered for orders, invoices, and credit notes. It makes sense to keep all settings the same, so that your customers constantly see the same display of calculated taxes.

The last part of this settings page contains a special function named **Fixed Product Taxes**. This is used when you need to apply a tax on your product, where the amount depends on the product, and not on the product price. An example would be the European Waste Electrical and Electronic Equipment Tax, which consumers need to pay when purchasing new equipment. We'll not discuss this specific topic any further here, but if you need more information about it, please refer to: `http://theblog.enova-tech. net/2011/04/magento-weee-and-fpt-fixed-product-tax- tutorial/` and `http://en.wikipedia.org/wiki/Waste_ Electrical_and_Electronic_Equipment_Directive`.

Product Tax Classes

The usage of **Product Tax Classes** is rather simple. You need at least one if you want to calculate all taxes:

By default, Magento has already created two for you: **Shipping** and **Taxable goods**. When do you need more? Well, for instance, if in your situation you are selling products in different groups, where different tax rates are applicable. Often you'll see that products such as food have a lower tax rate than other goods, such as apparels and hardware. If you are going to sell both the categories, you simply need to create an additional Product Tax Class here, which is as simple as providing a name for it.

Customer Tax Classes

It's not enough to simply set up a Product Tax Class. This is because the tax you're calculating does not only depend on the product, but also on the customer you're selling it to. This is where the **Customer Tax Classes** comes in. You can find it in the **Sales | Tax** menu;

By default, there's only one tax class created, the **Retail customer** class. This could be enough if you're only selling to consumers, but in the case of "business to business sales", you often need more than one. Also here, the Customer Tax Class is just a name, that will be easy to add. The functionality is defined somewhere else, which we'll see in a minute.

Customer groups

A quick side step to Customer groups will be used to create several groups of customers. More on using these will follow in *Chapter 6, Customer Relationships*, but for now it is important to know that they exist. A Customer group is connected to the Customer Tax Classes. A Customer group can only have one Customer Tax Class associated to it. A Customer group will be assigned to every future (registered) customer and therefore influences the way taxes are calculated for that customer. You can find the Customer groups in the **Customer** menu as follows:

Managing tax zones and rates

In here it becomes more important; this is the area where you'll define the different rates that Magento needs to calculate. Click on **Sales | Tax | Manage Tax Rates** in the menu and you'll see that Magento by default already has two predefined rates as seen in the following screenshot:

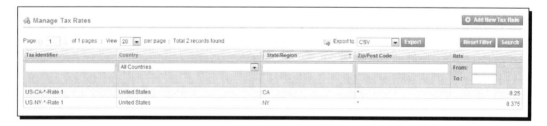

In fact these are only examples and if you do not need them, just delete or change them and create your own. But let's have a look at what's available, just to explain what you should do:

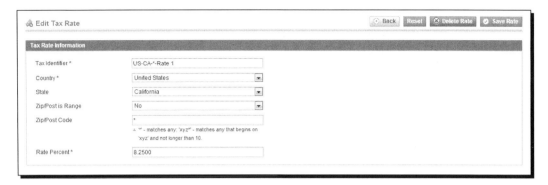

The identifier is something you can choose yourself. In here, it was chosen to use the abbreviation of the county, state, zip code, and the rate it will be used for. This comes in handy when you have to read the codes, but it isn't mandatory to do so. If you select a country where using the United States isn't applicable, the field will automatically become unavailable. The rate field determines the percentage that will be calculated.

There are situations where you will have to enter a lot of tax rates. For instance, if you need to enter all tax rates for the United States it might take you a while. We found a blogger on the net offering a `csv` file that you may import, but be careful, since the file is a bit older and we cannot guarantee that the rates didn't change since then: `http://rricketts.com/magento-us-tax-csv-file-all-50-states/` and read more on the United States taxes here at: `http://en.wikipedia.org/wiki/Sales_taxes_in_the_United_States`. If you are using a `csv` file, use the Sales | Tax | Import/Export Tax rate menu to import your file. You may even create your own if that is convenient in your case!

Managing tax rules

In the last screen (which is actually at the top of the **Sales | Tax** menu) we need to bring everything together by entering our **Tax rules**:

In here, there's also one default record. Let's take a closer look at that one:

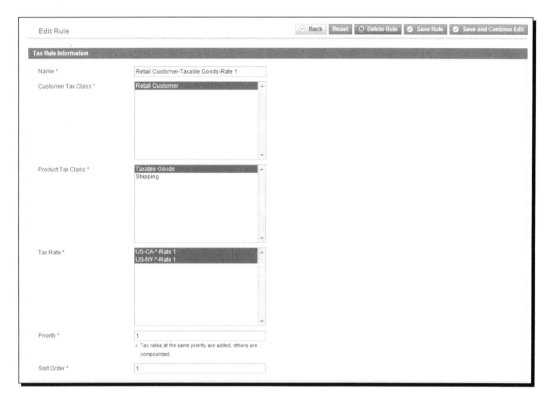

The first field is just a name again, that you can use to describe your tax rule. A tax rule contains one or more **Customer Tax Class**, one or more **Product Tax Class**, and one or more **Tax Rate**.

In the previous example this means that:

If a product is sold to a customer in the **Retail** group and the product has been assigned the "Taxable goods" class, the rate for the corresponding state will be applied. By going through the setup in the same order as we discussed it here, you should be able to define your own rates and use them in the way you need to.

EU business to business VAT

In the EU, there's a special situation for businesses selling goods to each other. So this last paragraph is only applicable for businesses in the EU. Besides that, you only need to read on if you're selling to businesses (B2B), not when you're selling to consumers. Since Magento Version 1.7, a feature has been added to Magento to support business doing international sales.

This is the situation:

- ◆ VAT is charged if the buying company is in the same country as the selling company.

- ◆ VAT is not charged if the buying company is not in the same country as the selling company, but both are in the EU and they both have a valid EU VAT ID (the VAT ID is a kind of Tax registration number). This is because the VAT being charged is a special rate, which is currently zero percent.

The problem with the former versions of Magento was: how do you know if the buyer has a valid VAT ID? Well, in the past, extensions could have been be used to do the verification, but currently, this has become a standard function for all Magento versions.

Time for action – using VAT validation

Perform the following steps to use Magento's VAT validation function:

1. Create customer groups, so that you can put a customer in a certain group, depending on a valid or invalid VAT ID number. You need to create four different customer groups for it.

2. Navigate to **System** | **Configuration** | **Customers** | **Customer Configuration** and expand the **Create New Account Options** section as shown in the following screenshot:

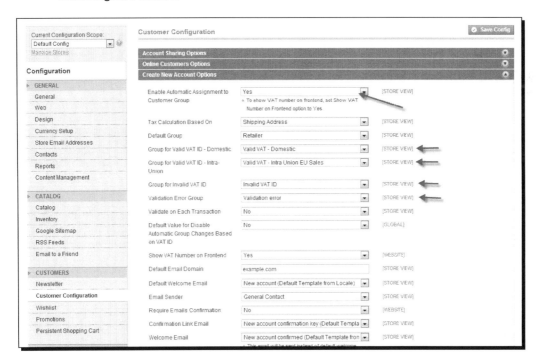

3. Enable the function for automatic VAT ID validation and set the **Customer Group** value you just created. From that moment on, new customers will be asked to enter their VAT ID at the account creation, after which it will be validated automatically. Depending on the validation result, the customer will be added to the correct customer group and assigned to that customer group is the Customer Tax Class, which gives you the possibility to define the needed tax rates and also create corresponding tax rules.

Please note that as an owner, you also need to supply and validate your own VAT ID to use this functionality. Navigate to **System | Configuration | General** and enter your **Country** and **VAT Number** to validate it. Please note that you should leave out the first two characters that determine the country. Just select your country, enter the VAT number, save, and then click on the **Validate** button:

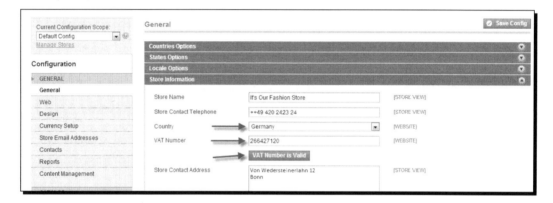

Summary

In this chapter we performed several tasks that are needed to prepare our online store. We made several general settings and spent time on setting up the correct Tax rates. But there are many more settings that affect the behavior of Magento, which we'll be discussing in the upcoming chapters. In the next chapter, we'll start preparing for our product catalog and have a close look at Magento's strong ability to use product attributes.

3
Categories and Attributes

Now that you have already done the basic configuration of your store, it's time to start thinking about products. Magento has everything you could wish for built-in. But the extended possibilities also mean that you need to carefully plan and execute your product catalog. Therefore, we're using multiple chapters to explain Magento's product functions.

This chapter will cover:

- ◆ Creating the right product settings for your store
- ◆ Understanding the way Magento handles products
- ◆ Setting up your own product attributes and attribute sets
- ◆ Working with categories to create logical structures for your products

What you need to know

Although Magento is preconfigured to immediately start entering your products, we recommend that you take some time to think about your product catalog before you do so. Of course it's easy to just start and see where you'll end up, but if you are serious about setting up your store, you must take some time to prepare it.

Let's first quickly have a look at the meaning of the various Magento keywords we'll use throughout this chapter:

- ◆ **Catalog defaults**: These are the settings in Magento that influence the behavior of your products.

- **Product categories**. This is the simplest one to understand. Your products will be put into a product category used for navigation purposes by your visitors and to create a logical structure of products throughout your store. As an example, a clothing store could have two main categories: men and women. Underneath those you would find shirts, trousers, underwear, and so on.

- **Product attributes**: Simply speaking, these are the fields you'll use to create your products. You have products in the Shirts category? Then it makes sense to use a field named **Color** and a field named **Size** for instance. In Magento, we call these fields **attributes**. You have complete flexibility here to determine what fields you want to use and you can create your own fields as well.

- **Attribute sets**: Fortunately you do not have to choose the fields you want to use for every product over and over again. This is where the attribute sets come in. An attribute set is a combination of various attributes, setting all the fields you'll need for a certain type of product. When creating a product, you'll select the attribute set it belongs to. By doing so, all the fields you need will automatically become available. Maybe this is still a bit theoretical, but we'll soon see the power of this principle in practice.

- **Product catalog**: This is your product database containing all the products for your complete Magento installation. Remember that we spoke about websites and store views earlier in *Chapter 2, General Configuration.* Product attributes can differ as per the level and it is possible to make your products visible or invisible as per the website.

All together you'll have complete control over your product catalog. And even if you are running multiple online stores using one Magento installation, it is still possible to use products in such a way that it isn't necessary to create any duplicate products, just because you would like to display different information in the various stores you are running.

Before you continue, remember that it is important to carefully think about your attributes and attribute sets. Once a product has been created, it's no longer possible to change the attribute set of that product! Besides that, your attributes will be used by visitors when browsing your store. Features such as Magento's famous layered navigation and comparison function heavily rely on a proper setup of your attribute sets.

An example category structure

Let's say that we are running an online store selling apparel, such as trousers, shirts, dresses, and shoes. We first have to create a logical category structure that makes sense for our visitors. Remember that your visitors will use your category structure to browse through your store and find the products they are looking for. So, try to think from the customers' perspective when creating your category structure.

Our example isn't very difficult, we see these kinds of online stores all the time and most of them are more or less following the same approach.

The following structure is what we could create. We kept the structure rather simple. Not everything will be in it yet, but this example is just used to explain what you can do using Magento:

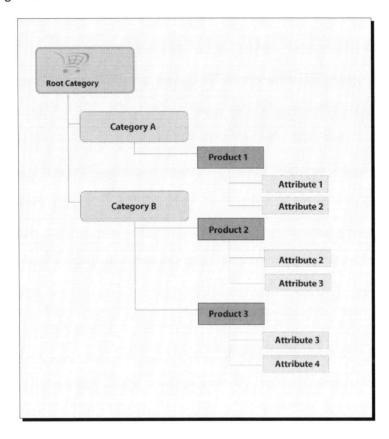

This example shows you the category structure we created, but also shows some products in it, which have different attributes. To be able to create the products, we would need different attribute sets for every possible combination of attributes.

Catalog defaults

Now that we know what we'd like to achieve, it's time to start preparing it. Let's first have a look at the Magento settings that will influence the behavior of your products.

Time for action – catalog settings

The catalog settings can be found in your menu by navigating to **System** | **Configuration** | **CATALOG** | **Catalog**. The first part is completely covered with the settings that will influence the way your products will be shown on the frontend to your visitors:

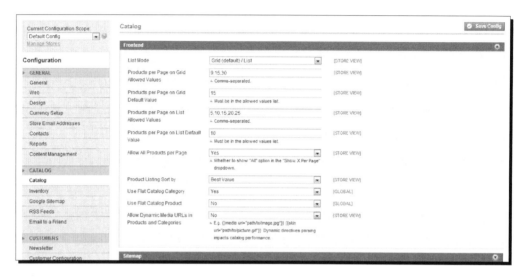

We made a few changes to the defaults, but whether you need to do the same differs from case to case. So, let's look at what you can achieve here.

The first five fields let you decide how the products should be displayed and how many of them. You can choose to use a grid view, a list view, or both. The following example shows the default Magento demo store, which has a Grid view (left) as well as a List view (right) for the same products. Generally speaking, you could say that visitors are used to Grid views and they like them, but of course, there can be circumstances to decide differently.

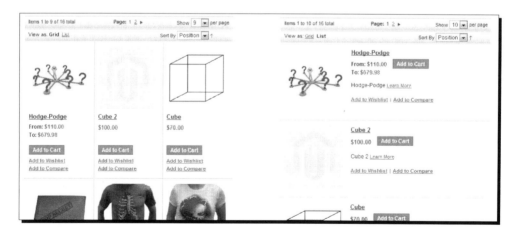

It's clear that the Grid view gives the possibility to show more products in a smaller area, whereas the List view delivers more room for product details. Using these fields, Magento lets you decide how you want to display your items and how many should be visible per page by default.

I like to see a lot of items on the same page personally, so I make these changes:

- The **Products per Page on Grid Default Value** field has been changed from **9** to **15**
- I have the **Allow All Products per Page** field changed from **No** to **Yes**

This last setting gives the user the possibility to show all products within the chosen category on one page. By default, **15** will still be shown, but we put the user in control.

There are a few settings on this page of which the meaning might not be very clear:

- **Product listing Sort by**: This determines how your products will be sorted. The default **Best Value** setting gives you, as an administrator, the maximum flexibility as you can set the ordering per category yourself when creating your products.

- **Use flat catalog category**: The structure of Magento caused category information to be stored in various tables. By changing this setting to **Yes**, Magento will create one flat catalog table for your categories, which improves performance. It is recommended to set it to **Yes**.

- **Use flat catalog product**: Something similar can be done for the product tables, but you only need to set this to **Yes** if you have 1,000 products or more in your catalog.

- **Allow dynamic media URLs in products and categories**: Setting this field to **No** can improve performance, but it gives you less flexibility when using images in the description fields of your products and categories. However, often it isn't necessary to use images in your descriptions (there are other ways to manage images), so it could be an option to switch to **No** if performance is important.

By expanding the other parts of this section that holds the settings, we'll see that there's much more that can be set as shown:

Use Tree Like Category Sitemap: If this is set to **Yes**, the automatic category sitemap that Magento can create for you will be shown in a "tree style", where subcategories are shown underneath their parent category. Set it to **Yes** if you have a lot of categories (but more than 15).

Allow Guests to Write Reviews: Leave this field with the value **Yes**, to make it as easy as possible for buyers to leave a product review.

Below this area you'll see a number of fields that can be used to send product alerts to the site owner or employee maintaining the product catalog. These product alerts will help you to keep track of changes in your catalog. By default product alerts will not be sent. If you enable them you also have the possibility to set how often they will be sent and to whom. Further on it's possible to select the layout of those messages using transactional e-mail templates. To read more on the topic of transactional e-mails, please refer to *Chapter 9, Customizing Your Store's Appearance*. For a small shop the default settings will do. Product alerts will become more important once your company and/or product catalog grows.

Expanding the next sections gives the possibility to set specific placeholder images. These are the images that are used by Magento when no product image has been set. Although we recommend always using multiple product images, it might happen that you temporarily do not have one. In such a situation, a Magento logo will be shown to your visitors. It's better to replace those using your own, for instance, with a watermark of your logo.

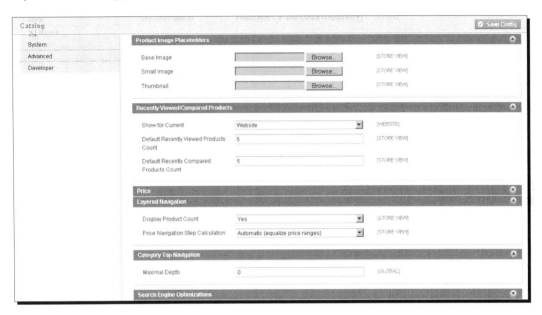

Magento has the functionality to show your visitors the recent products that they just viewed or compared with each other. You can set what the scope for this function will be, and how many products should be shown by default.

We are skipping the **Price** section. Using it makes it possible to set your currency to **Global**, which would mean that all websites within your installation must use the same default currency.

Using the settings in the **Layered Navigation** section gives the possibility to influence the behavior of another strong Magento functionality. The layered navigation can be used by visitors to select a product by, for example, the price range. But you can also use other product attributes in the layered navigation or even create your own. An example on how to do that will follow later on in this chapter, when we're discussing product attributes.

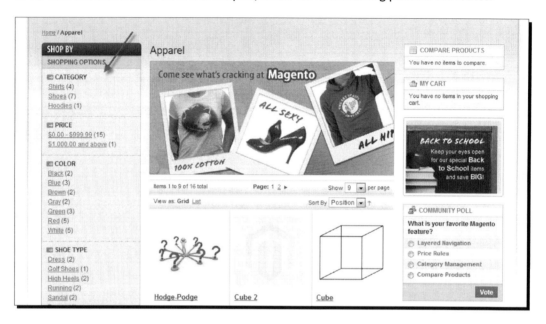

The default layered navigation shown in the preceding example of the demo environment gives the possibility to select a product by category, price range, color, or shoe type. In other words, the layered navigation can be used to narrow down the results of the product listing. Using the catalog settings, you can override the number of products that is shown by default. It's also possible to choose a method for putting products in price ranges.

Moving downwards on our **Catalog** settings page, there are a couple of areas left, starting with **Category Top Navigation**. By default, Magento will create menus based on your category structure. If you created a structure with many levels, this could become a problem for your users, depending on the way your menu works. By setting a maximum level, the menu will not drill down deeper than that. The default is zero, which means all levels will be shown.

The section holding **Search Engine Optimizations** immediately draws our attention, because we all want to be on the first page of Google, don't we? Well, the bad news is: there is no golden rule or setting that you can apply to get there. All the work you do in your store contributes to the results you'll reach in the search engines. There's really a lot you can do, and you might want to refer to the following article for further information:

```
http://www.boostingecommerce.com/tag/seo
```

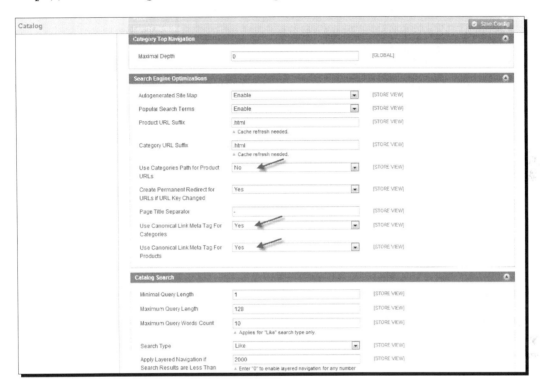

Although speaking about SEO settings always leads to a discussion, there are a few things that we would change looking at the defaults:

- ◆ **Use Categories Path for Product URLs**: Leaving this field as **Yes** would mean that your URLs would, for example, look like this:

    ```
    http://myfashionstore.com/women/shoes/boots/tall-buffalo-boot-woman-black.html
    ```

    Setting this field to **No** would simply take out all the categories and leave `http://myfashionstore.com/tall-boot-buffalo-boot-woman-black.html`. As long as the URL for your product contains some keywords, this would work just as well and deliver a much shorter URL.

◆ The last two settings are for handling canonical link meta tags. Set these to **Yes** to prevent duplicate content.

What is duplicate content?

Duplicate content means that the search engines are finding multiple (in Magento often even more than two) pages holding the same content. That's bad news, because this means that the search engine will split the ranking it would give to that page, and divide the score for your page in two (or three, or more parts). Duplicate content issues can really ruin the SEO of your site and bring you low rankings. This is something you would like to stop from happening of course! Read more on Magento SEO, duplicate content, and canonical links at `http://yoast.com/articles/magento-seo/`.

Leave all other SEO settings as they are when you're just starting your online store. Of course you want to start in the right way, but the area of SEO is complicated and always changing. Do not expect to become an expert without spending a lot of time in this area. Once your store is live and you're starting to perform some sales, we recommend working with experts in this field for further optimization.

Under the **Search Engine Optimizations** section, we'll find some parameters to influence the behavior of Magento's **Catalog Search** function. For now you may keep the default settings.

The last part of this settings page gives the opportunity to set the behavior of downloadable products. These are digital files that you might want to sell, take for example, photos or music files. The defaults are fine to get you started in this area. If you'd like to start working with downloadable products, please refer to *Chapter 5, Beyond Adding Simple Products*, for more information.

Now that we have discussed a lot of product-related settings, it's time to start entering our attributes and categories.

Working with attributes

As mentioned we can consider product attributes to be the "fields" of your products. It's good to think about all the data that you need to store for your products. Making changes at a later stage is possible, but can be very time consuming. Let's have a look at a few examples:

◆ **Product**: TV

Possible attributes: These include the brand, type, screen size, TV dimensions, weight, warranty, price, description, item number (SKU), and so on.

- **Product**: Shoes

  Possible attributes: These include the brand, type, size, color, heel height, price, description, item number (SKU), and so on.

> Did you notice that we're mentioning the shoe size as a product attribute? Yes, this means that if you're working with sizes, you will have to create a single product for every unique item in your store. This could easily grow your product catalog to a lot of items. But it is necessary, because it is likely that you want to keep track of stock levels per size. Fortunately, it's very easy in Magento to create those additional products. More on this topic will follow in *Chapter 5, Beyond Adding Simple Products*.

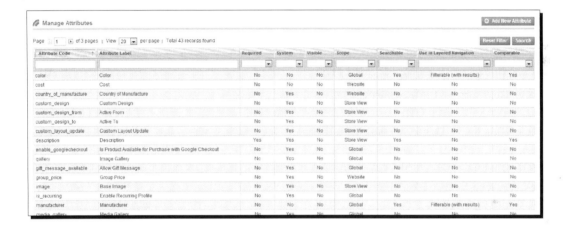

Now that we know what attributes are, let's first have a look at the attributes that Magento already has available by default. Navigate to **Catalog | Attributes | Manage Attributes**. Note that depending on your installation, the number of attributes that is available may differ. If you installed the demo content, there will be more attributes available, which you may not need yourself. In an empty installation, Magento currently offers 43 attributes by default. Most of those are system attributes that are needed to let Magento function properly. You cannot delete those.

You may click on an existing attribute to have a look at its settings, but we'll create our own attribute to explain all the possible settings.

Time for action – creating your own attribute

We are going to create an attribute to be able to enter TV screen sizes, from our previous example.

1. Click on the button in the top-right corner, **Add New Attribute**:

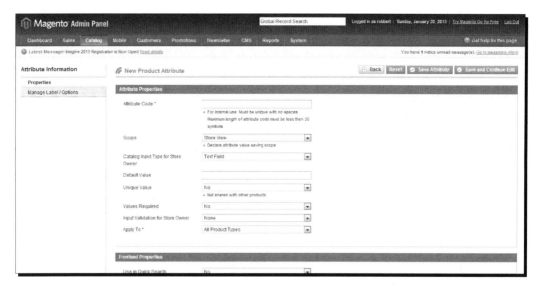

2. A new form appears that is divided into two parts: the **Attribute Properties** and the **Frontend Properties**. We'll start with **Attribute Properties**:

1. First, choose a name for your attribute, in the **Attribute Code** field. Use a name that makes sense: that describes what this attribute will be used for. The name must be unique. In our example, we use **screensize** for the screen sizes of the TVs we are going to sell. Do not use capitals or spaces in your name.

2. Next, select the scope for your attribute. Now, at the first thought you would think, if the screen size of a TV is 42 inches on one website, it is likely that it will have the same size if I use the product on a different website, isn't it? Well, yes, but don't go too fast. If I'm selling my TVs in more than one country, it could be that in one of my stores I'll show the screen size in inches, whereas in another store I'll show it in centimeters. I don't want risk that now so I'll leave the **Scope** field to **Store View**:

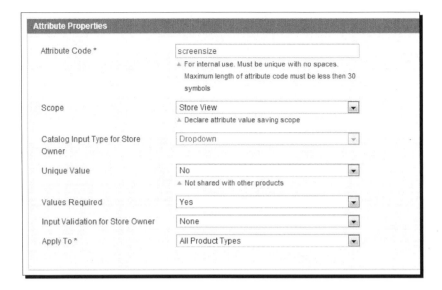

3. The third field, **Catalog Input Type for Store Owner**, is an important one. Using this setting you determine how the values for this field should be entered, once you're going to create products with this attribute in it. You may choose between a **Text Field** or **Text Area** types; for list prices you use the **Price** type. Or use a simple **Yes/No** (Boolean) type for your attribute.

Note that not all types can be used for layered navigation. The **Dropdown** field that we've chosen here can be used for layered navigation. But even more important, it gives us the possibility to preenter the possible values, so that no typographical errors will be made. TV screens generally come in fixed sizes. A TV screen is, for instance, 32, 40, or 42 inches. I've never seen one of 35.5 inches. Because of this behavior the **screensize** attribute is an excellent candidate for the **Dropdown** field.

4. Next, we set the **Unique Value** field to **No**. If you set it to **Yes**, every product using that attribute will need a unique value in that field, so no duplicates are allowed. A typical example of such a field is the item number (SKU).

5. **Values Required** simply determines whether a field can be left empty when creating a product. If this field is set to **Yes**, the user must make a choice.

6. **Input Validation for Store Owner** is not required in our example, but this field can be used to make sure that the entered value follows a certain rule. For example, if the value entered by the user needs to be a number, you may choose to check for **Integer** (a number without any decimals) or **Decimal** (a number that can include decimals) input validation.

7. Finally, the **Apply to** field lets you decide for which kind of products this attribute could be useful. We'll explain more on different product types in *Chapter 4*, *Simple Products*, and *Chapter 5*, *Beyond Adding Simple Products*. For now, just keep the default value, which makes the attribute available for all kinds of products.

3. The next part of our attribute form contains the frontend parameters. Using these we can set the behavior of our attribute and decide what the website visitor can and cannot do with it:

   ❏ To let the user search for this product attribute, set the fields **Use in Quick Search** and **Use in Advanced Search** both to **Yes**.

   ❏ Set the **Comparable on Front-end** field to **Yes** to let the user compare several products using this attribute. In our example, it makes sense to let the user compare various TVs, where the screen size is one of the fields that will be shown in the comparison.

   ❏ We also chose to set the **Use in Layered Navigation** to **Filterable (with results)** field. This means that the visitor of the website can use Magento's layered navigation function to select all products with a specific screen size, which makes the product selection user-friendly. There are two other possibilities for this field, which we will explain:

   ❏ **Filterable (no results)** has almost the same result. The difference being that, in our situation, the layered navigation would show all screen sizes available, even those for which we have no products.

   ❏ **Filterable (with results)** will only show screen sizes for which we actually have products. The third possibility for this field is **No**, which simply means that the attribute will not be shown in the layered navigation on the frontend.

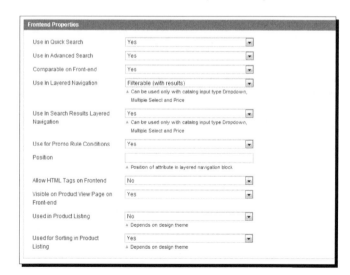

❑ If **Use In Search Results Layered Navigation** is set to **Yes**, Magento adds this attribute to the layer navigation panel on the frontend when products bearing this attribute are displayed in the search results.

❑ We haven't spoken yet about Magento's possibilities to organize promotions/discounts. By setting the **Use for promo Rule Conditions** field to **Yes**, it would in our case give us the possibility to do a promotion that says, "10% Off on all 40" LED TVs!" We want to keep that option open, so we say **Yes**.

❑ The **Position** field can be used to sort the various attributes in the layered navigation in a particular order. Does it make sense to let a user first select the screen size, and then further drill down by price? Set a number in this field (the lowest number shows on top).

❑ **Allow HTML Tags on Frontend** is especially helpful if you have text fields that could be filled using HTML codes (such as a description, for example). In our situation we do not need it.

❑ **Visible on Product View Page on Frontend** will be set to **Yes** to make sure that the screen size is actually visible to users looking for specifications for our products. An example of those product details can be found in the following screenshot.

 Please note that setting this field to **No** means that the attribute can still be used, but the visitor of your website won't see it in the frontend. The following example shows three more product attributes: the Description, the Contrast Ratio and the Response Time for a computer monitor.

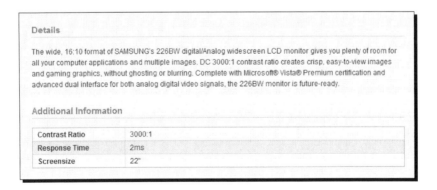

❑ The last two fields can be used to determine if your attribute will be visible in the List view and if your attribute can be used to sort products. We set the last field to **Yes**, because it sometimes makes sense for visitors to sort TVs from a smaller to a larger screen size.

Please note that its working actually depends on your Magento theme. In the standard theme, it will be no problem of course, but in custom themes, this function (among others) must actually be added by the programmer of the theme.

4. Aren't we there yet? No, although we just need to take the last steps. We've done everything for our attribute besides two things: we haven't specified the labels yet. The attribute label is the name that the user will see in the frontend. It makes sense that this can differ from store view to store view, especially when you are working with multiple languages. Besides that, we also need to specify the possible values for our drop-down list:

The preceding example shows what you should do. First, specify the labels. Of these, the label for the Admin area (that is the Magento backend) is mandatory. If you ever use this attribute in a store view for which no label has been defined, the Admin value would be used.

Underneath the labels, we can specify all options for our drop-down list. Click on the **Add Option** button to add a new row and fill all values according to your needs.

Note that it is possible to enter the values per store view again. In the preceding example, this means that if the user creating the product selects a value of **22inches**, our visitors in the frontend will actually see **22"**. And if I had a second store view, I could easily show **56cm** to visitors from a country using that particular metric.

5. That's it. Just click on **Save Attribute** on the top of the page.

If we were to really start selling TVs, we probably also would want to create additional attributes such as dimensions, weight, type, and so on. In that case, just repeat the process mentioned to create the needed attributes.

Using attribute sets

An attribute is useless if it doesn't belong to an attribute set. When creating products you do not individually choose attributes that you need. The very first step when creating a product is always to tell Magento which attribute set you want to use. As already mentioned, you cannot change the attribute set of your product later on. To be able to use our freshly-created attribute, we need to add it to a set. Yes, of course, it is possible to use one attribute set only and just add all attributes to that one. But that won't be smart, because it would mean that suddenly for my TV the heel height could become a mandatory field. And it would even be shown to our visitors! No, that's not the way to do it, you need to create an attribute sets per product group, for items using the same attributes.

Navigate to **Catalog | Attributes | Manage Attribute Sets** to check what's already available:

Nothing much, right? Just one default set. If you installed the Magento demo content, you'll have additional sets predefined. These sets are more than what you need and in that case, you might even need to clean them up before setting up your own.

Time for action – creating your attribute set

We are going to create a new attribute set for our TV product group using the following steps:

1. Click on the **Add New Set** button on the top-left corner.

2. When creating a new attribute set, it always has to be based on an existing one, to make sure that all mandatory (system) attributes are copied in automatically. Just enter a name that makes sense for your set and save it.

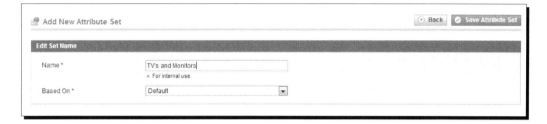

3. In the following screenshot you'll see all available attributes. Most of them have already been selected. Those were copied from the default set:

Those system attributes cannot be deleted from the attribute set. If you're carefully looking at the list, you'll notice that the attribute named **Cost** can be deleted. It doesn't have that red stop sign on its icon. Adding and deleting attributes is as simple as dragging-and-dropping them.

4. In our case we are going to add our **screensize** attribute. And we'll add the Manufacturer as well. In your situation there can be other attributes that you'd like to add to the set. Note that it's possible to create groups of attributes so that everything that logically needs to stay together can be grouped. A practical approach would be to put your own attributes all together in a group named **Custom** as shown in the following screenshot:

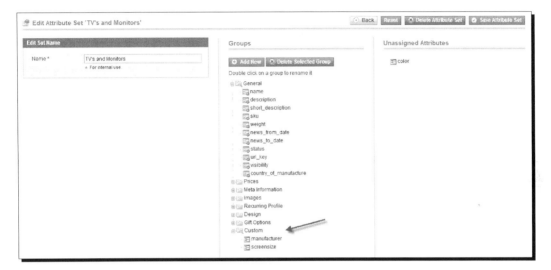

5. Once done, just save your attribute set for later use when creating your products.

It's possible to change attribute sets, even if there are already products created with them. But be careful with deleting attributes from an existing set. Doing so could cause a loss of data!

Using categories

Now that we're done with attributes and attribute sets, we are going to take the last step before we can finally start adding our products. We need to create a category structure to logically put our products in a tree.

Navigate to **Product Catalog | Manage Categories**. In the page that opens, your category tree is on the left-hand side. The right part of the screen is used when you create a new or edit an existing category.

A category tree in Magento always starts with the top level, the root category. Under the root category the subcategories on the top level will follow, which will also be the first level that will become visible in your Magento menu:

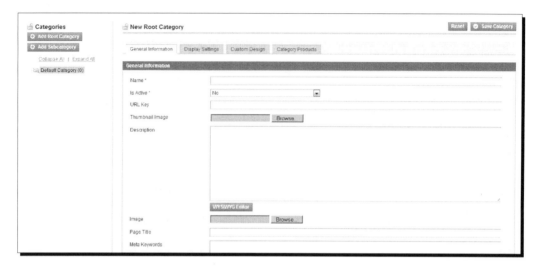

Remember that your root category is connected on a store level to your online shop? Store views within that particular store will all use the same root category and thus category structure.

In an empty Magento installation there's only a default (root) category available. You must create all categories under that one, or start with a brand new root category if you want to. If you installed the demo content, there will already be a couple of categories and subcategories available. Again, if this isn't what you need then starting from scratch is easier.

Continuing our example, we create a number of categories that we can use for our store. But let's start with one to explain the available fields.

Time for action – creating your first category

We are going to create the main category for our TVs, which will be a category named **Video**:

1. We start with renaming our **Default** root category to something that is more descriptive. Just click on the name, change it on the left and save your category:

2. Next, click on the top-left corner on the **Add Subcategory** button. Even your main categories are named **subcategories** in Magento!

3. Fill in the name of your category in the **Name** field and keep in mind that it will be visible to your audience. If you set the **Active** field to **Yes**, the category will immediately become visible for your visitors. Next, you may enter a URL key for your category in the **URL Key** field that will be used to create the URL for your category page. If you leave it blank, the URL key will be filled automatically by Magento, based on the name you entered.

4. Whether or not to fill the **Thumbnail Image**, **Description** and **Image** fields depends on your theme. Using the default Magento theme these will be used, but we often see themes that do not use these fields.

5. The **Page Title** value is shown in the search engines and important for your SEO. Keep it short, but use the relevant keywords in it. The **Meta Keywords** values are hardly used anymore by search engines. You may put in a few, but do not expect any positive results of it anymore. On the other hand, the **Meta Description** value is still important for the search engines. Carefully create a short description with your most important keywords included. Finally, if you want to show this category in the navigation menu for your visitors, keep the **Include in Navigation Menu** field on **Yes**.

6. Save your category and continue on the second tab:

In here, you can make the following choices: **Display Mode** lets you decide what should be shown on the category page. The default is **Products only**, which will indeed only show products to your audience (below the description and image if you've chosen to use those). It's also possible to select a static block. This gives the possibility to show other content instead of products. And it is possible to use as well a static block and products below that. More information on using a static block is available in *Chapter 9, Customizing Your Store's Appearance*.

1. The **Is Anchor** field is used for the layered navigation. If it is set to **Yes**, the layered navigation will show the subcategories under this category. The **Available Product Listing Sort By** field lets you decide which sorting options you want to give to your visitors when they are browsing this category. It makes sense to keep all options open and leave the default, but if you want to change it, you may switch off the checkbox and enable the sort options you'd like to give to your users.

2. The same applies to the **Default Product Listing Sort By** field. The default is a value that makes sense, but you are able to change it by switching off the checkbox and selecting a different one.

3. For **Layered Navigation Price Step**, enter the size of the price range to be used when calculating the price ranges for the layered navigation. This is determined by the catalog configuration we saw earlier in this chapter, but you can clear the checkbox to specify a price range size for this category. Normally, you do not have to change it.

The **Custom Design** tab has settings that give control over the theme layout for this category page. Since we haven't spoken about any layouts and themes yet, we do not discuss the possibilities here. For now, you may keep the defaults. You'll learn more on this topic in *Chapter 9, Customizing Your Store's Appearance*.

The last tab, named **Category Products**, shows which products are connected to this category, so when we create it, everything will still be empty. From within this tab it's also possible to quickly add products to this category, giving you a shortcut instead of opening and adding products one by one. Since we are just building our category tree now, we'll not yet add any product.

Once you create subcategories, it's easy to get them in the right place in the hierarchy by selecting the main category first. Alternately, if they show up in the wrong spot, you can drag-and-drop them to the right place. Note that your main and subcategories often directly impact the top navigation of your store in most themes.

After saving your category once more, you may simply continue adding more categories on different levels. Please note that it is possible to reorganize the categories by simply dragging-and-dropping them the way you want.

The final result for our store could look as follows, where more categories could be added once our product range starts expanding:

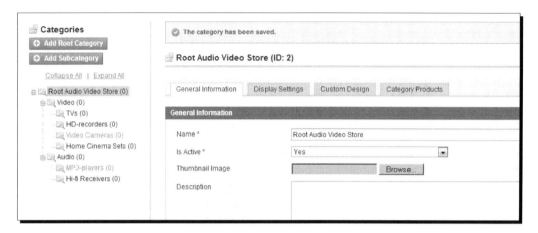

Summary

You've learned what product attributes are and how to use them in an attribute set. Next, we created a category structure for our store. From here, everything is in place to start adding our first products, which we'll do in our next chapter.

4
Simple Products

All preparations for our product catalog have been done. We have made the settings we needed, created attributes and attribute sets and we created a tree structure of categories. Finally, we'll be able to add our very first products.

In this chapter we will learn:

- Creating simple products, the easiest and most used product type
- Understanding all product attributes that you'll need to create simple products the right way

Within Magento you may use various types of products. You'll need them depending on what your store is going to offer. The more complex product types will be discussed in *Chapter 5, Beyond Adding Simple Products*. In this chapter we'll only discuss the simplest type: **Simple Products**. A typical example of a Simple Product is one that does not have any options for the buyer. This could be our TV from the previous chapter, a phone, bag, office supplies, and so on. The Simple Product is the most used product type in Magento, especially because other types use the Simple Product to create a new one.

Adding a Simple Product

Adding a Simple Product requires several steps. We are going to use the TV example for these steps.

Step 1 – creating a product and assigning an attribute set

Navigate in the top menu to **Catalog** | **Manage Products** and the following dialog will open:

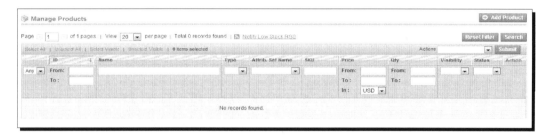

If you're in a Magento instance including the demo content, a list of already existing products will be shown here. In our case we started empty, so we have a completely empty product catalog.

In the top-right corner, click on the **Add Product** button.

The first thing you need to do know is to select the **Product Type** and **Attribute Set** that this product will belong to. So, leave the default value of **Simple Product** and select the **Attribute Set** field for your product as shown in the following screenshot. You cannot change that later on!

Lastly, click on **Continue**.

Step 2 – the General tab

Next, the product maintenance screen appears, starting with an empty page. This is the first tab on the left of the screen, named **General**. In total there should be 13(!) tabs, giving you a lot of opportunities to do what you need for your product. But, in our situation, we see one additional tab, which isn't there by default, named **Custom**. This tab exists because we defined it that way in our attribute set for TVs and monitors in the previous chapter. So, the number of available tabs will not always be the same; it depends on the attribute set. We'll not discuss every single tab and field here, but focus on the things that we'll absolutely need to know to be able to create our products.

But let's first focus on our **General** tab and fill that one with the necessary data. In the following example screenshot, we have already filled in some data to make clear what the fields are used for:

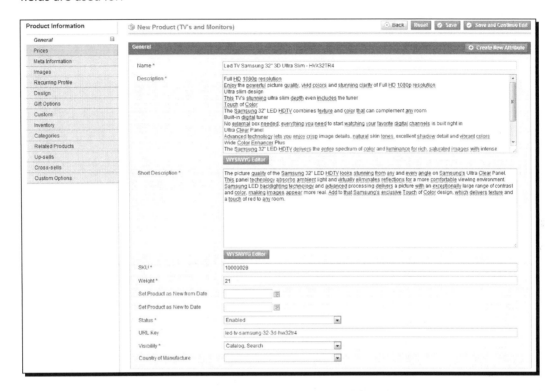

Time for action – filling the General tab

1. The fields **Name**, **Description**, and **Short Description** are all very important. They are used to introduce the product to your visitors, but they are also important for the search engines.

 Note that the **Short Description** field is used before the **Description** field on your product page! Somehow Magento decided to switch the sort order here in the **General** tab.

2. Let's have a look at where we'll see these fields in the frontend of your store:

 Often in software programs or websites, the *mandatory fields* are all marked with an asterisk (*). These fields are required. If you leave one of them empty, you will not be able to save your product. If you try to save the page, the tabs on the left of the screen turn red indicating that there are one or multiple mandatory fields that have not been set.

Looking at the example screenshot, it's clear that we still need to set fields such as images and pricing, but that's something we'll do in a minute. For now, take a look at where the **Name**, **Description** and **Short Description** values are used.

Let's go back to our product in Magento and we'll fill those fields with our data:

❑ Start with filling your **Description** and **Short Description** fields. Note that below these fields, there's a **WYSIWYG** (What You See Is What You Get) button. Click on it to open an editor that gives a way to create a better looking text using, for instance, bullet points, bold or italic text, and so on. It's even possible to add images here, but we recommend that you don't use those in your description fields. Magento offers a better way to work with images on your product page, and having an image in your description fields might not be the best choice.

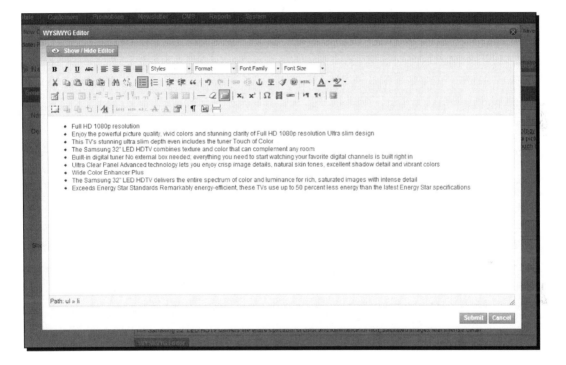

SEO Tip

Do not just copy and paste description and titles that you received from your vendor(s). Create your own unique content; search engines will reward you for it!

- ❑ Fill the **SKU** field. **SKU** stands for **Stock Keeping Unit**, also often referred to as an "item or article number". The **SKU** field must be unique in your Magento installation.

  Although there's a lot that can be said about using these codes, concerning whether or not to use a meaningful code, we don't do it and just use a number value for the field. However, using alphanumeric values is also possible and you could even decide to keep the exact code as your vendor does.

- ❑ The **Weight** field is mandatory as well and can only contain a numeric value. The strange thing is that it is unknown whether this is in lbs or kg. On the other hand, that's good, so you can decide for yourself.

  But be aware to use it consistently throughout your shop, because the weight of a product can be used to calculate shipping prices. Therefore, it makes sense to enter a weight including packaging material and not only the weight of the bare product.

- ❑ The **Set Product as New From Date** and **Set Product as New To Date** fields can be used to mark a product as New! in your shop, just to emphasize it. You could also use this function to show a list of new products in your store.

  The way it looks for your visitors completely depends on your theme. Because it makes sense to do this only for a limited time period we recommend to immediately fill the **End Date** field if you want to use this function.

- ❑ Set the **Status** field to **Enabled** to make sure your product is visible to your audience. A disabled product will never be visible in your store.

- ❑ The **URL Key** field can be set automatically when you save your product, but it is possible to set it manually as well. Just make sure that you do not use any spaces or capitals, and use your most important keywords for this product in it!

  The **URL Key** value is used by Magento to create the link to this particular product page. It's better to keep the **URL Key** field unique as well, but Magento doesn't warn you if you don't.

- ❑ The **Visibility** field is mandatory, but it is set by default. For regular simple products, you do not have to change it. We'll see later on in the next chapter why it might sometimes be necessary to use a different value.

- ❑ The **Country of Manufacture** field is optional and is sometimes needed by companies for mandatory reporting.

Step 3 – the Prices tab

Magento offers extended possibilities to work with sales prices for your products. There are two mandatory fields in this tab, so we always have to visit this tab when creating our products.

Time for action – filling the Prices tab

1. The **Price** field is mandatory and contains your regular sales prices. If nothing fancy is needed and you just want to quickly set one sales price only, use this field for it. The extended currency is filled automatically based on the settings you made earlier in *Chapter 2, General Configuration*.

2. The **Group Price** field can be used if your store is servicing different customer groups that need different sales prices. As an example, you could think of a shop with members, where the members receive better prices than a casual visitor.

   More on working with customer groups will follow in *Chapter 6, Customer Relationships*. We do not use the group price in our example, but if you want to, just click on the **Add Group Price** button, select your customer group and enter the sales price. The **Prices** tab would look something like the following screenshot:

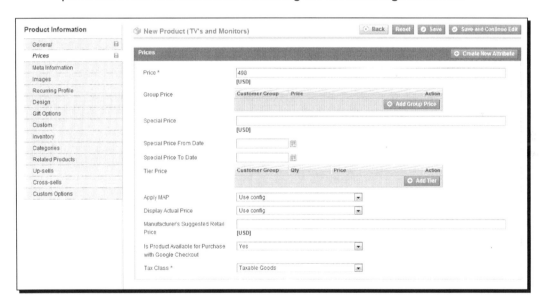

3. The **Special Price** field can be used to offer a special (usually lower) price. In the frontend of your store, you'll see both the prices, where the current, lower price is emphasized. The exact way that it is shown depends on your theme. This field is often used together with the **Special Price From Date** and **Special Price To Date** fields, so that the temporary price will only be valid for a limited time period.

4. The **Tier Price** field is interesting, because you can use this to calculate a lower price, depending on the number of products a customer buys. Tier pricing is especially useful in cases where you want to do a "*Buy 5, pay for 4*" promotion or anything similar. In our TV example, we do not need it of course, but if you want to use it, click on the **Add Tier** button, select a customer group, minimum quantity, and special price.

5. The last really important field of this tab is **Tax Class**. Remember that we discussed **Tax Class** earlier in *Chapter 2*, *General Configuration*. This is the field to connect **Tax Class** to your product. Often, all of your products will be in the same tax class, but if you need to calculate various tax rates, which depend on the product, this is the place to set it.

Step 4 – the Meta Information tab

We have already slightly touched the topic of **Search Engine Optimization (SEO)** in this book, but in this tab things become important. The **Meta Information** tab holds a couple of fields that will become visible in the search engines directly.

Time for action – filling the Meta Information tab

There are three fields in this tab, of which only two are important:

◆ The **Meta Title** field will be used by search engines to display our product. Use your most important keywords at the beginning. This title will be used by the search engines as the heading of your product listing. Create an informative title that describes your product and do not use more than 70 characters.

◆ The **Meta Keywords** field was important for search engines in the past. The more keywords you put in, the better it was. But almost all search engines are ignoring this field nowadays and you may just as well leave it empty.

◆ The **Meta Description** is important, because this will appear in the results of the search engines again. Keep it short and attractive though! Unfortunately, Magento doesn't assist you here, but generally you could say that the search engines will only show the first 160 characters. The **Meta Information** tab looks like the following screenshot:

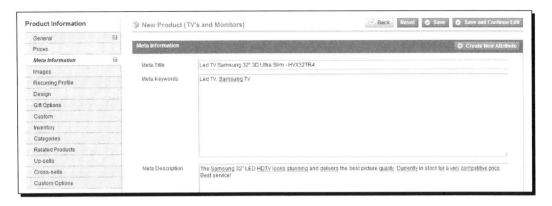

Step 5 – the Images tab

Not only is an image worth a thousand words, images (together with reviews) are the most important part of your product page. Without good images you're very likely to fail in the process of selling your products. Working with images is not always simple for beginners though. Especially when you have to create your own images, it's not always easy to create good results. When you're not used to tools such as Photoshop, PaintShop Pro, Gimp, or any other photo editor, you should definitely spend the time learning it. Believe me, it's worth it.

Magento works with different image sizes, named **Base Image**, **Small Image**, and **Thumbnail**. Let's first go through what these different images are used for:

- **Base Image**: This will be the main product image in the highest quality. It is used on the product page and you should give your audience the possibility to zoom in. There are no real fixed rules for sizing this image type, but generally we could say that anything with a width of around 800 pixels could be suitable. Smaller image sizes will be accepted and will work, but your visitors will not be able to zoom your images when the width is lower than about 300 pixels. Whether or not the 800 pixels are enough depends on the product you are selling.

- **Small Image**: The Small Image is used on the product grid and list pages, where multiple products per page will be shown. The needed size depends a bit on your theme (how many image images will be displayed next to each other), but on average we could say that an image between 150 and 300 pixels width should be OK.

◆ **Thumbnail**: This is really a tiny image, only used to display your products on the cart of your store, or in a list view such as "New Products" or "Most Popular Products". Generally, an image width of around 80 pixels should be more than enough.

You will use these three image types usually with the same image, just using different sizes! Besides these three images, it's also possible to add additional images to your product, to show different angles or a really detailed photo, for example. The three images are needed, but you are not limited to those.

The file size of your images is very important. The larger your image files, the slower your website will respond. Verify in your favorite image editor how to obtain the smallest images sizes, without delivering too low quality images. You may also use online tools such as **SmushIt** (`http://smushit.com`) that can help reducing the file size of your images.

Time for action – filling the Images tab

1. Opening the **Images** tab shows an empty screen for a new product. Click on the **Browse Files...** button to start selecting your images:

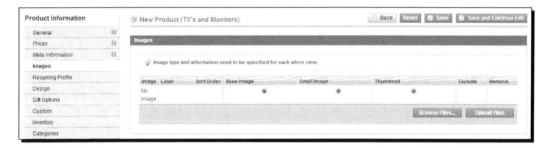

2. Select the first file you'd like to add using your operating system and open it. Click on the **Upload Files** button to add your image to Magento. When you're just starting, we recommend you do this image by image. Once you're familiar with this function, you may just as well upload multiple images at once. Magento allows you to do so.

3. Now that your image has been uploaded, you can see it on the left of the table by hovering over it with your mouse cursor. You should set the correct radio button for your image type. In this example, I just added our largest image, so I select the **Base Image** radio button. Technically it's possible to also switch on the other two buttons and only use one image file. However, we recommend that you create separate images for every type, to keep the file size and quality of the images as good as possible.

4. Fill the **Label** field of your image since it will be used as the image's **Alt** attribute. And that's another field that is important for the search engines. Do not underestimate the power of this field and always enter those labels.

5. Add the two other images as well (for the Small Image and Thumbnail) and set the radio buttons accordingly. Next, click on the **Exclude** checkbox for these two images; otherwise they will be used on the product page as well. If you do not exclude them, you would see three similar images on the product page, but in different quality. Look at the result of our example to see how your fields should be set:

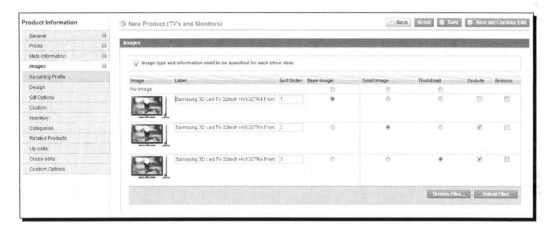

6. If you made a mistake with one of your images and added the wrong one, you can remove it again by clicking on the **Remove** checkbox. Your image will not be deleted immediately; this will happen once you save your product.

7. If you have them available, add additional images as well. Normally, these additional images will appear on your product page under the main image. It makes sense to use a higher resolution (preferably 800 pixels of width or more) for these images, so that these can also be used for zooming by the user.

 Note that there should always be a balance between picture detail and image size. For these additional images, you do not click on any radio button or checkbox.

The final result could look something like the following screenshot:

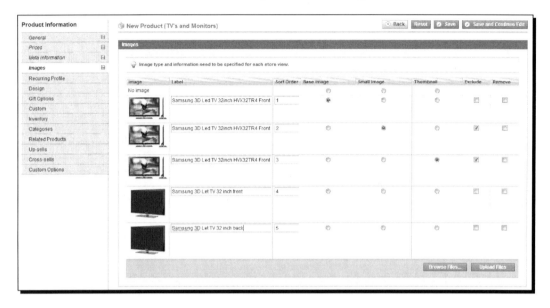

Once our product has been saved, the result in the frontend looks good. Note that the default Magento zoom function will not win any prizes. This is something that can be improved by your theme or by using an extension.

What just happened?

You took the very first steps in creating a product in Magento. You created descriptions, price information, and meta tags for the search engines and images. But we aren't there yet, there are a couple of additional tabs that you should fill before your product will be visible.

For a beginner's guide, the **Recurring Profile**, **Design**, and **Gift Options** tabs are out of scope, but we would still like to mention them briefly, so that you know what they could be used for:

 ◆ **Recurring Profile**: This is a function that can be used to handle recurring payments, for instance, if you're selling a subscription service, where your customers have to pay a monthly fee. The **Recurring Profile** function gives the possibility to do that, but it's currently only working in combination with the payment method PayPal Express checkout.

 ◆ **Design**: This tab can be used to give the product page for this product a different design compared to the one that is used by default in your theme. This could be useful when you need to create a landing page or special promotion. However, using this technique is not so easy, because you need deeper knowledge about XML and the way Magento themes are built.

 ◆ **Gift Options**: This tab holds only one field, which you can enable to let your customers add a special text to the product. For instance, when they are ordering the product as a gift for someone else. Just set the field to **Yes** if you want to use it.

Step 6 – the Custom tab

The **Custom** tab will or will not be there, depending on the steps you take when creating your own attribute sets. We've defined a special group named **Custom** in our attribute set, and it appears here in our product creation page. It even holds a mandatory field, because we defined it to be mandatory, so we cannot ignore it here. But be aware that by default this tab does not exist in Magento.

Time for action – filling the Custom tab

1. There are only two fields in our example attribute set as shown in the following screenshot, but yours could have much more, or it might not even exist. In here, we have two fields that we need to set: **Screensize** and **Manufacturer**. The values that are available have been set during the maintenance of our attributes:

 Note that it is even possible here to create additional instant attributes with the top-right button named **Create New Attribute**. If you do so, the attribute maintenance form will pop up, giving you the possibility to create additional fields on the fly. However, although this is possible, we do not really recommend it. You should think about your attributes and attribute sets thoroughly before starting to add products.

Note that we've now filled all mandatory fields. This means you may now save the product. Do that, to prevent any loss of data. It has already happened a lot to me that when I was creating items in Magento, the phone rang; I had to do something else and was logged out of the system after a while. Don't let that happen and regularly save your work!

Use the **Save and Continue** button to save and stay on the same page. If you click on the **Save** button, your work will be stored as well, but you'll leave the current page and return to the product overview page. Of course, you can always come back to your product and add any missing data.

Step 7 – the Inventory tab

The next tab we'll need to look at is the **Inventory** tab. Do you need to keep track of stock levels in Magento? And if yes, how? What will happen if an item is no longer in stock; can we still sell it and take a backorder or should we prevent the user from buying such an article? Having a clear inventory status of your products is not only important for you, but your visitors will appreciate it as well if it is completely clear for them whether an item is available on stock or not.

Time for action – filling the Inventory tab

1. First of all, you will see that a lot of fields in the **Inventory** tab have been defaulted to the configuration settings. This means that, by default, Magento will use the settings you made as the default value for these fields.

If it is more convenient for you to change the defaults, go to **System** | **Configuration** | **CATALOG** | **Inventory**. Since we did not discuss these default settings in *Chapter 2, General Configuration*, we'll do it here. Just remember that if you're changing the fields below very often, it might be easier to change the defaults for your situation.

To be able to change the contents of the fields on the item level, first deselect the **Use Config Settings** checkbox and then change the value of your field of choice.

2. The **Manage Stock** field is pretty clear: do you want to keep track of stock levels for this product, **Yes** or **No**? If you set it to **No**, a lot of other fields will disappear, because they are no longer relevant in that case. The **Inventory** tab looks like the following screenshot:

3. If managing stock levels, you must enter a starting stock value in the **Qty** field.

Remember that this value is in the unit of measure you're selling your products in. As an example, if you have 900 pairs of socks in stock, but sell them only in packages of three pairs, you would enter 300 here.

4. The **Qty for Item's Status to Become Out of Stock** field is a minimum value that you can use to have some control levels in your stock. By default this is set to zero, assuming that you can sell every single piece you have available.

5. **Minimum Qty Allowed in Shopping Cart** is clear: if there's a minimum number of products your customer should buy, enter it here. Please note that this is on the product level, it has nothing to do with a minimum order value.

6. **Maximum Qty Allowed in Shopping Cart** will block any customer from buying more items in one order than the value in this field.

7. **Qty Uses Decimals** will be needed if, for instance, you're selling something by weight or length. Do you allow the customer to buy 5.5 meters of loudspeaker cable? If yes, set this value to **Yes**.

8. The **Can be Divided into Multiple Boxes for Shipping** field is a new field in Magento 1.7 and can be used for more complex shipping solutions, where it is important to know how to handle the product at shipping. You may leave the default for now.

9. The **Backorders** field is important to set the behavior of Magento when you're running out of stock. You may decide to not accept backorders, accept backorders, or accept backorders including a notification to the customer that the products are actually no longer in stock.

10. The **Notify for Quantity Below** field holds the threshold value for the aforementioned field. A customer will only be notified if the stock value drops below the value of this field.

11. The **Enable Qty Increments** field is used in special circumstances. Set it to **Yes** if you're, for instance, selling wine in boxes of six. If you set this field to **Yes**, another field will appear, which you can use to set **Quantity Increments**:

By setting this to 6, for example, Magento will let your visitors know that they have to buy six or a multiple-of-six items. Trying to order something else will fail and Magento will warn the visitor, explaining that they must order the correct quantity.

Note that if you're selling in boxes of six, and you have six boxes on stock, the **Qty** field should still be set to 36 if you are using this functionality. Of course, we'll not use this function for our TV example, but there are a lot of products where this function comes in handy.

12. Don't forget to set the last field, **Stock availability**, to **In Stock**, otherwise your product might not be visible in the frontend of your store! As soon as you're running out of stock, Magento will automatically change the value of this field. So, remember that whenever you're adding a new stock in Magento in the **Qty** field, you must also check if the **Stock Availability** field has the correct value. Just changing the **Qty** field isn't enough.

> Depending on the configuration of your Magento environment, you may have an additional tab between **Inventory** and **Categories**, named **Websites**. This tab is only visible if you define multiple websites, and this gives you the opportunity to assign the same product on multiple sites.

Step 8 – the Categories tab

If you have already set up your categories before starting to add products, this is an easy step. Just assign the correct categories to your products. It's possible to select multiple categories. If you do not select any category at all, your product will not be visible for visitors through the regular site navigation.

Time for action – filling the Categories tab

1. Just one step here. Open your category tree by clicking on the category folders and select one or multiple categories within it. Magento will show the number of products in a certain category, but will only update that number if you save your product.

> Note that it is also possible to add an item to a category from the **Category Maintenance** page. This is especially helpful if you need to assign a lot of items to one specific category. Instead of opening every single item one by one, you can go to the **Categories** function and add them all at once.

What just happened?

And that completes the final mandatory tab that we had to go through, to create our product. If you did everything correctly, your product should now be visible at the frontend of your store, seen as something like the following screenshot:

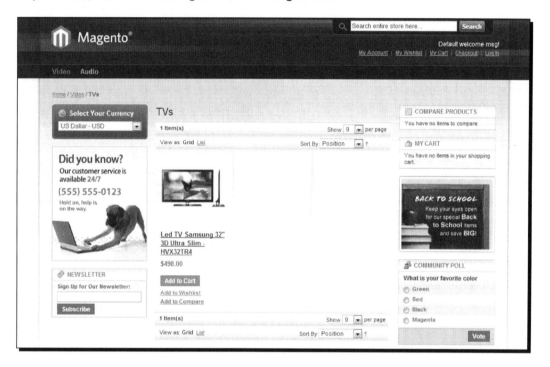

However, we haven't seen all the tabs yet and there are still some interesting functions that we will discuss in the remainder of this chapter.

Before we do so, consider, what if the product you created did not become visible in your store? There can be a number of reasons for this and sometimes it can be frustrating when you're just starting and cannot find the reason. The following are some tips that should help you out:

- First check if your product's **Status** field, within the **General** tab, is set to **Enabled**.
- Just below that, check if the **Visibility** field has the value **Catalog, Search**.
- On the **Inventory** tab, check whether you set the **Manage Stock** field to **Yes**. If you did, make sure you have a **Qty** value more than zero and you set the **Stock Availability** field to **In Stock**.
- Check if you assigned your product to a category in the **Categories** tab.

◆ If you're running multiple websites, you will also see a **Websites** tab. Make sure that your product is assigned to the website, as you need your product to appear in it.

Does everything seem to be correct, but your product is still not showing? Sometimes, it is necessary to rebuild your indexes or flush the Magento cache. Visit **System | Index Management** or **System | Cache Management** to rebuild or flush, if the aforementioned steps do not deliver the desired result. More information on using the index and cache management functions can be found in *Chapter 11, Maintaining and Administrating Your Store*.

Related products, up-selling, and cross-selling

Before looking at the way you can set up related products, and up- and cross-sells, let's first take a closer look at what these actually are and how you can use them in your store to sell more items or products with better revenue.

Related products are—as the name already states—related to another product. To give a few examples: a mouse could be related to a keyboard, video cables could be related to a TV, and ink cartridges could be related to a printer. Related products can also be used to show alternative products within the same product range, although often the up-sell function is used for that purpose.

Generally, in Magento, related products are shown on the product page in a sidebar at the right of the screen. However, the exact position of related products may vary depending on your store's theme.

Up-sell products are used to show your visitor alternative products, generally in a higher price range. The goal is to let the customer view alternatives as well. Generally speaking, a higher sales price means more revenue for the seller. Often, the more expensive products are combined with one cheaper product, to get a more balanced product overview, still pointing your visitor in the direction of buying a product with a higher sales price. Take a look at the products in the following example:

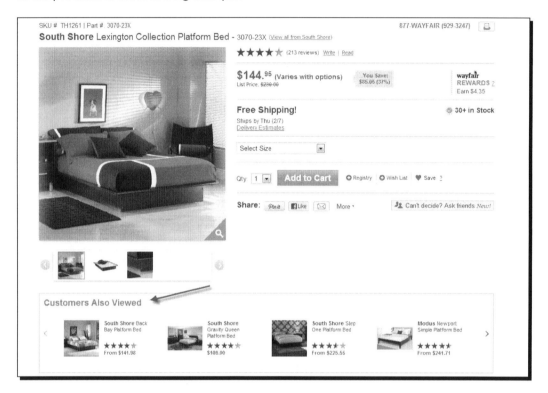

Up-sell products are shown on the product pages, in most cases under the product that you selected. A text such as "Other visitors also bought..." or "These items could be interesting for you..." will help to encourage the visitor to click on those items as well.

Cross-sell products aren't shown on the product page directly, but are shown in the cart or just before checkout. This is the moment when it's possible to sell some additional accessories to your customer, by giving them the possibility to easily add them to their cart. So, where the up-sell tries to sell a similar product, but a different one, the cross-sell tries to add last-minute additions to your cart. For an instance, when you're in the supermarket and see some nice cookies offered just when you're waiting in line to check out your groceries. The following example shows a Magento store that is holding the demo data. Although the shown cross-sell products are not the ones you would expect here when buying a camera, the idea is clear: let the user quickly add additional items just before starting the checkout:

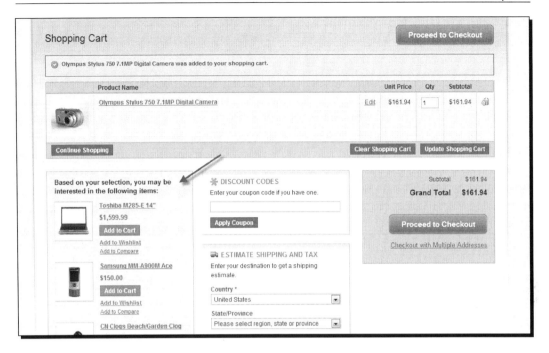

These ideas aren't new and they work online just as well as in real stores. Magento offers the possibility to use them. Whether or not to use them all or just a few depends very much on the product range you are offering.

Adding related products in Magento

The principle of adding related products, up-sell and cross-sell products is the same. Therefore, it's sufficient to show you the procedure for related products.

Adding up-sell products and cross-sell products works exactly the same. You just need to do it on a different tab of your product maintenance page.

 Whether or not related and up-sell items will be shown depends on the Magento theme your store is using. In the default theme, they will be there, but for other themes it completely depends on the creator of the theme if they will be shown.

Time for action – adding related products

Let's return to our TV example, which we created in this chapter. If needed navigate back to it using the menu: **Catalog | Manage Products** and open your product. On the product page, select the **Related Products** tab as shown in the following screenshot:

By default there's an active filter, showing products that have already been set as a related product for this one. Since we haven't set a related product yet, we'll see an empty screen. The easiest way to solve this is to click on the **Reset Filter** button on the right-hand side of the screen. After that, all the products in your store will be visible again:

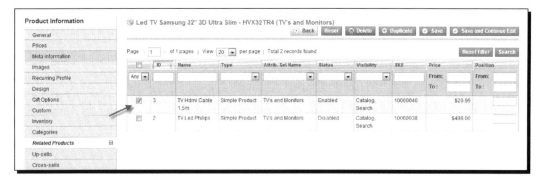

Now it's easy to add a product as related, just click on the checkbox in front of that particular product as shown in the preceding screenshot. It's possible to add multiple products at once. If you already have a lot of products available in your store, you may filter your list by entering a part of the description, for example, and click on the **Search** button. Don't forget to save your product once you're done, otherwise your changes would be lost.

Adding up-sell products and cross-sell products is just as simple as repeating these steps on the other tabs of your product.

Summary

In this chapter you've added your very first products in Magento, congratulations! Having to go through a complete chapter just to add one simple product seems a lot of information and an ineffective process. However, you'll soon learn to quickly create products by just repeating these steps for a couple of products.

In the next chapter we'll go one step further. Magento offers other product types as well, which enables you to sell more complicated products. However, a good knowledge of the simple products is mandatory to be able to follow along.

5
Beyond Adding Simple Products

In the last chapter we added Simple Products to Magento's catalog. It is possible that Simple Products do not suit what you want completely. In that case, some of Magento's other more complex product types may be useful for you.

In this chapter we will discuss the following product types:

- **Virtual product** and **Downloadable product**: This is used to sell a nonphysical or downloadable product
- **Grouped product**: This is used to allow a customer to add multiple products to his/her cart at once
- **Configurable product**: This is used to sell a product that consists of multiple variants where each variant can have its own inventory and product code (**SKU – Stock Keeping Unit**)
- **Bundle product**: This is used to allow a customer to quickly configure and order a whole set of products that belong together

Grouped and Configurable products will receive the most attention as these are in general the product types that are most used besides Simple products. After the different product types have been discussed, the final part of this chapter will explain more about what the three types of product relations (cross-sells, up-sells, and related products) are in Magento as well as how to set them for a specific product.

By the end of this chapter you should know enough to completely set up your store's catalog!

Virtual products and Downloadable products

Virtual products are used to facilitate nonphysical purchases such as house cleaning, a service contract, or an hour of consultancy. Adding a Virtual product is much like adding a Simple product as described in the previous chapter. In the Magento admin, by using the default Magento settings, the most noticeable difference when adding the Virtual product is the absence of the attributes weight, color, and manufacturer.

Adding a Virtual product

In your store's frontend, the difference between a Virtual product and a Simple product can be seen in the checkout process. When a customer orders a Virtual product, the step to select a shipping method will be completely gone!

The first step when adding a Virtual product is to go to **Catalog | Manage Products**. On this screen, click on **Add Product** in the top-right corner. You will be taken to the first step of adding a product: choosing the attribute set and product type. So far, this should be familiar from *Chapter 4*, *Simple Products*. However, now choose **Virtual Product** from the **Product Type** drop-down list instead of **Simple Product** and click on **Continue**:

As stated earlier, the next screen will be much like the product edit screen for adding a Simple product, with the main difference being that some attributes are not available. In this example, we will be adding a Virtual product with the name **House cleaning**.

The easiest way to find your product on the frontend of your store is by searching your store for the product's name. If you cannot find your product in your store, check if the product is enabled, check if it has stock and stock availability is set to **Yes**, and check if the product has been added to the website you're searching on in the **Websites** tab of the product edit screen.

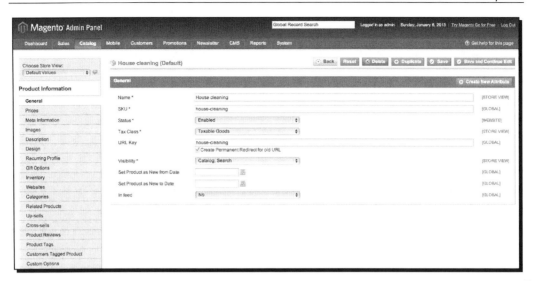

All information pertaining to this product can be filled in in the same way you would do for a Simple product. In the frontend, the resulting product page looks much like a Simple product:

The big difference with a Simple product can be seen in the checkout. First, add the product to the shopping cart. Choose **Proceed to Checkout** when you are in the shopping cart. You will arrive at Magento's one-page checkout process as usual, but look at the checkout steps and you will see that the entire step of choosing a shipping method will be gone.

As a rule more people will finish the checkout if your checkout process is shorter, so always be careful to choose the right product type when adding products, as that way your checkout flow will be as smooth as possible.

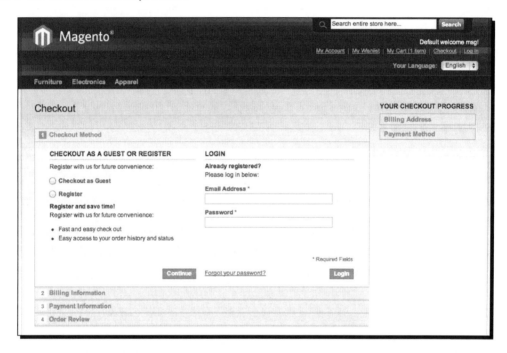

Time for action – adding a Downloadable product

Downloadable products are used to, as the name implies, sell anything that can be downloaded. Examples are e-books, MP3s, videos, images, and software. The process of adding a Downloadable product is much like that of adding a Virtual product, with the addition of a tab on the product edit screen where the download options are set.

1. First go to **Catalog | Manage products**. In this screen, click on **Add Product** in the top-right corner. You will see the screen asking for an attribute set and product type. Now choose **Downloadable Product** from the **Product Type** drop-down list and click on **Continue**:

In this example we'll add a Downloadable product called **Top secret document**. In the left column the final tab is **Downloadable Information**. Compared to the Virtual product, this is where you fill in the additional information pertaining to the download options.

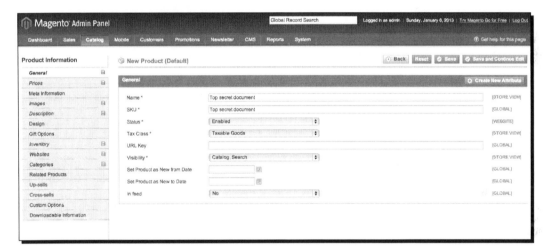

2. Fill in all product information as usual, and proceed to the **Downloadable Information** tab. In this tab, you will see two sections: **Samples** and **Links**. **Samples** are not mandatory; using the **Samples** section you can make a preview of the Downloadable product available on the product page in your storefront. Filling in the **Links** section is necessary; otherwise your Downloadable product will appear out of stock.

3. In this example we shall fill in the **Samples** and **Links** sections. Click on the **Samples** section to expand it. You will see an input field for the title of the sample and an empty table with the headings **Title**, **File**, and **Sort Order**:

4. Magento allows you to add multiple sample files. We shall be adding one; the process is similar if you want to display multiple sample files. To add a sample file, click on the **Add New Row** button in the **Sample** section. You will see a row appear containing an input field for the title of this specific sample row and an input section for the location of this sample row's file. Fill in the general title for the **Sample** section and the title for the sample row. We have picked **Sample of secret document** as the title for the sample section and **First paragraph of secret document** as the sample row's title. Next, Magento should know which file to offer as a sample. There are two choices, either a file upload or a URL. By default the radio button for file upload is selected. A file upload works by pressing the **...** button next to the text saying **File:**, which opens your computer's file browser. Double-click on the file you want to upload and you will see the file's name appear in the row (**sample** in the following example):

5. This does not yet save the file to Magento! The final step is to click on the **Upload Files** button, after which the row slightly changes in appearance to signify the file is uploaded.

The final two columns of a sample row are the sort order and a delete buttons (the delete button is the red button with an X). By using sort order you can adjust in which order samples appear by filling in whole numbers signifying the row's position, if you have used multiple rows. The delete button deletes a sample row.

6. Now save the product and visit it in the frontend of your store. You will see the product is out of stock because the **Links** section is not yet filled, but you can see the information you filled in under the **Samples** section already present!

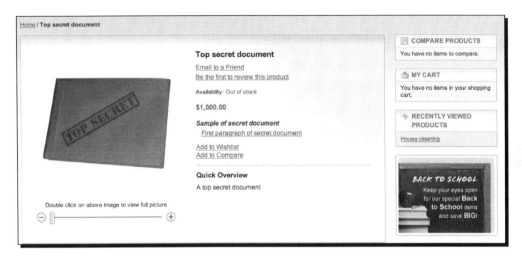

7. Head back to the Magento Admin and open the Downloadable product again. In the **Downloadable Information** tab, the **Links** section will be expanded by default. The first input field in the **Links** section is for the general title of all the links, where we have filled in **The secret document**. The second is a choice whether the downloadable files you add in the **Links** section can be purchased separately or not. We will get back to this choice after discussing the **Links** section so we can show the effect of this choice better.

8. The most important part of the **Links** section is the table where one or more downloadable files can be set. In general, this table functions similarly to the downloadable files table in the **Samples** section. We will be adding two files to the **Links** section: Part 1 and Part 2 of our top secret document. Because we are adding two files, click on the **Add New Row** button twice. This results in the following view:

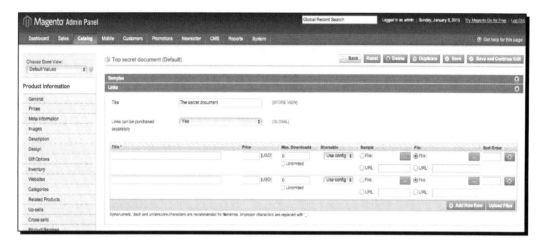

The **Title**, **File**, and **Sort Order** columns have the same purpose as in the **Samples** section. The same goes for the delete buttons. The columns that differ from the **Samples** section are **Price**, **Max. Downloads**, **Shareable**, and **Sample**.

♦ Under **Price**, you can fill in an additional price for a specific downloadable file. For instance, if the base product price is 1000 and we would want to give Part 1 of our top secret document an additional price of 100, the customer would have to pay 1000 + 100 = 1100 for the purchase of Part 1 of the top secret document. Filling in this price is not required and the input field should be left empty unless specific downloadable files, which you are adding, have specific additional costs to your customers.

♦ Under **Max. Downloads** you can set the maximum number of downloads for each downloadable file by filling in a whole number greater than zero in the input field. Magento automatically selects the **Unlimited** checkbox for you if you do not do anything with this column.

◆ Under **Shareable** you will see a drop-down that lets you set the product to be shareable or not. Setting this to **Yes** means that your customers can share the URL of the Downloadable product with others. Generally, this is not desired. The default setting for this drop-down menu is **Use Config**, and Magento's default config value is to not allow sharing of downloadable files. We recommend you to leave it at the default settings and do not change anything in this column.

◆ Under **Sample** you have the option of uploading a specific sample of the downloadable file. This is not mandatory and you can see that no radio button is selected by default.

If you are already using the **Samples** section, filling in the **Sample** column in the **Links** section can be superfluous and confusing to manage. We recommend that you either use the **Samples** section or the sample column in the **Files** section unless you have a solid reason to use both. In our example we have added sample files for download in the **Links** section to be able to show how it will render on the frontend. If you choose to add a sample for a downloadable file in the **Links** section, make sure to click on the radio button for **File Upload** or **URL**, otherwise your sample will not get saved even if you have uploaded the sample file or provided the URL for the sample file.

After filling in the titles and choosing the files for the samples and actual downloads, the table looks as follows:

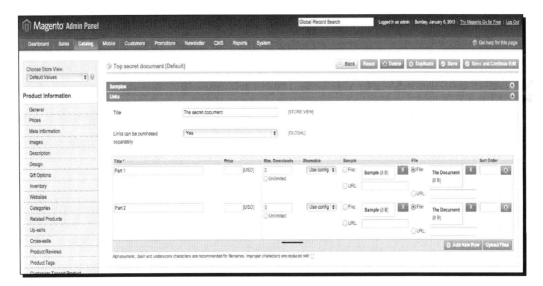

Now the files have to be uploaded by clicking on the **Upload Files** button. After that, the layout changes to the view shown in the following screenshot:

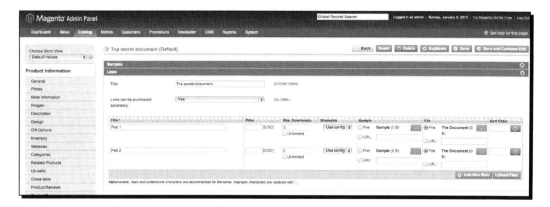

 Uploading a file does not work if the directory permissions for your store are not set correctly. If you are using a local installation, we recommend that you set your full Magento directory open for read and write access from all users. In the Mac section of *Chapter 1, Installation*, we provided some more information about that. If you are using a Magento installation hosted by a hosting provider, please contact your hosting provider for information about fixing directory permission issues.

Finally, after saving the product, the **Downloadable Information** section of our top secret document looks like this:

What just happened?

The storefront will now display the product as shown in the following screenshot. An **Add to Cart** button is now available, and there is a new section called **The secret document**, which is what we filled in as the title for the **Links** section in the **Downloadable Information** section of the product edit screen. Inside the **The secret document** section there are two rows displaying the two downloadable files we added in the backend, including sample links after their titles:

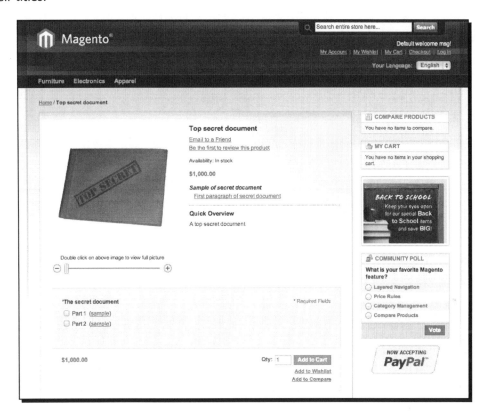

Finally, it's time to discuss the **Links can be purchased separately** option that can be found in the **Links** section of the **Downloadable Information** section of the product edit screen.

By default this drop-down menu is set to **Yes**. Looking at the preceding product page screenshot, you will see checkboxes in front of each downloadable. This happens when the **Links can be purchased separately** drop-down box is set to **Yes**, and means your customers have to select the checkbox for each file they want to order. Setting the drop-down menu to **No** results in a product presentation as shown in the following screenshot, meaning customers do not need to select checkboxes, and they will be able to add all downloadable files to the cart:

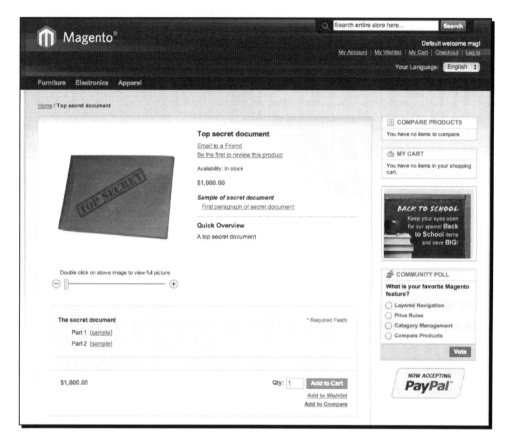

The shopping cart reflects the files that were chosen: both in the following screenshot. After clicking on **Proceed to Checkout**, Magento's one-page checkout appears. Like the checkout for a Virtual product, the shipping method step is gone. There is a difference with the checkout for Virtual products however. Magento links the Downloadable products to customer accounts. Because of this there is no possibility to checkout as a guest anymore!

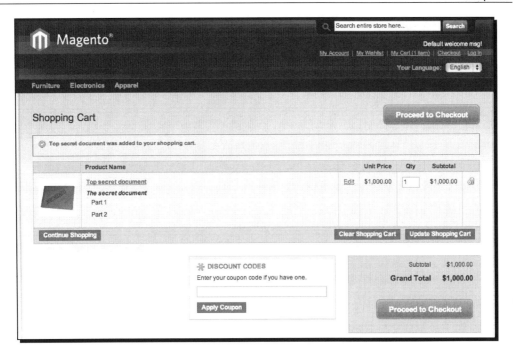

After placing an order, your customers can go to their customer account to get access to their Downloadable products in the **Downloadable Products** section. In it, customers can see which files they have ordered, if they are available and how many downloads are remaining. By clicking on the hyperlinks behind the entries in the **Title** column, customers can download their files.

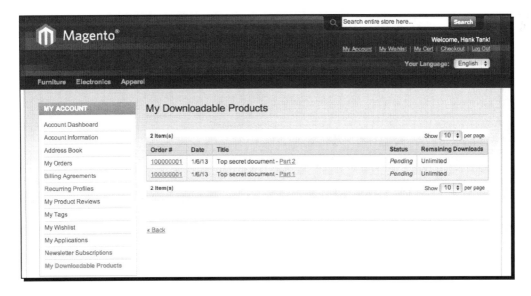

The general configuration settings for Downloadable products can be found at **System | Catalog**, in the **Downloadable Product Options** section:

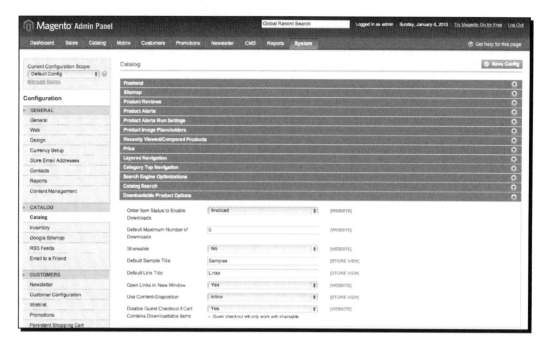

We advise you to leave these options to their default values. The first option is important to be aware of: by default Magento makes downloadable files available to your customers only after your customer's order is invoiced.

> Set the **Links can be purchased separately** choice to **No** if you only have one row in the **Links** section of the Downloadable product. Otherwise, your customers have to mark the checkbox for that single file before they can add the product to their cart, reducing the effectiveness of your product page!

Grouped products

Grouped, Configurable, and Bundle products have in common that they comprise a combination of other products. A Grouped product is displayed in the frontend as a product page where your customers can choose to order multiple individual products in different quantities, in one go. For example, the Magento Red Furniture Set from Magento's sample data displays an order form where quantities for three different products can be filled in. These three products exist as individual products in the store; the Grouped product is a way to present them together. A Grouped product is useful for showing your customers which products go together well:

Time for action – adding a Grouped product

Adding a Grouped product starts in **Catalog | Manage Products**. Click on the **Add to Cart** button and in the next screen, choose **Grouped Product** and click on **Continue**:

The product edit screen that is now displayed should look familiar, with the exception of three things:

 ◆ It is not possible to enter a price for the Grouped product as the purchase price is determined by the underlying products that the customer chooses to add to his/her cart

♦ It is not possible to enter a stock quantity for the Grouped product as the stock information is kept in the underlying products

♦ There is the **Associated Products** tab, where the products that should be displayed in the "add to cart" form in the storefront for this Grouped product should be set

We will name our product "Phone and/or House Cleaning". The products that will be displayed in the "add to cart" form for this Grouped product will be a phone and the House Cleaning Virtual product that we created earlier.

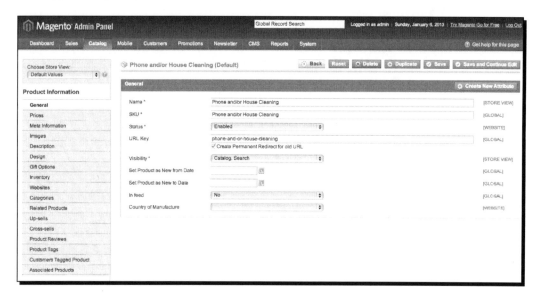

After filling in the regular product information and setting the **Stock Availability** field to **In Stock** in the **Inventory** tab, open the **Associated Products** tab (located at the bottom of the left column). The **Associated Products** tab will show a product grid containing all Virtual and Simple products in your store. This has two implications:

♦ You can only associate Virtual and Simple products to a Grouped product

♦ If you do not have Virtual or Simple products in your store, you cannot display any choices in the Grouped product's add to cart form

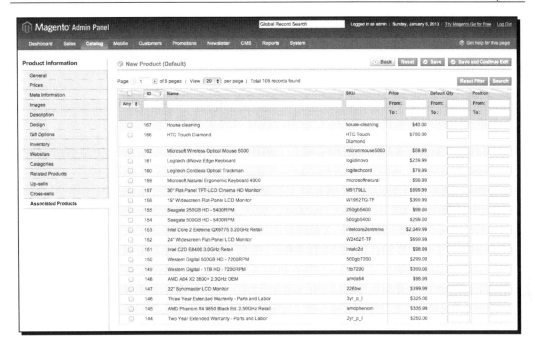

The grid that is displayed in the **Associated Products** tab functions much as other Magento admin grids. It has pagination above the table, and the table has several fields:

- A column with checkboxes
- ID
- Name
- SKU
- Price
- Default Qty
- Position

In the header above the column with checkboxes, you see a drop-down menu, which is set to **Any** when you are adding the Grouped product. The next time you open your Grouped product (after saving), this drop-down menu will be set to **Yes**. The grid will then only show Simple and Virtual products that are already associated to the Grouped product. In that case, set this drop-down menu to **Any** or **No**, and press the **Search** button in the top-right corner to display all or all non-associated products inside the grid.

The **ID**, **Name**, and **SKU** fields display the corresponding Simple and/or Virtual product information. The **Default Qty** field allows you to set a default order quantity for each associated product. By default Magento displays a zero in the add to cart form, if you want some products selected for purchase by default in your Grouped product, you can fill in a one or higher. In the **Position** column, you can enter a non-negative whole number value to indicate the position of the product inside the add to cart form on the product page.

The **ID**, **Name**, **SKU**, **Default Qty**, and **Position** columns are searchable. You can enter a value in each column's header cell and press the **Search** button to look for specific products according to the values you entered.

The product grid in our case displays a heap of Simple products from Magento's sample data as well as the "House Cleaning" product from our discussion of the Virtual product. Associating a Simple or Virtual product with our Grouped product can be done by selecting the checkboxes for the products we want to associate. In our example, we have done so for the "House Cleaning" and "HTC touch Diamond" products.

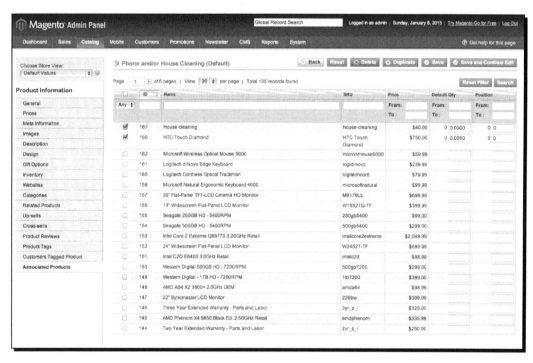

After saving, you can view the product page on the frontend. It should look similar to our example. Fill in a quantity of one, and click on the **Add to Cart** button. The cart will look exactly the same as it would if we had added these products to the cart separately from their respective product pages:

The final screen would be shown as follows:

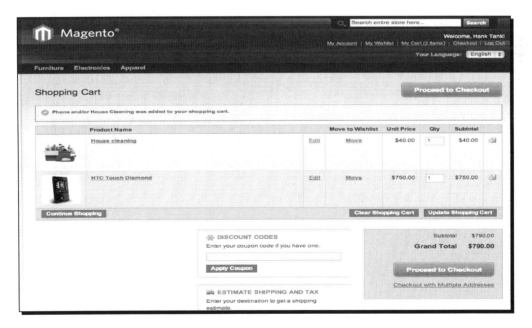

Configurable products

A Configurable product is a product that comprises multiple variants. Each variant in the Configurable product is a separate product in your store as well, and thus can have its own stock management and SKU. A good example for this is clothing, let's say for t-shirts. The Magento sample data contains a t-shirt called "Zolof The Rock And Roll Destroyer: LOL Cat T-shirt". This t-shirt is available in sizes small, medium and large, and in colors green and red. This means there are six Simple products to track stock for:

- Size small, color green
- Size medium, color green
- Size large, color green
- Size small, color red
- Size medium, color red
- Size large, color red

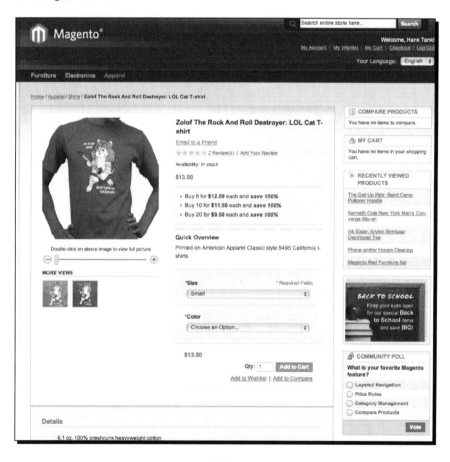

Usually as a store owner you do not want to display all these Simple products as separate products inside your categories. Instead, generally you want to display the Zolof t-shirt once in your catalog and to offer size and color choices (drop-down lists) on the product detail page. This is the use of a Configurable product; the Configurable product only displays color and size combinations that are in stock.

Setting Configurable products in the Magento admin can take some getting used to. A thorough understanding of Magento's attribute system as discussed in *Chapter 4*, *Simple Products*, is very important. If necessary we advise you to (re-)read that chapter before continuing with the following discussion of adding Configurable products.

Time for action – creating a Configurable product

To be able to add Configurable products, you will need product attributes with **Type** set to **Dropdown** and **Use To Create Configurable Product** set to **Yes**. In our example, we will use a product attribute called color, which comes by default in Magento and can be found under **Catalog | Manage Attributes**. The color attribute has a number of possible values that were set by importing the Magento sample data, the values can be seen in the following screenshot. In our example we will use the color values **Red**, **White**, and **Blue**.

 If you do not have the Magento sample data installed, you should go to **Catalog | Manage Attributes**, open the **Color** attribute and add the colors yourself. Additionally, if you do not have the sample data installed, go to **Catalog | Manage Attribute Sets**, open the attribute set called **Default**, drag the color attribute inside it and save the attribute set.

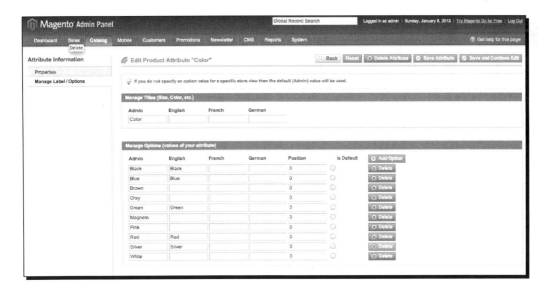

As usual the process of adding a product starts from **Catalog | Manage Products**. After clicking on the **Add Product** button, choose **Configurable Product** and click on **Continue**. The next step will not be the product edit screen yet, but a screen asking you on what attributes the variants of the Configurable product will be based. These attributes are called the **configurable attributes**. In our case this is just color. If you have more attributes in your store that are set to be usable in a Configurable product, check the checkboxes that apply and click on **Continue**. If you were adding a "Zolof The Rock And Roll Destroyer", for example, you would choose the t-shirt size and color here.

This means that in order to work with Configurable products, you first need to know exactly which choices (drop-down lists) you want to display to your customers on the Configurable product's page in your storefront. Only after creating all necessary attributes and their values is it possible to continue with the following steps:

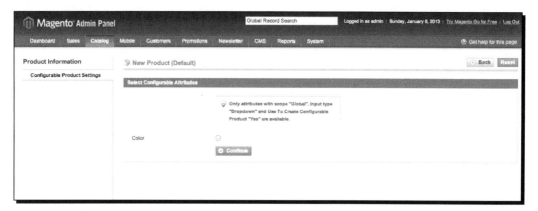

After you have chosen the configurable attributes for your Configurable product, you will arrive in the product edit screen. For this example, we will add a product called "Cube", which will be available in colors red, white, and blue.

Most of the tabs in the left column of the product edit screen are as expected, but just as with the Grouped product, an **Associated Products** tab is present for the Configurable product. Fill in the product's information as usual and proceed to the **Associated Products** tab. This will look like the following screenshot, though your product grid at the bottom of the page may be empty; ours is filled with Magento sample data:

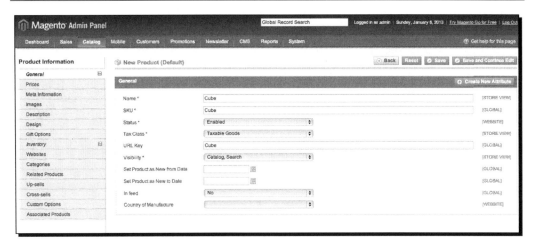

Click on the **Save and Continue Edit** button. Your screen will refresh and you will end up back in the **Associated Products** tab, which will now look differently because a **Quick simple product creation** section has been added:

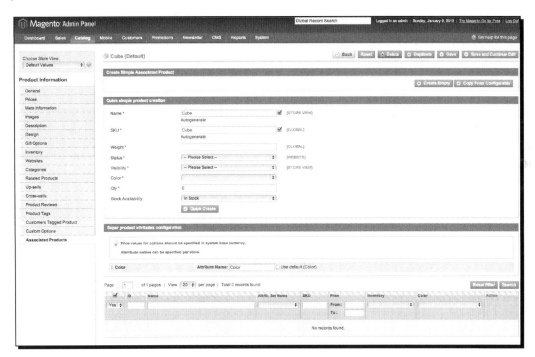

There are two options for associating products to the Configurable product:

- The Simple products you want to associate to the Configurable product *don't* already exist

- The Simple products you want to associate to the Configurable product already exist

Simple products don't already exist

If the Simple products do not already exist, the **Quick simple product creation** section helps greatly. Using this section you can let Magento create the Simple product variants that should be associated to your Configurable product. The different options are as follows:

- **Name**: This is the Simple product's name; we suggest that you leave the checkbox selected (meaning Magento will take care of the naming).

- **SKU**: This is the Simple product's SKU. Often you will want to use your own SKU for the Simple product variants. In that case, uncheck the checkbox and fill in the SKU for the Simple product that you are creating.

- **Weight**: This is the weight of the Simple product.

- **Status**: This is the product status for the Simple product that will be created.

- **Visibility**: This is where the Simple product, which will be created, can be found in your store. We advise setting this to **Not visible individually** as your Configurable product will already be able to be found.

- **Color**: In our case, this is the configurable attribute. If you have chosen other attributes as configurable attributes, you will see them here. After choosing a value, you will be able to specify an additional price for the option. For instance, if size XL costs 40 more than size L for your t-shirts, you can input 40 here. You can specify these as a fixed increase of the product price or as a percentage increase of the product price.

- **Qty**: This is the number of units that are in stock for this Simple product.

- **Stock Availability**: You can choose whether or not the Simple product that is being created is in stock.

After you have set the options to your liking, click on the **Quick Create** button. When you have pressed the button, you can see the **Quick simple product creation** form has remembered all settings except for the configurable attributes' values. Choose the next value (**Blue** in our case) for your configurable attributes and press Quick Create again.

After doing the same again for the **White** option, our page looks like the following screenshot. As we are creating a Configurable product with three variants: **Red**, **White**, and **Blue**, we have three associated products. These can be seen in the product grid of the **Super product attributes configuration** section. In the Zolof t-shirt example previously mentioned, there are three sizes and two colors. In that case, six associated products would need to be created: one for each possible combination.

In the **Super product attributes configuration** section you can see that it is possible to add additional costs for each variant, if you forgot to do so during the quick creation of Simple products. As we have created all the products we want to associate to the Configurable product through **Quick simple product creation**, we don't need to use the product grid further. As a final step, do not forget to save your Configurable product now that the Simple products are created.

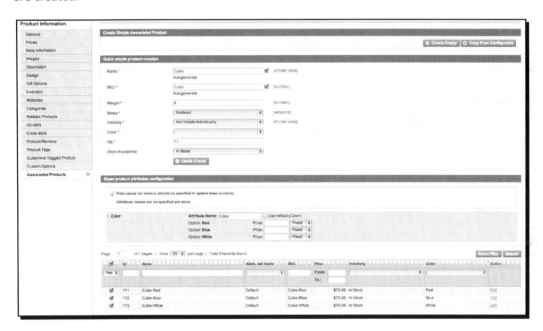

Simple products already exist

If the Simple products already exist in your store, logically it is not necessary to create them using the **Quick simple products creation** tool anymore. Instead, you can associate the Simple products to the Configurable product through the product grid in the **Associated Products** tab. To follow the steps given, please ensure that you have followed the previous section using the **Quick simple product creation** tool, and use the same configurable attributes as you did when following the previous section. That way you will have available the Simple products that you previously created.

To demonstrate associating Simple products that already exist to the Configurable product, we will be adding a second Configurable product called "Cube 2". Add the product using the same steps as previously mentioned: go to **Catalog | Manage Products**, click on **Add Product**, choose **Configurable Product**, click on **Continue**, choose your configurable attributes and click on **Continue** again:

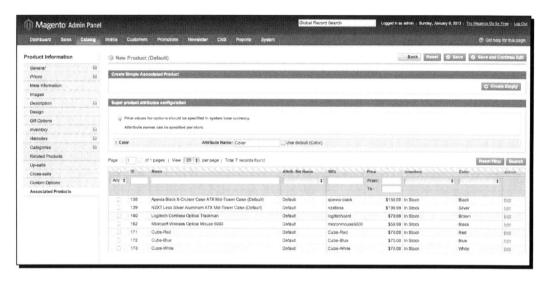

Fill in the product edit screen as you would normally, go to the **Associated Products** tab again and click on **Save and Continue Edit**. As you can see from the screenshots, the product grid can show some products before clicking on **Save and Continue Edit**, but will display none after saving. This is because the product grid is set to only display associated products after saving. In the header cell of the first column of the product grid, set the drop-down menu, which says **Yes**, to **Any** and click on the **Search** button.

Associating the Simple products to the Configurable product now works as it did for the Grouped product mentioned earlier: check the boxes in front of the rows of the Simple products you want to associate to the Configurable product, and click on the **Save** button. In our case, we have checked the boxes for the **Red Cube**, **White Cube**, and **Blue Cube** Simple products.

After that, head back to the product edit screen and the **Associated Products** tab will look the same as in the previous Configurable product, where we used the **Quick simple product creation** tool!

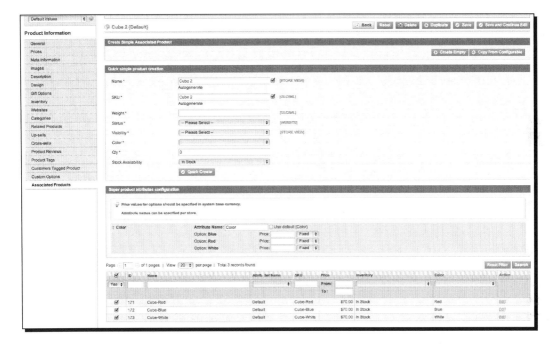

What just happened?

In your storefront, the Configurable product will now show one or more drop-downs menus that reflect the Simple products that are associated to your Configurable product. When the product is added to the shopping cart, the shopping cart reflects that a product with an option that is added to it by displaying the chosen option below the product's name. After proceeding to check out and completing an order for the Configurable product, you can see that the inventory for the option you have chosen will have decreased. In our case, the stock of the Simple product called **Cube** will decrease by one after our purchase:

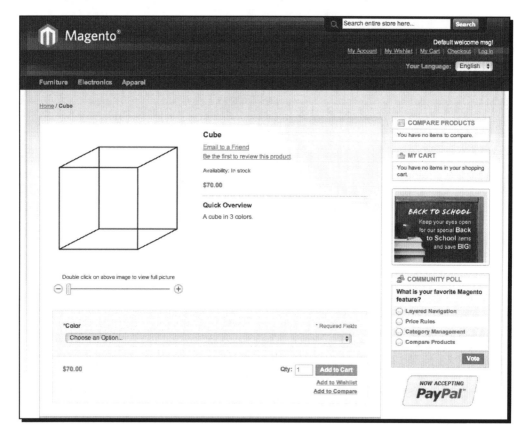

Bundle products

A Bundle product can be used to allow a customer to quickly configure and order an entire set of products that belong together. This is also the thought behind a Grouped product, but a Bundle product takes the concept much further, which is best illustrated with an example from Magento's sample data:

Time for action – creating a Bundle product

As you can see in the screenshot, the Bundle product is very well suited for build-your-own type products, in the example, a personal computer. There are multiple options presented in a different way (radio buttons, drop-down menus, checkboxes, and so on) depending on what is necessary for each option. For instance, it is possible to select multiple peripherals for the computer, but only one choice can be made for the amount of RAM (memory). Every choice that a customer can make for this computer is a Simple product itself and as such able to be sold separately in the store as well.

Besides, the more advanced presentation of the different choices, a Bundle product also differs from a Grouped product because some of the Bundle product's attributes such as its price and weight can be set for the Bundle product itself and item options can be set as required.

Adding a Bundle product starts in the usual fashion, by going to **Catalog | Manage Products** in the Magento Admin Panel. Click on the **Add Product** button, and in the next screen, choose **Bundle Product** in the **Product Type** drop-down menu and click on **Continue**:

The product we will be adding will be called "Hodge-Podge". Most of the input fields should be familiar, but a Bundle product differs from Simple products here:

- ◆ **SKU**: There's an extra drop-down menu where you can choose if the SKU is **Fixed** (the Bundle product will always only have the SKU you specify) or Dynamic (the Bundle product's SKU inside an order placed by a customer comprises the SKUs of the items that were selected when the customer configured the Bundle product). You always need to set a value for the SKU no matter the choice, **Fixed** or **Dynamic**.

- ◆ **Weight**: The **Fixed** versus **Dynamic** drop-down menu is also present here: whether there is one weight for the Bundle that always applies or the weight of the Bundle is determined when a customer is placing his/her order. If you choose **Dynamic**, no weight needs to be entered.

◆ **Price** (in the **Prices** tab): Again, the **Fixed** versus **Dynamic** drop-down menu is present. Here, a fixed price means there is a single price that is always applied to the Bundle, while dynamic means that the price to be paid by the customer is determined based on the items chosen when a customer chooses the Bundle options.

◆ **Price View** (in the **Prices** tab): This specifies if the product's price is shown as only the least expensive (**As Low As**) or as a range, from the least expensive component to the most expensive (**Price Range**).

◆ **Bundle Items** (a new tab): Here all the Bundle product choices are set.

When you get to the **Bundle Items** tab, the first input section is for specifying how the Bundle's items are shipped. The **Ship Bundle Items** drop-down menu has two choices: **Together** and **Separately**. **Together** means that in determining the shipping methods that apply, Magento will consider the entire bundle as one shipment. If the drop-down menu is set to **Separately**, Magento will consider the Bundle product order as an order for multiple separate products for the purposes of showing relevant shipping methods:

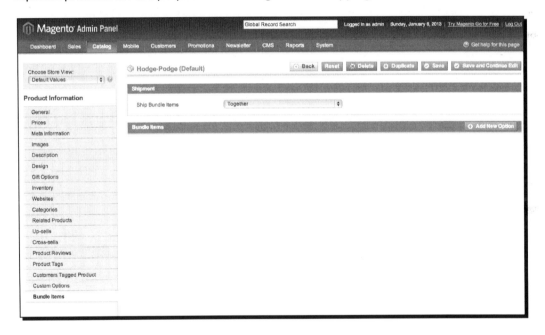

The **Add New Option** button starts the process of adding Bundle options. Taking the multitude of ways a Bundle product can be set up into account, our discussion of adding these options will be relatively short. We will demonstrate adding a checkbox and drop-down Bundle option and leave exploring the other types of Bundle options as an exercise to the reader:

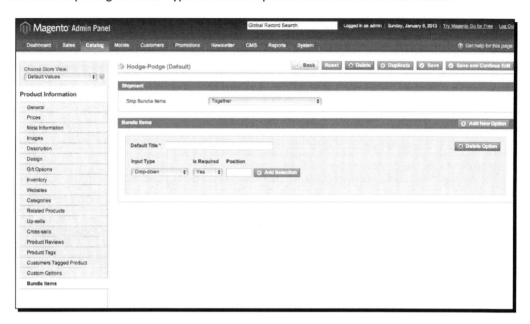

After clicking on the **Add New Option** button, a form section opens showing the following input options:

- ◆ **Default Title**: This is the title of the Bundle option you are entering that will be shown in the frontend. We will choose Hodge here.

- ◆ **Input Type**: This is how the Bundle option is presented on the frontend, either as a drop-down menu, a multiple select element, radio buttons, or checkboxes.

- ◆ **Is Required**: If the Bundle option is mandatory in the frontend; you will have to choose **Yes** or **No**.

- ◆ **Position**: This is a whole number greater than or equal to zero, signifying the position of the Bundle option on the Bundle product's detail page. This is not required to be set.

After clicking on the **Add Selection** button, a product grid appears, which functions in the same way as the product grids we saw earlier. Click on the **Search** button to start searching for products:

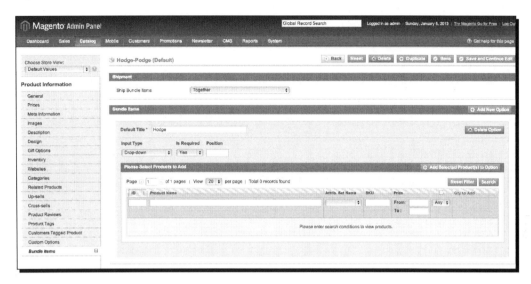

After clicking on **Search**, you will see a list of products. Associating a product to the Bundle option is done by selecting checkboxes for the products you want to associate, and by clicking on the **Add Selected Product(s) to Option** button after that:

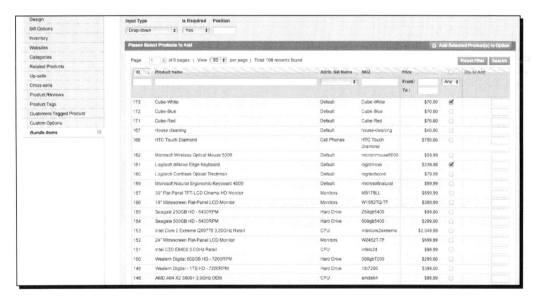

In our case, we will add the Cube-White and the Logitech Keyboard to our first Bundle option. If you do not have these available, you can pick any other products to follow along. The **Bundle Items** section will now show the products you selected inside the Bundle option, along with some final extra configurations inside the product rows, such as what is the default quantity (**Default Qty**) for that specific product, if a customer can specify how many of the product they want (**User Defined Qty**), the position of the product in the list of products within the Bundle option, and whether or not the product is the default choice within the Bundle option. The **User Defined Qty** input is only available for Bundle options of the type **Radio Button** or **Dropdown**.

We will repeat the aforementioned steps for a second Bundle option of type **Checkbox** with the name **Podge**. We have chosen the House Cleaning product and a monitor as the products to associate with this Bundle option:

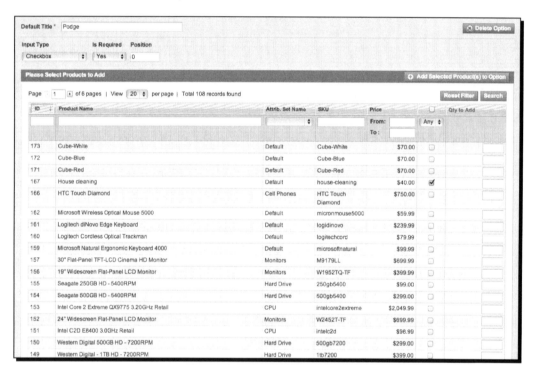

Again, click on **Add Selected Product(s) to Option** and save the product. The end result of your **Bundle Items** section should look similar to this:

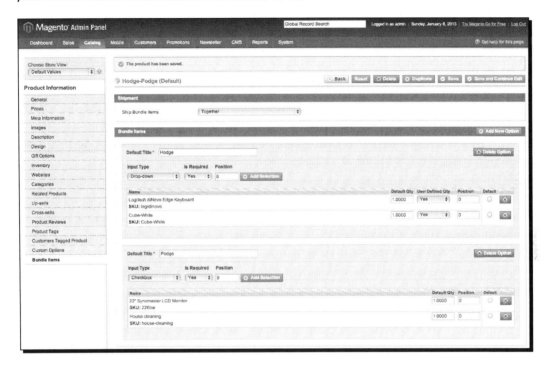

What just happened?

In the storefront the Hodge-Podge product is displayed as expected, with a drop-down menu for **Hodge** and checkboxes for **Podge**. After choosing some options and adding the product to the shopping cart, the shopping cart will reflect the options that were chosen. Of course, using Bundle products will require some planning up front. We threw together some non-related products in order to demonstrate how Magento lets you set up a Bundle, but actually creating a Bundle such as the computer shown earlier requires extensive knowledge of what you sell and how you want to present it to your customer.

Summary

In this chapter we looked at more advanced product methods and techniques. We discussed how to add nonphysical or downloadable products (such e-books). We went through how to allow a customer to add multiple products to a cart at once. We also looked at configuring products that consist of multiple variants as well as allowing customers to bundle a whole set of products together. Now that managing products should be clearer, in the next chapter we will show you how to manage your customers through Magento.

6
Customer Relationships

Settings related to the way Magento sends e-mail and manages customer accounts are often overlooked during initial set up of Magento. Unjustly so, however, as omissions in these configuration sections can lead to things such as strange address forms for the region where you are active, your order e-mails getting sent from non-existing addresses, to a non-working contact form! In this chapter we will first discuss setting up the most important configuration options related to communication and customer accounts. After that we will show how customer accounts look in the frontend and how to manage all customer accounts in your store from the backend.

In this chapter, you will learn:

- ◆ Setting up guest checkouts
- ◆ The basics for sending out newsletters
- ◆ Configuring contact details
- ◆ Adding new and amending existing customers' profiles

Setting up guest checkout

Magento differentiates between orders placed by guests and orders placed by registered customers. The big difference between the two modes of order placement is that the order information (such as billing and shipping information) for guest orders can only be found by opening the actual order under **Sales | Orders**. A customer that places an order by logging in or registering has a customer account, where all the order information also can be found, that is, you can find the customer and her or his order under **Sales | Orders** and **Customers | Manage Customers**.

Another way to think about it is: guest orders are one-off orders and do not allow Magento to tie the order to a customer account. Orders by logged in customers are tied to a customer account.

Customers, who have a customer account but then place a guest order, will not have that order shown in their customer account. This can create a bit of confusion for your customer service as well as customers. It is because of this, that it should be carefully considered if you want to allow guest checkouts or not. On the other hand, offering a guest checkout option has been shown to increase the number of sales in some stores to a great deal, even 40 percent increases are reported due to guest checkout options!

The first step in Magento's standard one page checkout is the choice for guest checkout (if enabled), logging in or registering.

Magento offers a configuration setting located in **System | Configuration | Checkout | Checkout Options**, called **Allow Guest Checkout**. If you set this to no and save it, all of your customers will have to either log in or register during checkout. However, allowing guest checkouts can (greatly) increase the number of customers who successfully place orders in your store, so we generally advise to keep the option for guest checkout turned on as follows:

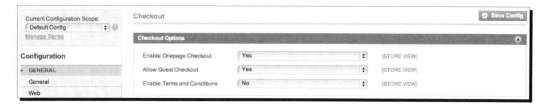

Newsletters

Even though some entrepreneurs consider e-mail marketing out-dated, a lot of consumers complain about marketing e-mails. Thus, newsletters are still a highly effective customer communication tool. The key to effective e-mail marketing is only approaching your subscribers with relevant information and only subscribing people who can reasonably expect to receive e-mails from you. E-mail marketing should be used with great care as spamming your customers is detrimental to your image!

A good way to fine-tune your messages to what your subscriber wants to read is to measure your e-mails' open rates and the number of clicks per hyperlink in your newsletter.

Magento's newsletter feature is not recommended as it does not offer the many essential features that a dedicated newsletter tool should have. Of course you should still let people subscribe through your Magento site, but for the actual sending of newsletters a tool like MailChimp (`www.mailchimp.com`) is recommended. MailChimp is not the only newsletter system available; there are many others as well. We shall simply use MailChimp as an example here. It serves as a useful example because there is a free Magento extension available that synchronizes your Magento subscribers with MailChimp. Without such an integration, you would have to manually ensure that the subscribers within your Magento installation are present in MailChimp, for instance, by copy pasting. It should be clear that that quickly becomes cumbersome:

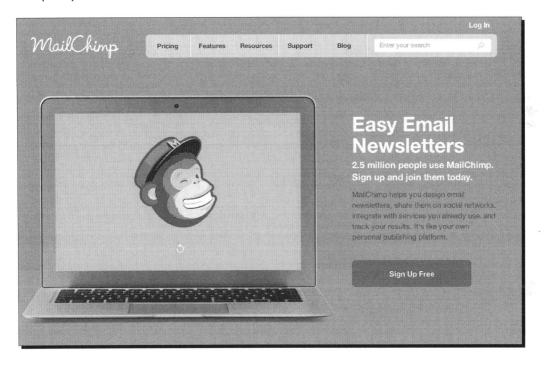

As MailChimp is an external system, the subscribers within Magento need to be synchronised with it. As mentioned, there are many more e-mail service providers; MailChimp is a user-friendly tool with a good feature set and the lowest price tier is completely free. Because of that it is excellent for small and medium-sized stores.

Registering an account with MailChimp can be done by browsing to its website and by clicking on the **Sign Up Free** button. Follow the steps shown and after you are logged in, MailChimp will show you how to get started by creating a list of mailing subscribers and a newsletter template:

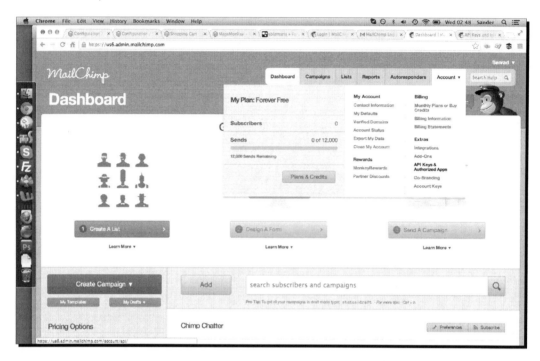

To fill your MailChimp subscriber list with the people who subscribe through your Magento store, you need a so-called "API key" from MailChimp. To find that, go to the **Account** menu in the top-right corner, and click on the **API Keys & Authorized Apps** option. In the next screen, click on the **Add A Key** button and the screen will update with an API key. In the following screenshot, we have hidden the API key because it is sensitive information. After you have followed MailChimp's instructions for creating a mailing list and e-mail template design, create the API key and save it. The API key will be needed within Magento later:

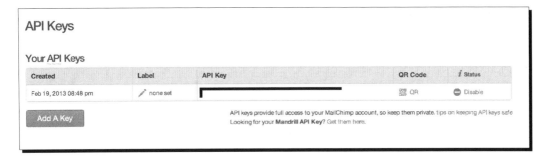

There is a Magento extension that sends your newsletter subscribers over to MailChimp automatically here: `http://www.magentocommerce.com/magento-connect/mage-monkey-mailchimp-integration-4865.html`.

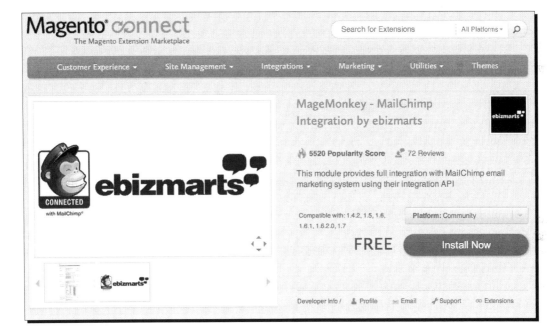

This module is available through MagentoConnect, which we can install using the MagentoConnect manager in the Magento admin. First you need the extension key for the MailChimp module. Retrieve the extension key by going to the MagentoConnect page mentioned and clicking on the **Install Now** button. You need to log into the Magento website before you are shown the extension key. If you see a choice for which version of MagentoConnect you'd like the module for, choose **MagentoConnect 2.0**. After you have the extension key, go to **System | Magento Connect | Magento Connect Manager** in the Magento admin. Log in again using your admin credentials, and in the **Paste extension key to install:** input field paste the MailChimp module's extension key:

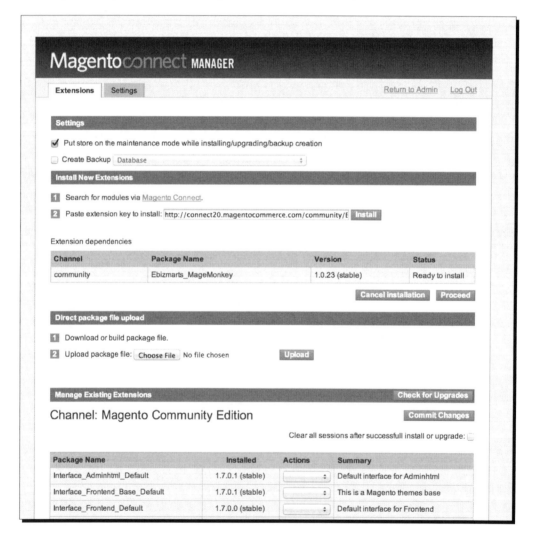

Click on the **Install** button and after that click on the **Proceed** button that just appeared and the module will be installed for you. When the installation process is done, click on the **Return to Admin** link at the top of the page and you will be back to your regular Magento admin.

Next, we can head over to the new configuration section in **System | Configuration | MailChimp**. If you get a 404 error page after installing this module through MagentoConnect, this is usually fixed by logging out and logging back into the Magento admin. In this configuration screen, paste your API key in the input field with the corresponding name, set the module to **Enabled** and save the configuration. After that, you will be able to set additional parameters, the most important one being **General Subscription**, which is the mailing list your Magento subscribers will get synchronized to within MailChimp. Another recommended setting is to set **Subscribe on Checkout** to **Yes**, which lets your customers subscribe to your mailings during the checkout process in your store. Other settings related to the MailChimp module will not be discussed further as they are too detailed for the broad discussion of e-mail marketing here. More information on this module can be found on `http://ebizmarts.com/forums/view/1`.

Configuring contact options

You can find the configuration of the e-mail addresses used by your store under **System | Configuration | Store Email Addresses**. There you will see several sections representing different e-mail senders:

- **General Contact**: By default, this is used to send out general e-mails such as the confirmation e-mail that gets sent out when a customer account is created.

- **Sales Representative**: This sender is used to send out sales-related e-mails such us order confirmations and shipment updates.

- **Customer Support**: This sender sends out e-mails such as password reminders.

- **Custom Email 1**: This is an extra sender that you can use if the distinction between **General Contact**, **Sales Representative**, and **Customer Support** is not enough for you.

- **Custom Email 2**: This is an extra sender that you can use if the distinction between **General Contact**, **Sales Representative**, and **Customer Support** is not enough for you.

- The tab looks like the following screenshot:

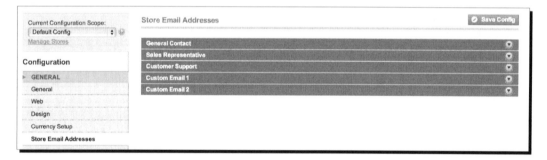

After clicking on each section, a form appears with input fields for **Sender Name** and **Sender Email**. In the **Sender Name** input field is the name that will appear in your customers' inboxes when an e-mail is sent by the sender you are editing, while in the **Sender Email** field is the e-mail address from which the e-mail will be sent. If you are a small company, it can help to set the **Sender Name** and **Sender Email** fields to the same name and address for all the different e-mail senders previously mentioned, as you will have to manage fewer addresses. It is essential to fill in proper **Sender Names** and **Sender Email** addresses for the **General Contact**, **Sales Representative**, and **Customer Support** options as all of those are used by default in Magento:

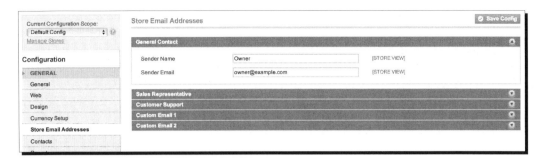

There are several places in Magento's configuration where you can set which senders are used for particular e-mails. We shall show the most important ones only: where to set the sender for customer account information and where to set the sender for sales e-mails.

In **System | Configuration | Customer Configuration** there are several sections such as **Account Sharing Options** and **Online Customer Options**. Later in this chapter we will discuss configuring some of these customer-related settings.

To set the e-mail sender for e-mails that get sent out when a customer account is created, click on the **Create New Account Options** section within the **Customer Configuration** section of the Magento Configuration. Here you will see an **Email Sender** drop-down list containing the sender options as previously described. By default, this is set to **General Contact**, but for instance, you can select **Customer Support** to ensure that customer account creation e-mails are sent out using the **Sender Name** and **Sender Email** input fields configured for the **Customer Support** section in **System | Configuration | Store Email Addresses**.

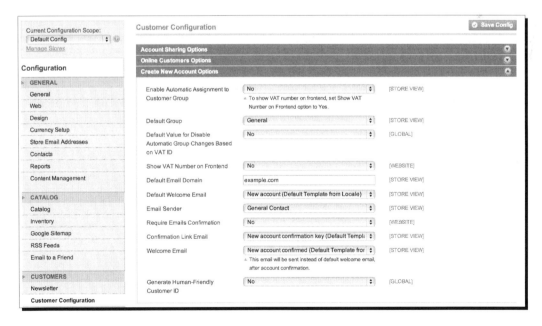

To set the sender for other customer account related e-mails, simply click on the other customer configuration sections in **System | Configuration | Customer Configuration** and look for the **Email Sender** drop-down list. The drop-down list to select e-mail senders always applies to the section you are looking in. For instance, in the **Password Options** section the **Forgot and Remind Email Sender** drop-down list applies to e-mails related to passwords:

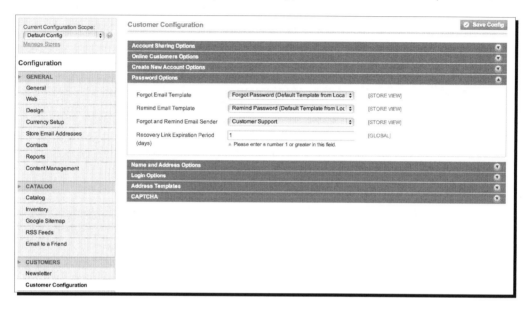

To set e-mail senders related to sales e-mails, go to **System | Configuration | Sales Emails**. The process is like that for customer account related e-mails: click on the different sections such as **Order, Invoice**, and **Shipment**, look for the **Email Sender** drop-down list and set it to the desired value. Changing the contents of transactional e-mails will be shown in *Chapter 9*.

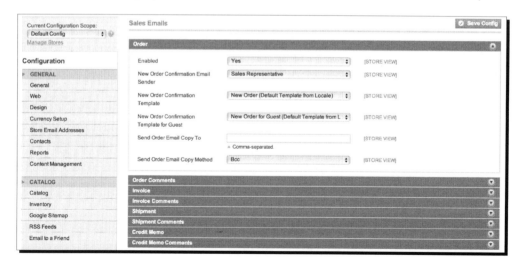

Configuring customer options

In the previous section of this chapter, we already briefly touched upon the **Customer Configuration** section of Magento, located at **System | Configuration | Customer Configuration**. Magento allows a lot of fine-tuning in the way your store is set up. Because of that there are many different configuration sections for each part of Magento, including customer account management. We will only describe the settings we believe are important to think about when starting with your store.

When you click on the **Create New Account Options** section, a relatively big group of settings appears. Some of those are the following:

◆ **Default Email Domain**: This is the domain that shows us the example domain in various parts of your website.

◆ **Default Welcome Email**: This is the e-mail template that is used when sending your customers the welcome e-mail after they have registered on your website.

◆ **Require Emails Confirmation**: Whether or not to require confirmation by new customers that they really want to create the account on your website. If this is disabled, anybody can make an account for any e-mail address and it will be active immediately.

◆ **Confirmation Link Email**: This is the e-mail template used when sending the account confirmation link.

◆ **Welcome Email**: As the small note below the input field says, this e-mail template is used instead of the Default Welcome Email, if e-mail confirmation for new customer accounts is necessary.

In the **Password Options** section, you can set the templates to e-mail the customer when he or she requests a new password (**Forgot Email Template**) and also for the actual password reminder (**Remind Email Template**). For the security of your customers' information, it is very important that you make your own **Remind Email Template** and set it here. Magento's default password reminder e-mail contains customers' passwords in text format. Because e-mail is an unsafe medium, if you do not edit this e-mail template all passwords sent through password reminders can be intercepted! The same goes for the welcome e-mails that are sent after a customer registers on an account. Magento also sends passwords in those e-mails and they should be changed.

In the **Name and Address Options** section, there are some relatively straightforward settings like how many address lines a customer can use, if customer properties such as gender and date of birth are required to be filled in, and whether to use prefixes and suffixes along with customer names.

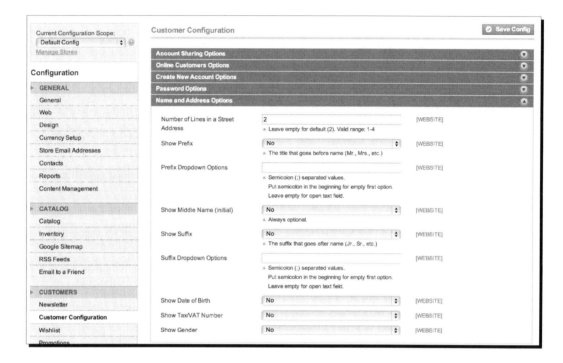

Customer accounts on the frontend

It's time to look at how a customer can manage his/her account in your store, meaning from the frontend of your website. A customer can get an account in two ways:

1. By registering from the **My Account** section of Magento.
2. By registering during the purchasing process.

Time for action – registering for an account

Registering for an account is a fairly straightforward process for your customers, as can be seen in the following steps:

1. Registering from the **My Account** section is straightforward and starts when you click on the **My Account** button, located at the top of the page in a default theme. After that, click on the **Create an Account** button in the left column:

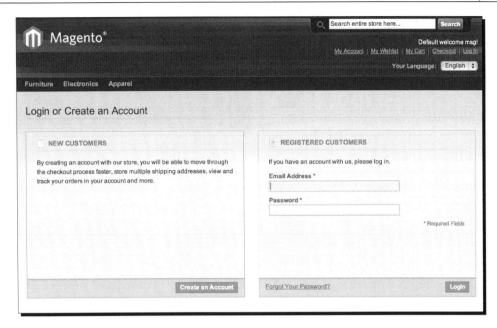

2. The next screen shows us the **First Name**, **Last Name**, **Email Address**, **Password**, and **Confirm Password** fields. Magento recognizes a customer account solely on the basis of supplied e-mail address, so later when logging in only the e-mail address and password are needed:

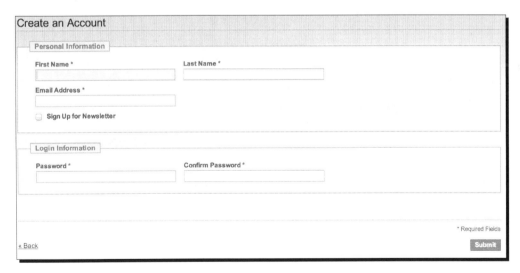

3. Submit the form. Now there are two options. The first is that the newly created account needs to be confirmed, which will be indicated with a message. You will get an e-mail containing the confirmation link, and after clicking on that you will have access to the customer account. The second option is that the account confirmation is not necessary; your customers will have access to their account immediately after registering in that case. As mentioned earlier, as a store owner you can set whether account confirmation is needed in **System | Configuration | Customer Configuration | Require Emails Confirmation**.

What just happened?

After clicking on the **Submit** button, you will be taken to the customer account, where the first thing your customers will see is the customer dashboard. The dashboard displays the customer's general contact information, newsletter subscription, and address information.

The left-hand menu is the main navigation of the customer account and allows your customers to go to the different sections of their customer account. We will discuss the various menu options relatively briefly here; it is wise to get familiar with them by experimenting with the various forms and settings a customer can use, since those customers will have questions about it. It also gives you a better feeling of what you are doing when you are changing customer information from Magento's admin panel. You cannot break anything related to the functioning of the store by clicking around in a customer account from the frontend. The most important sections are:

- **Account Information**: This allows a customer to change their first name, last name, e-mail address, and password.

- **Address Book**: A customer can enter a new address here. After saving the first address, a customer can choose to use different addresses for billing and shipping by clicking on the **Add New Address** button.

- **My Orders**: This gives us an overview of all placed orders, regardless of their order status. From this section the customer can also click through the invoices and shipment information.

- **My Product Reviews**: This is a list of all reviews placed by the customer who is logged in.

- **My Tags**: This is a list of all the tags a customer has entered into the store.

- **My Wishlist**: This is a list of items the customer has marked to save on her/his wishlist.

- **Newsletter Subscriptions**: Here a customer can subscribe to or unsubscribe from your newsletter.

- **My Downloadable Products**: This is the collection of downloadable products available to your customer.

As you can see in the following screenshot, there are more sections. However, these are features much less used by most stores and/or customers.

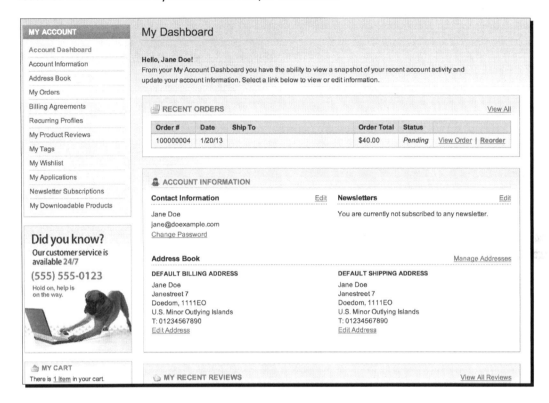

Customer accounts in the backend

Now that you are more familiar with the customer account in your storefront, it is also useful to know how you can manage customer information from the admin panel. Under **Customers | Manage Customers**, you can find all your customers' accounts. After going there you will see a standard Magento grid, which functions the same way as the other grids in the Magento admin panel: pagination above the grid and the header row allows you to search for specific customers by filling in information about the customer you are looking for in one of the header cells.

Time for action – adding a customer

Sometimes it's necessary to add or manage customer information yourself, for instance when helping out somebody who is having a difficulty in using your website. Here's how:

1. At the top-right corner of the page, there's an **Add New Customer** button. By clicking on a row in the results grid, we get the customer's details. We will show the process of adding a new customer briefly because you will generally open already existing customer accounts from the customer grid:

2. After clicking on the **Add New Customer** button, the **New Customer** screen appears containing two sections: general account information and customer address(es). The first section contains the only mandatory fields: **Associate to Website**, **Customer Group**, **First Name**, **Last Name**, **Email**, and **Password**. In the **Associate to Website** drop-down list you can choose which website you are registering your new customer to. It's possible to make the customer account available in all the websites that are present in your Magento installation by choosing **Admin**.

3. The e-mail address you enter cannot exist yet within the store to which you are adding the customer. In the **Password** form you have two choices: either supply a password yourself by entering the new customer's password in the input field, or have Magento send an automatically generated password by ticking the **Send auto-generated password** checkbox. If you choose to supply a password yourself, do not forget to let your customer know their password!

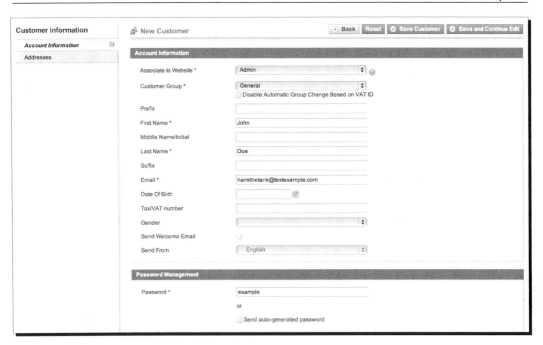

4. In the **Addresses** section, not surprisingly addresses can be added for the new customer that is being created. Click on the **Add New Address** button to start adding an address. A form will appear where you can enter the standard address input Magento requires. As a reminder, you can adjust some of the address requirements in the configuration section under **System | Configuration | Customer Configuration | Name** and **Address Options**.

5. Two radio buttons will also appear after clicking on the **Add New Address** button: **Default Billing Address** and **Default Shipping Address**. By clicking on these radio buttons you can set the address you are entering as the default for billing and or shipping. Setting these makes checking out a little faster and easier for your customer.

6. You can make the form switch between the different addresses you are entering by clicking on the small round icon containing horizontal lines as shown in the following screenshot. After you are done filling in the customer details, click on the **Save Customer** button and the customer grid in your admin will show the new customer!

What just happened?

We just added a customer and optionally provided an address for the new customer as well. It is possible to create multiple address for your new customer, by clicking on the **Add New Address** button again. A new block also containing the **Default Billing Address** and **Default Shipping Address** radio buttons will appear, though you will not see a new address form:

The other, non-mandatory, inputs in the **Account Information** section are mostly self-evident. The **Disable Automatic Group Change Based on VAT ID** option below the customer groups drop-down list in the **Account Information** section is related to the business-to-business feature included in Magento, which is mostly interesting to European companies. It is best left alone for beginning business-to-consumer stores.

Managing an existing customer

More often than adding new customers yourself, you will be looking at or changing their existing information.

Managing existing customers starts by clicking on a row from the customers grid in **Customers | Manage Customers**. The **Customer Information** page will open with the **Customer View** section visible:

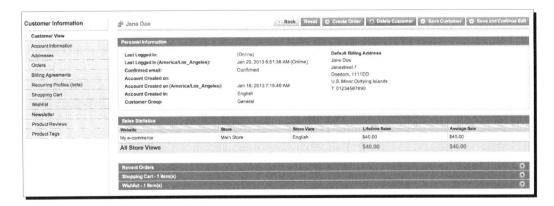

Some general information about your customers' activity in your store can be found there. The other sections found in the left-hand column are:

◆ **Account Information**: This manages your customers' general information, and works as described above when adding a new customer.

◆ **Addresses**: This manages your customer's address(es) , and works the same as described above when adding a new customer.

◆ **Orders**: These are the orders your customer has placed.

◆ **Billing Agreements**: This is a feature used to arrange recurring billing with PayPal. It is not recommended for use while starting Magento shops, as it is not user-friendly and stable enough at the time of writing.

◆ **Recurring Profiles (beta)**: Recurring profiles are used to facilitate recurring billing, and are still in beta status. As such, it is not recommended to use at the time of writing.

◆ **Shopping Cart**: These are all items currently in your customer's shopping cart.

◆ **Wishlist**: These are all items currently placed on your customer's wishlist.

◆ **Newsletters**: This manages your customer's newsletter subscriptions.

◆ **Product Reviews**: This shows all reviews placed by the customer.

◆ **Product Tags**: This shows all tags added to products by the customer.

The **Orders** section is a standard admin order grid, and clicking on an order inside the grid takes you to the order detail screen for that particular order. The last column of the grid has a reorder link. By clicking on that link, you will be taken to an order creation screen for a new order that has the same items as the original order already added to it:

In the **Shopping Cart** section a product grid will be visible if your customer has products placed inside the cart. Clicking on a product row in this grid takes you to the product edit screen for that product. The last column of the grid contains **Configure** and **Delete** links. The **Configure** link is greyed out if the product cannot be configured, otherwise it allows you to set the product's options for your customer (their cart will reflect the options you set from the backend). The **Delete** link behaves as expected, removing the product from the customer's shopping cart:

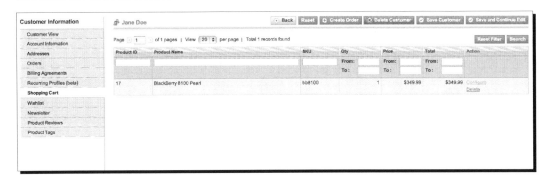

The product grid containing all products on the customer's wishlist, found in the **Wishlist** section, behaves similarly to the product grid in the **Shopping Cart** section. Clicking on a row takes you to the product edit screen for that product and the same **Configure** and **Delete** links are present:

In the **Newsletter Information** section you can tick or untick the checkbox, **Subscribed to Newsletter** to subscribe or unsubscribe the customer to or from your newsletter, respectively. There is also a grid showing which newsletters have been sent by Magento to this customer. However, as mentioned at the start of this chapter, we do not recommend using Magento's newsletter sending component:

Under **Product Reviews**, a standard grid shows all reviews placed by the customer, either pending or accepted. By clicking on a review you open the review edit screen for that review, where you can take further actions such as approving or deleting the review.

The **Tags** section follows a similar logic, allowing you to click through a tag added by the customer and from there either approve or delete a tag.

You have now seen all of the many features and options available in customizing an account. All in all, the bulk of your work when dealing with customer information will be changing general information, (re-)sending passwords, and editing addresses. These can all be done from the **Account Information** and **Addresses** sections, and can function the same for new and existing customers.

Pop Quiz: default address

Q1. When adding your customer's address, which of the following are true?

1. A customer can have more shipping addresses than billing addresses.
2. A customer can have different default addresses for billing and shipping.

Summary

In this chapter we briefly looked at some overlooked but vitally important customer management features of Magento. These features are critical to your store as every sale counts! We looked at adding guest checkout and then went through adding newsletters with MailChimp. We then explored the configuration of contact options before moving on to seeing how our customers experience signing up for our store. We then finished this chapter by going over the many features and options available to you when you add or administrate new and existing customer profiles. In the next chapter we will be looking at how to configure your payment methods.

7
Accepting Payments

The payment methods you offer in your checkout can make or break your store. You should strive to offer ways of payment that make you appear as trustworthy as possible, and that provide the least hassle to your customers. Which payment methods you should set up for your store depends on which countries you will be active in and in which market you are going to sell. In this chapter you will find out how setting up payment methods in Magento works. Magento has a few payment methods available by default, which will be tackled first. After that other payment methods and **Payment Service Providers** *(PSPs) will be discussed.*

In this chapter, we will learn:

- What common payment methods are supported by Magento
- Setting up the default payment methods in Magento
- What a payment service provider is
- Setting up a payment service provider

Common payment methods

It is essential to offer the right payment methods for your market and geography. As an example of tailoring to the market you are in: if you are selling beds with a long delivery time, a lot of customers will want to pay upon delivery instead of up front. On the other hand, if you're selling standard goods such as DVDs, which are shipped very quickly, requiring payment up front is much more accepted.

With regards to the country you are operating in, each country can have one or more highly specific payment methods. For instance, in Germany an up-front bank transfer payment method called **Giropay** is big, while its equivalents are called **iDEA** in the Netherlands and **Mister Cash** in Belgium. If you are selling in the United States, the most important payment methods to arrange are payments made by credit card and PayPal! There are many different payment methods available world-wide and because of that, it's not possible to discuss each one of them within the scope of this chapter.

By default Magento includes these common payment methods, which can be found under **System | Configuration | Payment Methods**:

- **PayPal**: PayPal is a company that offers a number of different payment methods. By far, their best known payment method is **PayPal Payments Standard** and in this chapter we will only discuss this payment method as the other options that PayPal offers are generally not used by starting/smaller online stores. In order to use PayPal Payments Standard, any customer can register at www.paypal.com and when they have a PayPal account, they can use that account to pay for orders on any website that accepts PayPal payments. Making a PayPal payment only requires logging into PayPal with a username and password, which is one of the reasons it has become an internationally popular payment method so quickly.

- **Credit card**: Using this mode of payment, your customer supplies his/her credit card details, and is charged for the purchase on his/her credit account at the end of the month. Credit cards are issued by companies such as VISA, MasterCard, and American Express.

- **Check / money order**: This is primarily used in the United States; this payment method involves your customer sending you a check through regular postal mail in order to pay for his/her order.

- **Bank transfer**: Your checkout displays information about how to wire the money to your bank account. The order is usually only fulfilled after the customer performs the transfer.

- **Cash on delivery**: In this mode of payment, the customer pays when the goods are physically delivered to his/her doorstep. The manner in which the customer can pay differs as per the fulfillment partner; some only support cash payments when performing cash on delivery shipments while others accept cards.

  This payment method involves a risk for the store owner especially when the shipment involves customized goods, as the goods will be produced and shipped before funds are received.

◆ **Purchase order**: In stores, a purchase order is a document that indicates that a buyer wants to buy a list of products from the store against the prices listed in the order. Purchase orders are mostly used in business-to-business settings where the buying company has arranged for a purchase order number internally to benefit its financial administration. The seller usually sends the buyer an invoice containing the purchase order number.

The configuration of each payment method listed will be discussed in the upcoming sections. Other payment options that can be found in the **Payment Methods** section of the Magento configuration are **Zero Subtotal Checkout** and **Authorize.net**. Zero Subtotal Checkout is not an actual payment method but a payment option that Magento only displays when a customer's order total is zero. With this payment option a customer is not required to input any payment details. It is advised to leave this payment method turned on as a zero subtotal order can occur frequently when you are running promotions and supplying discount codes to your store.

Authorize.net is a PSP, of which there are many. Authorize.net is a PSP that is included by default; for most other PSPs you will need to install a Magento extension. The process of installing a PSP extension and configuring it will be shown toward the end of this chapter. Like most parts of Magento, the payment processing part of Magento can be adjusted to meet your specific needs. You will almost certainly need a development partner for that (refer to *Chapter 11, Maintaining and Administrating Your Store*, for further tips on working with a development partner). It's recommended to leave it as close to default as possible.

Setting up Magento's default payment methods

In the payment configuration section located at **System | Configuration | Payment Methods** you will find all of the payment methods Magento includes by default. Inside this part of the Magento configuration you will also see that PayPal gets a lot of attention, and the configuration section for PayPal is expanded by default. This is because Magento is owned by eBay and PayPal is owned by eBay as well. More information about the relationship between eBay and Magento can be found in *Chapter 1, Installation*.

Before starting with the configuration of your payment methods, it is advised to open the first configuration section titled **Merchant Location** as shown in the following screenshot and to set the default country there:

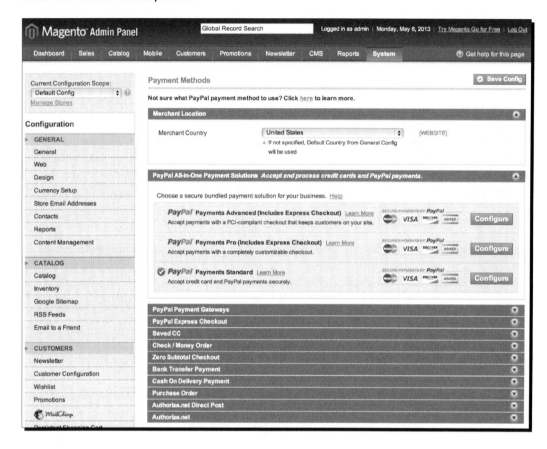

Every payment method discussed in the chapter can display one of the following settings, which will not be discussed separately for each payment method:

 ◆ **Enabled**: This specifies whether the payment method is active or not.

 ◆ **Title**: This is the name of the payment method as it will be displayed to a customer during checkout and inside order e-mails and order summaries.

◆ **New Order Status**: This is the status that an order with a particular payment method will get immediately after the order is placed successfully. In a standard Magento installation, this drop-down menu will either display only **Pending** or it will display **Pending** and **Processing** as choices. **Pending** is the only choice when the payment method you are configuring is one where a manual look at the order is necessary to determine if it needs further financial handling. A few examples of such payment methods are bank transfers and purchase orders.

◆ **Sort Order**: This displays a number that indicates the position of this payment method in the list of all the payment choices during the checkout process.

◆ **Payment Applicable From**: This is sometimes also called "Payment from Specific Countries": in which countries you are willing to offer the payment method you are configuring.

◆ **Minimum Order Total**: This specifies that the payment method is available for orders from this amount and up.

◆ **Maximum Order Total**: This specifies that the payment method is available for orders below this amount.

Setting up PayPal Payments Standard

As mentioned earlier, the company PayPal offers multiple payment methods. The methods most often found are titled PayPal Payments Standard, PayPal Payments Pro, and PayPal Payments Advanced. The standard PayPal merchant to start with is appropriately named the Payments Standard option.

If you do not yet have a PayPal account, we advise you to start with the PayPal Payments Standard method, which even medium to large size stores regularly still use. This is also the only PayPal merchant option we will discuss as the Pro and Advanced options can be relatively confusing and complex to set up without detailed knowledge of PayPal's terminology. Pro and Advanced also cost more money than the Standard account. Of course, PayPal Payments Pro and PayPal Payments Advanced do have some advantages, the main one being that a customer will not be redirected to PayPal for payment if you have Pro or Advanced. A comparison between Standard, Pro, and Advanced can be found at `https://www.paypal.com/webapps/mpp/compare-business-products`.

In the payment configuration of Magento you will also see sections titled **PayPal Payment Gateways** and **PayPal Express Checkout**, which provide even more possibilities for accepting credit card and PayPal payments. We advise you to leave those alone for now.

Time for action – starting to sell through PayPal

As mentioned, PayPal offers multiple payment methods. In the following steps we will go through how to get their most-used method available:

1. **Creating a PayPal seller account**: The first thing that's needed to start selling through PayPal is a PayPal seller account. To create this, head over to `http://www.paypal.com`. On the home page, there is a big blue **Sign Up for Free** button as shown in the following screenshot:

After clicking on this button, you will be taken to the first step of the account creation wizard. Click on the **Get Started** button in the **PayPal for business and nonprofits** block and go through the form:

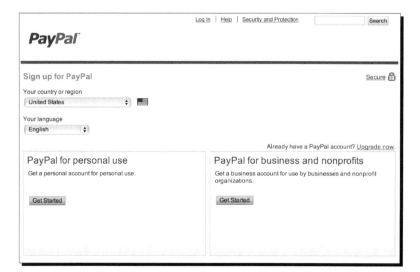

2. **Verifying your PayPal account**: After you have successfully submitted the form, it is advised to verify your PayPal account by clicking on the **Get verified** link below the welcome message in the top of the screen, as shown in the following screenshot. This ensures that PayPal knows who you are and can safely handle your transactions. Not getting verified means you can have trouble accepting payments. After signing up and getting verified, you are ready for configuring PayPal Payments Standard in Magento!

    A PayPal account looks like the following screenshot:

3.   **Configuring Magento for PayPal payments**: After going to **System | Configuration | Payment Methods**, click on the **Configure** button in the PayPal Payments Standard row. More input options will appear, the most important one being **Email Associated with PayPal Merchant Account**. Fill in your PayPal seller account's e-mail address there, and set the **Enable this Solution** drop-down menu to **Yes**. Now your Magento store is ready to accept payments through PayPal. The following screenshot shows what the input section, where you can input your e-mail address, looks like:

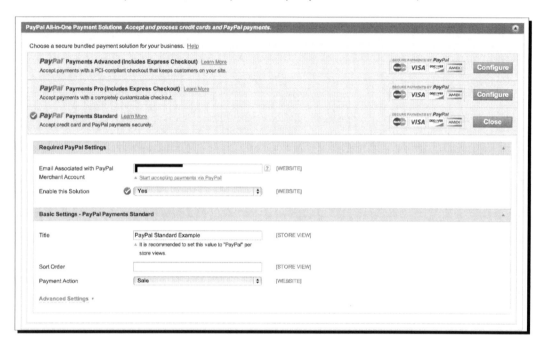

Besides the general payment configuration options **Title** and **Sort Order**, which are explained at the start of this chapter, another (not required) setting that can be found in the PayPal form is **Payment Action**: this is set to **Sale** by default, but can also be set to **Authorization**. Setting it to **Authorization** means that you will not receive money after the customer finishes his/her order, but instead you as the store owner will have to complete the transaction at a later time by performing a "capture" of the payment (either through PayPal's system or through invoicing in the Magento admin). We recommend that you leave this set to **Sale** unless you have a good reason for a deferred payment through the **Authorization** option.

Clicking on the **Advanced Settings** orange link displays some final setup options, all of which you are advised to leave to the default settings:

- **Sandbox Mode**: This specifies whether or not you are using PayPal's testing grounds (sandbox) or the live merchant environment.

- **Transfer Cart Line Items**: If this is setting is set to **Yes**, Magento will transfer information about the products inside the order to PayPal, so you can see what was ordered from within PayPal.

- **Debug Mode**: This is primarily useful for somebody with technical expertise, for when detailed troubleshooting of the PayPal integration is necessary.

- **Enable SSL verification**: This specifies whether or not to check the integrity of the secure connection between PayPal and Magento.

In the following screenshot you can see what the basic and advanced settings for PayPal Payments Standard look like:

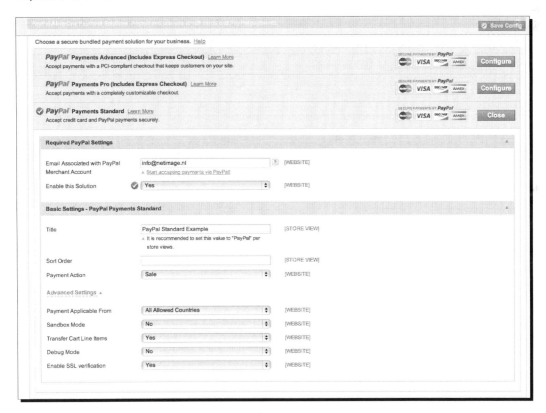

Remember to save the config after setting everything to the desired values. As a rule, it's best to save as soon as you're done with a certain section. After setting up PayPal, it will look like the following screenshot in your checkout:

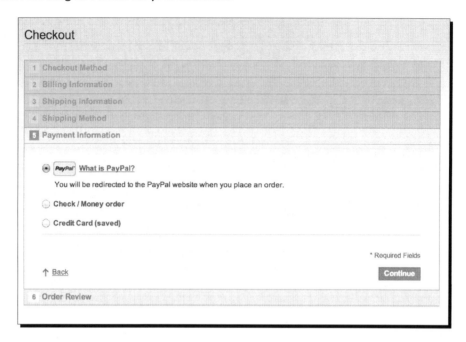

Pop quiz – the bare minimum for PayPal Payments Standard

Q1. What is the minimum amount of information needed to input into Magento in order to accept PayPal Payments Standard? Choose the right answer from the following options:

1. Your PayPal merchant e-mail address, basic settings related to sort order, and authorization mode.

2. Your PayPal merchant e-mail address and password, basic settings related to sort order, and authorization mode

3. Your PayPal merchant e-mail address and password.

Setting up saved credit cards

Saved credit card (saved CC) is Magento's way of allowing you to capture credit card payments out of the box. It should be noted that this payment method is not a particularly good way of offering credit card payments on your website. In fact, we advise you to look for other options if possible. The main drawbacks of the saved CC payment method in Magento are as follows:

♦ It saves your customer's credit card details inside your own system, which places the burden of securing that data on your shoulders. You should go in for a secure hosting provider because a store always handles private customer data, but credit card details are more sensitive than regular customer data. Storing credit card details also means you will have to comply with e-commerce industry standards for credit card processing (called **PCI compliance**). Attaining PCI compliance is not easy.

♦ The saved CC payment method saves the credit card details inside Magento, but no payment is made at that time. You have to manually process the payment through some other credit card payment processor.

A more usual way of accepting credit cards is by working with a payment service provider (PSP). Payment service providers will be discussed in more detail toward the end of this chapter. Authorize.net is a payment service provider integrated by default into Magento, which can be used to accept credit cards without having the issues previously outlined. The payment service provider will receive the money and transfer it to you automatically, and the customer's sensitive credit card data is handled and saved by the payment service provider as well.

A quick solution for shops that cannot arrange credit card payments through a payment service provider is naming the PayPal Standard payment option along the lines of "PayPal and credit card through PayPal". This works because customers can pay using their credit card through PayPal Standard as well, although it isn't as quick or easy to use as a dedicated credit card payment method.

All that having been said, if you want to go ahead with saved CC payments, these are the specific configuration options:

♦ **Credit Card Types**: This selects the credit cards for which you will process payments from here.

♦ **Request Card Security Code**: This sets whether or not Magento will ask for the credit card's security code. It is recommended to set this to **Yes** as it makes fraud a little harder.

◆ **3D Secure Card Validation**: 3D Secure is an additional security layer where the customer has to supply his/her credit card password before being able to complete a purchase successfully. If you are experiencing a lot of fraud, it is but wise to set this to **Yes**.

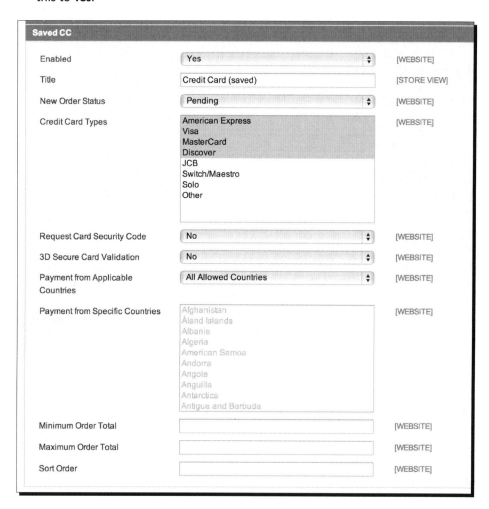

Enabling this payment method and saving the configuration results in the following payment method display in the checkout:

Setting up checks / money orders

The check / money order payment method has two configuration inputs:

◆ **Make Check Payable to**: This will take the name of the company that will receive the money for the order being placed.

◆ **Send Check to**: This will specify where the check needs to be sent for processing.

These are displayed in the following screenshot. Other than capturing the customer's order, Magento will not automatically arrange anything relating to the payment of the check / money order:

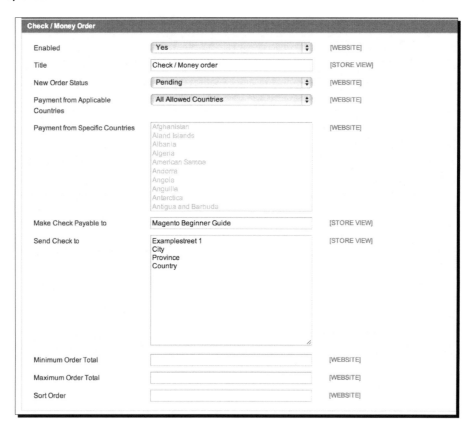

Setting this payment method results in the following display in your store's checkout process:

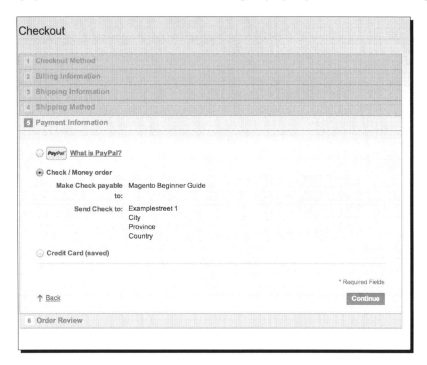

Have a go hero – activating check / money order

As an exercise in enabling a simple payment method, enable the check / money order payment method. It may be already enabled in your store if you have a completely default installation. Set it up so that it is only shown to U.S. customers through the **Payment from Applicable Countries** input field. After you are done, verify that it's done correctly by purchasing two products in two separate checkouts in your test store: one with the country selected as U.S. and one with the country as Belgium. In the latter checkout, you should not see the check / money order payment method, of course!

Setting up for a bank transfer

There is only one specific field to configure for the bank transfer payment method, and that's called **Instructions**. In this field, you should enter all relevant bank account details that your customer needs to transfer money to you.

 Note that Magento does not automatically handle anything related to bank transfer, so it is necessary to monitor your bank account to see if the customer really transferred the money.

Setting the bank transfer to active results in the following payment display:

After setting up the bank transfer settings, when you check out it is shown as follows:

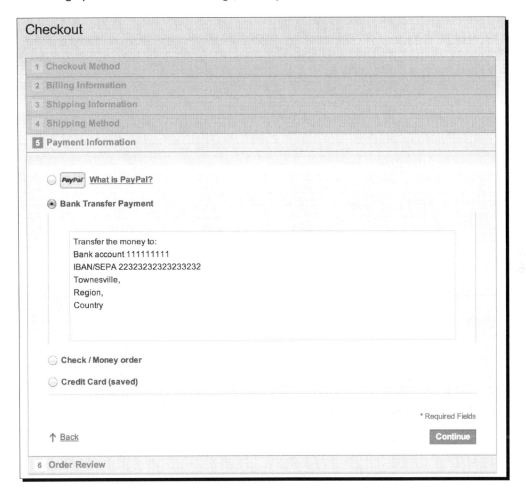

Setting up cash on delivery

This payment method also has only one specific setting called **Instruction**. Here you should list any information related to the cash on delivery payment, for instance, how your customer can pay (cash, debit card, credit card, and so on) when the goods are delivered. Often the delivery company charges extra for performing a cash on delivery shipment, and because of that often store owners charge customers extra for the cash on delivery shipment option as well. Unfortunately, a surcharge for cash on delivery is not possible through the default cash on delivery payment option in Magento, but there is a free module on **MagentoConnect** that does offer this. It's located at `http://www.magentocommerce.com/magento-connect/cashondelivery.html`.

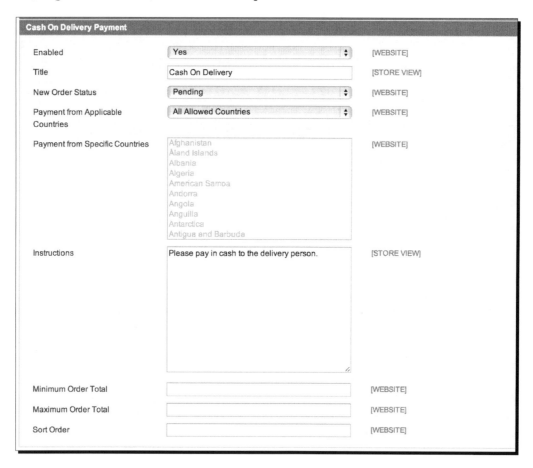

Activating cash on delivery results in a payment selection as follows in the checkout:

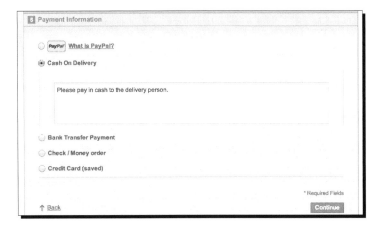

Setting up purchase orders

There are no specific input fields in the admin for purchase orders, just the general payment configuration fields that were discussed at the start of this section. This also implies that Magento will just save the order information when a customer chooses **Purchase Order** as their payment method; any additional actions will need to be performed by the store owner. Activating the purchase order payment method results in the screen shown, where it can be seen that the customer can input their purchase order number:

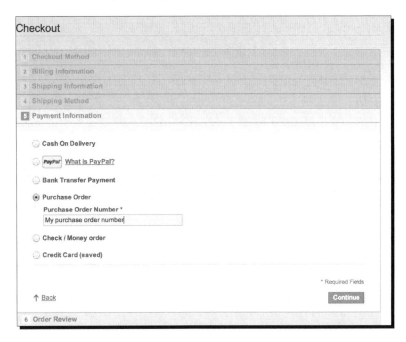

From the preceding screenshot it should be clear that most of the payment methods that are offered by Magento out of the box require manual processing to receive an actual payment and safely fulfill the order. The exceptions are the payment gateways PayPal Payflow Pro and Authorize.net, and the PayPal Payments Standard payment method. For stores that process multiple orders daily, the manual payment methods offered by Magento become cumbersome quickly.

Working with payment service providers

A payment service provider is a company that, as the name implies, acts as the layer through which payments are handled. A payment service provider has already made the connections to different payment methods and generally has a plugin available for Magento. This means that by installing the payment service provider's Magento plugin, you have access to all of the payment methods the payment service provider is connected to! This can help a great deal in serving all of the right payment methods applicable to your country and market. A payment service provider automates as much as possible, so using one ensures you will not have the same manual workload as you would with most of Magento's default payment methods.

An important distinction between payment service providers is whether they are collecting or processing. A collecting payment service provider will transfer the funds they captured for you once per period, while a processing gateway will immediately transfer the funds to your account. Per transaction, a collecting payment service provider is usually cheaper.

Usually the payment flow using a payment service provider works like this:

1. Your customer goes through your checkout and chooses to pay through a payment method that is handled by your payment gateway. Let's take a credit card as an example.

2. After pressing the **Place Order** button your customer is taken to the website of the payment service provider and enters his/her credit card credentials there.

3. The payment service provider communicates with the credit card processor and captures the payment.

4. The customer is sent back to your store and the payment service provider lets Magento know the payment has been fully handled.

The same would be valid for other payment methods as well: the payment service provider will notify Magento about the status of the payment handling of your customer's orders. Besides offering a multitude of payment methods, a payment service provider can also help you arrange the necessary contracts for accepting certain payment methods, such as credit cards, and is able to provide detailed reports about the transactions that have been performed for your store, which can be a huge administrative hassle otherwise.

Selecting the right gateway

Selecting the proper payment service provider can be difficult, especially without prior experience with them. It's advised to consult somebody with knowledge of your market and payment gateways. The most important questions that should be answered are as follows:

◆ Which payment methods does the payment service provider offer? Do they suit your website fully? Also, check if the available payment methods match your future plans, for instance, if you want to expand to other countries.

◆ What are the costs? Is there a starting rate? What is the monthly fee? What is the fee per transaction? The rates are often tiered, meaning they differ based on the number of transactions you have going through your store. It's best to calculate these costs with a longer time-frame in mind, so also to try to include the expected costs based on the number of transactions in six months to a year, especially if you have a starting store. Some payment gateways offer very low monthly fees but have higher transactional costs, which can suddenly become expensive when your volumes increase.

◆ Is a good Magento module available? What is and what is not included in this module? Are all the payment methods you need from the PSP available through the Magento module?

The last point warrants special attention as the PSP will be useless for you if you cannot integrate your Magento installation with the PSP. Judging the quality of a Magento module is best done by somebody with knowledge of the technical aspects of Magento extensions. These are the things to look out for, at a minimum:

◆ With which Magento version(s) is the payment module compatible? Is it compatible with your shop's Magento version?

◆ Can you include extra text or instructions for the different payment methods offered by the module?

◆ Are the payment settings able to be changed per website or store view in Magento? This is useful, for instance, to only show certain payment methods at certain domain names (such as only showing purchase orders on your business-to-business website).

◆ Is the payment module secure and is it properly maintained? In general, the more releases and the more information available per release, the better.

Most of these checks are useful for any Magento module you may wish to install! A good way to find out more about the quality of a payment gateway's Magento integration is to google the keyword "Magento" combined with the name of the payment gateway. If the module is available on MagentoConnect, browsing through the release history and reviews for that module is also a good idea.

Setting up a payment service provider – an example

As an example of working with a payment service provider that is not included by default in Magento, we'll install the ICEPAY payment module. ICEPAY (www.icepay.com) is a payment service provider that is especially strong in Europe. Their Magento module is available on MagentoConnect at http://www.magentocommerce.com/magento-connect/icepay-advanced-8489.html. The big advantage of situations like these is that you can take a look at their payment extension before deciding to do business with them. Ask the PSP you are considering if you can take a look at their extension beforehand as well!

Time for action – installing and configuring a PSP extension

Because ICEPAY has a module available through MagentoConnect, we can install the extension using the MagentoConnect manager in the Magento admin.

1. **Retrieving the extension key**: First you need the extension key for the ICEPAY payment module. The extension key can be retrieved by going to the **MagentoConnect** page previously mentioned and clicking on the **Install Now** button.

2. **Pasting the extension key into the MagentoConnect Manager**: Go to **System | Magento Connect | Magento Connect Manager** in the Magento admin. Log in again using your admin credentials, and in the input field saying **Paste extension key to install**: paste the ICEPAY module's extension key. An example of MagentoConnect with an extension key filled in can be seen in the following screenshot:

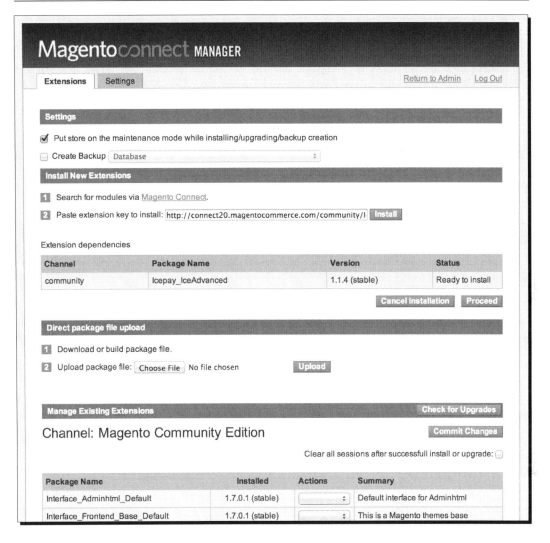

3. Let the MagentoConnect Manager install the extension. Click on the **Install** button and after that the **Proceed** button that just appeared, and the module will be installed for you.

4. Return to the admin and go to the configuration section.

5. When the installation process is done, click on the **Return to Admin** link in the top of the page and you will be back in your regular Magento admin.

6. Next, we can head over to the new configuration section in **System | Configuration | ICEPAY**. If you get a 404 error page after installing a module through MagentoConnect, usually logging out and logging back into the Magento admin will fix that.

7. Fill in the configuration settings specific to your PSP. If you have an ICEPAY account, you will have received a merchant ID and a secret code, which can be supplied in the configuration section. After saving those, we can click on the **Get paymentmethods** button and the payment methods we have available through ICEPAY will become visible and can be turned on and off individually. We will not go through all the configuration options the ICEPAY module offers as these are specific to the way ICEPAY have built their module.

The following screenshot shows a configured ICEPAY section:

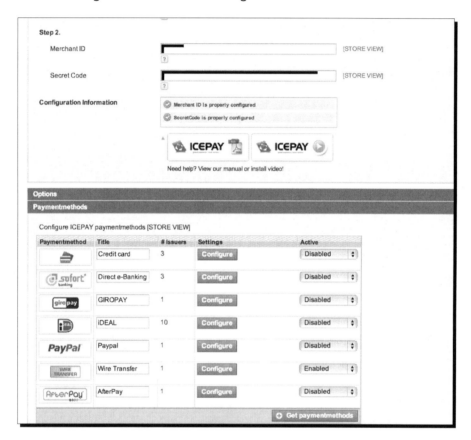

8. Activate your payment methods and save the configuration.

The payment methods that were activated will appear during the checkout process accordingly, of course. In the following example screenshot, we have only activated the **Wire Transfer** payment method of ICEPAY:

What just happened?

It should be noted that every payment module handles this in its own way the aforementioned example helps to get a feel for the process of using a non-default payment module. Magento extensions are not only offered through MagentoConnect, but are also distributed as standalone ZIP files. In the next chapter about shipping methods, we will discuss how to install a shipping module that is distributed as a ZIP file.

Summary

In this chapter we discussed how to set up different payment methods such as PayPal, check / money order, and cash on delivery. Besides that we discussed what a PSP does and how to integrate a PSP's Magento extension into your store. As general advice for your store, keep all the information you show your customers about payment methods as clear as possible and try to offer payment methods that are relevant for the country you are selling in, and which are most often used in your market segment. In the next chapter we will handle Magento's shipping options and discuss how Magento handles other aspects of logistics such as returns and purchasing as well.

8
Configuring Shipping

Most online shops send out physical products. The ways this can be handled are manifold, and the logistics chain encompasses many business processes. This chapter will give a brief introduction to those and after that we will discuss how you can set up shipping methods inside Magento. Finally some possible additions to Magento's default shipping functionalities will be discussed.

Logistics in Magento

Magento Community Edition supports part of the logistics processes that occur in online stores. Put simply, logistics is everything related to moving the goods within your business from one place to the next. This entails stocking your inventory, picking your products from stock when an order arrives, packing your goods for sending, and finally shipping the order to your customer. One important aspect of this is that your customers should pay you the correct amount for shipping to their doorstep. In order to arrange that Magento has some default shipping calculations included. In this chapter the following will be discussed:

- ♦ At a general level, what kind of actions and processes are involved in e-commerce logistics

- ♦ Setting Magento's default shipping methods and what you can do if those do not suffice

- ♦ Why some aspects of logistics are not fully supported by Magento and what you can do if you need more logistics functionality in your Magento installation

Shipping processes and shipping arrangements

The core of most retail is getting a physical product from one location (your inventory) to another (your customer). For stores, shipping a product after it has been ordered consists of a number of standard steps:

1. Picking the product from its stock location
2. Packing the product in a protective material
3. Offering the package to a transport company
4. (Optionally) handling returns

All of the preceding steps, especially handling returns, consist of many different details and substeps. For instance, for returns, a couple of substeps are inspecting a product to see if it can get added back to stock, boxing the product properly again, refunding a customer after the return is received, and so on.

You can decide how many of these steps you want your company to perform. There are many warehouses that offer e-fulfillment services, meaning that all you do is arrange for stock to come in and after that the warehouse handles everything including picking, packing, shipping, and handling returns. This is a model used by many stores as the store can keep focusing on advertising, website improvements, and customer service while not having to deal with all the complexities of logistics.

The most extreme case of this, called "dropshipping", does not even require you to purchase stock. Steps 1 through 4 will all be handled by another company (called the dropshipper) and the only thing you do is send your orders to them. You only pay for products that are actually ordered and have no inventory risk. While this sounds good, the biggest disadvantages of dropshipping are that the margins on orders become very thin, and managing your product catalog and shipping prices becomes complex when you are sourcing your products from multiple dropshippers. For a more detailed discussion on dropshipping, an excellent guide can be found at `http://ecommerce.shopify.com/guides/dropshipping`.

Regardless of how you choose to handle picking, packing, shipping, and returns, you will need a way to communicate and charge the proper shipping costs to your customers. Besides keeping your products' stock levels, this is the only logistics-related thing the Magento Community Edition facilitates by default. Below you will find how to utilize Magento's shipping methods as well as pointers on what to do if you need other kinds of shipping price calculations.

Default shipping methods in Magento

The default shipping methods of Magento can be found in **System | Configuration | Shipping Methods**. There are multiple shipping methods included by default in Magento, of which three can be used relatively quickly in a starting store:

- ◆ Free Shipping: This is a zero sum shipping rate.

- ◆ Flat Rate: Here all customers see the same shipping rate during checkout.

- ◆ Table Rate: Here your customers will see a shipping rate that is determined by a number of factors.

Setting these up will be discussed later. Apart from these, Magento also includes integrations with UPS, USPS, FedEx, and DHL.

Configuring free shipping

When you enable this shipping method, customers get an option to choose a shipping method that does not increase the price of the total order. In other words, a free shipping method. Most of the settings for this shipping method function in the same way as the input fields with the same name for the Flat Rate shipping method as discussed previously. The only specific input field is **Minimum order amount**. The number you set here is from the order subtotal, which your free shipping method will show to customers. For instance, if you want to offer free shipping for all orders of 50 and above, set this value to 50, as shown in the following screenshot:

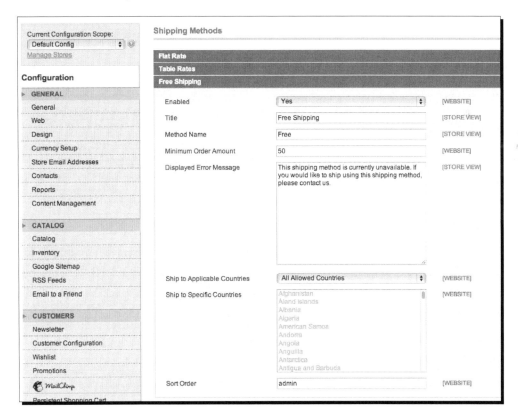

The free shipping method displays the following when it's applicable:

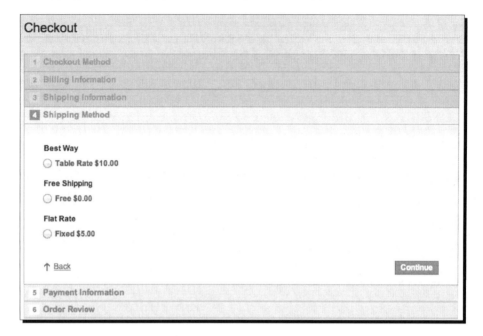

Configuring Flat Rate shipping

This shipping method is straightforward, both in presentation and configuration. Click on the **Flat Rate** configuration section in **System | Configuration | Shipping Methods** in the Magento admin. Here a number of settings shown:

- **Enabled**: This sets whether Flat Rate shipping is used at all in your store or not.
- **Title**: This is the text that displays next to the radio button, as the primary name of the shipping method.
- **Method Name**: This is an explanatory secondary title that shows after the shipping method is chosen.
- **Type**: This is either **None**, **Per Order**, or **Per Item**. This sets if the Flat Rate you enter is applied for the whole order or for each item in the order. The default is per item. As an example, if you have a Flat Rate of $5, and you have three items in your cart, the Flat Rate would be $15 if you set this type to **Per Item** and $5 if you set it to **Per Order**. If you set it to **None**, no Flat Rate is applied, effectively making this shipment method free.
- **Price**: This is the flat rate price.
- **Calculate Handling Fee**: This sets if the handling fee you specify is a fixed amount or a percentage surcharge over your Flat Rate price.

◆ **Handling Fee**: This is the additional handling cost you want to charge to the customer.

◆ **Displayed Error Message**: This message to show if something goes wrong.

◆ **Ship to Applicable Counties** and **Ship to Specific Countries**: This includes the countries you want to ship to. Most shops can leave this set to **All Allowed Countries**. In the configuration section in **System | Configuration | General** you can set which countries your visitors are allowed to pick in the shipping address form, which automatically limits the available countries for all your shipping options.

◆ **Sort Order**: This is a number that signifies the position of the Flat Rate shipping method within the list of all available shipping methods.

The Flat Rate shipping method configuration looks like the following screenshot:

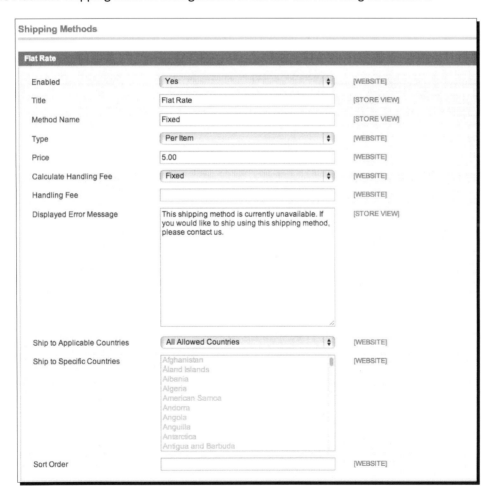

As an example, we've chosen a title of Flat Rate, "Bubble-wrapped parcel" as the method name, a Flat Rate of $5 and a fixed handling fee of $1, which results in the following presentation during checkout. It does not display as a choice with radio buttons because there is only one shipping method available, which Magento autoselects, as seen in the following screenshot:

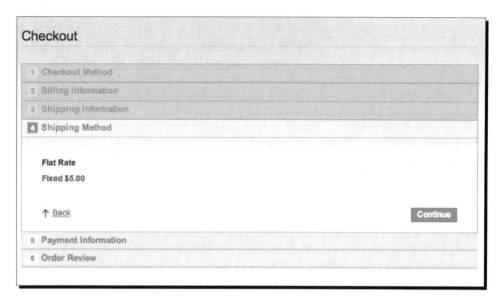

Table Rate shipping

It's also possible to set additional costs for handling the shipment. Using this shipping method you can save a table with shipping costs in the Magento admin, where the shipping costs are determined by one of the following combinations:

- Weight and destination
- Price and destination
- Number of articles and destination

It's also possible to set additional costs for handling the shipment. This is the most elaborate configuration of Magento's default shipping methods. Let's see how to do it!

Time for action – configuring Table Rate shipping

1. Selecting the right store scope.

   Go to **System** | **Configuration** | **Shipping Methods** and click on the **Table Rates** section. Magento's configuration has a drop-down list, which sets the store scope. By default, you are editing configuration values for all the Stores and Store Views in your Magento installation. If you want to configure this shipping method, you have to choose your website using the scope drop-down list in the top-left corner of the configuration section. You can't fully set up this shipping method if you have not chosen the Store or Store View for which you are editing the settings. The store scope drop-down list can be seen follows:

   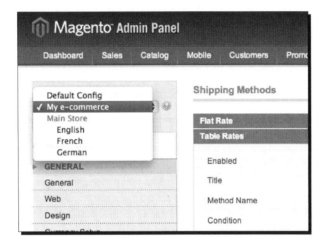

2. Exporting the CSV file.

   After you have set the scope drop-down list to the website, you can see a button for exporting a CSV file and a button for uploading a CSV file. A CSV file is a **Comma Separated Values** file and it is the file format often used in information systems to transmit rows of data.

   Select your desired way of determining the shipping price (either based on weight, number of articles, or order value), and click on **Save Config**. After that, click on the **Export CSV** button.

3. Opening and editing the CSV file.

The resulting CSV file can be opened in Microsoft Excel or other spreadsheet software such as LibreOffice. If you have chosen weight as the deciding factor, the CSV file looks like the following Excel screenshot:

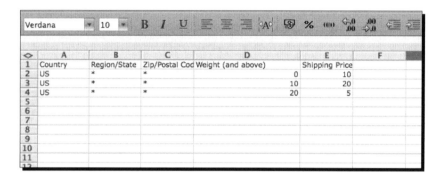

Each row is a different shipping rate for a combination of weight and destination. The **Weight (and above)** column signifies from which weight the shipping price is applied. In the example, orders with a total weight of 0-9 will get a shipping price of 10, orders with a total weight of 10-19 will get a shipping price of 20, and orders with a total weight of 20 and above will get a shipping price of 5. The units of weight can be anything you want such as kilograms or pounds. The important thing is that you use the same convention for all your products. The unit for the price you enter will be the base currency you have set for your store, in **System | Configuration | Currency Setup**.

4. Saving and uploading the CSV file.

When you are done setting the table rates in the spreadsheet, save it as a CSV file. After that you can go back to the admin in **System | Configuration | Shipping Methods**. Click on the Table Rates section, select the relevant store, and click on the **Browse files** button. A dialog similar to the one below will be shown:

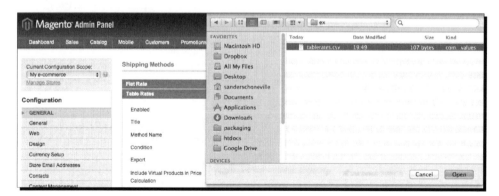

Select the CSV file and click on the **Import** button. After uploading the file, and enabling the shipping method, Magento will show the relevant rate to your customers. An example of an order with a weight of 1 can be seen in the following screenshot below:

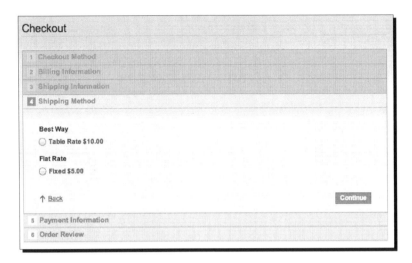

What just happened?

The Table Rate shipping method has many configuration fields that should be familiar from the Flat Rate shipping method. The following fields work in the same fashion as in the Flat Rate shipping method: **Enabled**, **Title** , **Method Name**, **Handling Fee**, **Displayed Error Message**, **Ship to Applicable Countries**, and **Sort Order**.

The CSV file that can be opened in Excel contains the following columns if you choose weight versus destination as the criteria for the Table Rate:

- **Country**: This is the two-letter country code for the country that this rate applies to (according to the ISO 3166 standard). You can find these country codes at: `http://www.iso.org/iso/country_codes/iso_3166_code_lists/country_names_and_code_elements.htm`. If the rate you are setting applies to all countries, you can enter a * character here.

- **Region/State**: If the rate you are entering applies to all regions within a country, fill in a * character here. If you need different rates for different regions of a country, in this column, an ISO 3166-2 letter abbreviation for the specific region has to be entered. You can find these letter combinations for each region quickest through this Wikipedia article: `http://en.wikipedia.org/wiki/ISO_3166-2`.

- **Zip/Postal Code**: This is the zip code for which the shipping rate is applied to. Usually inputting a * character will suffice here, which means that the zip code applies to all regions in a country.

- ◆ **Weight (and above)**: This is the weight for the shipping price of the zip code, region, and country of the particular row in the spreadsheet. Note that the "and above", means that when you input 1 as a value, the rate will apply to weights 1, 2, 5, 10, 100, and so on.

- ◆ **Shipping Price**: This is the price, entered as a regular decimal value without currency symbol.

When choosing the number of articles as the determining factor, the spreadsheet looks similar. The major difference is the **# of Items (and above)** column. In the following example, an order with 1 article will have a shipping cost of 10 and an order with 2 articles or more will have a shipping cost of 15. The following Excel screenshot shows a spreadsheet example with these values:

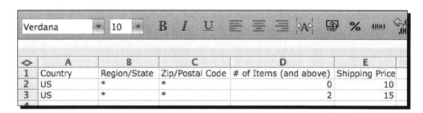

For the final possibility with Table Rates, base them on the order value, and the spreadsheet looks as follows. In this example, the important column is **Order Subtotal (and above)**. The following example would result in orders with a value from 0-49 having a shipping cost of 10 and orders with a value of 50 or higher having a shipping price of 5. This kind of construction is often employed by stores to drive visitors to higher average order sizes in order to reduce their shipping costs. See the following screenshot for an example of Table Rates spreadsheet based on **Order Subtotal (and above)**:

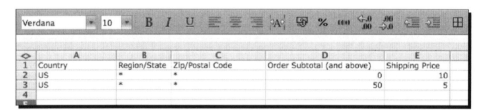

Have a go hero – add shipping costs for different countries

In our example, we added shipping rates for the US. Logically, the next step is to add shipping costs for other countries by yourself. Alternatively, try to make variants in shipping costs for different regions and zip codes. Remember to look up the ISO codes for countries and regions through the Wikipedia pages mentioned previously.

Pop quiz – vital conditions for Table Rates

Q1. There are several steps to take when setting Table Rates. For each of the following actions, indicate whether or not the action is mandatory:

1. Uploading your CSV file

2. Adding extra lines to the CSV file

3. Setting your store scope in the Magento configuration section

4. Opening the CSV file in Excel

Other ways of calculating shipping costs

It's possible that the default shipping methods included in Magento are not enough for you. For instance, if you are selling products that differ in size and weight and you need different shipping costs based on that, Magento's standard shipping methods are not enough. Another possibility is that your shipping costs need to be set as per product separately and need to be added together per product in your order. You will either need customizations or third-party extensions that arrange your desired functionality. One module supplier that has great expertise in Magento shipping methods is WebshopApps. You can find them here at: `http://www.webshopapps.com/`. Modules by WebshopApps are of a good quality and are relatively easy to install. If you are not exactly sure about your needs for a certain module, it is advised to mail them before you purchase it. As per the desire mentioned above, to input shipping prices per product they offer a free extension here at: `http://www.webshopapps.com/eu/product-flat-rate-shipping-extension.html`.

Presentation of shipping methods in your store

Just as with payment methods, it is crucially important that your shipping methods are presented in a crystal clear way. A lot of stores will only offer their customers one shipping method and one choice during checkout, but even in that case ensure that it is clear what costs are included in the shipping charge. For instance, handling, service fees, administration costs, and so on. If you communicate clearly what is included in your shipping price, your customer will also understand better why your price is what it is. Especially, if your shipping prices are higher than your competitor's but you offer additional services, be sure to make your customers aware of that!

It is possible to have several shipping methods in Magento active at once. Take care to test your settings thoroughly, otherwise undesired scenarios can occur. For instance, if you've set a Flat Rate of 4 and the Free Shipping method as well, the shipping methods will be displayed like this:

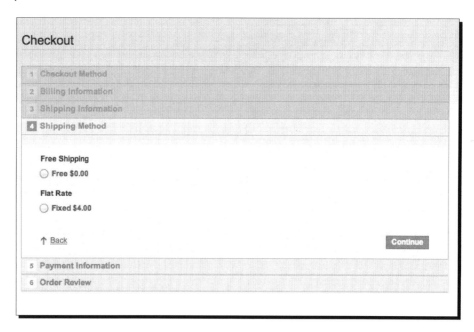

It's clear what your customers will choose! Again, always test your checkout process extensively. If you offer multiple shipping methods, list out the differences between each one of them and also describe the advantages of the more expensive ones.

Magento's blind spots

At the beginning of the chapter, we mentioned the shipping process from a bird's eye view. Before you can actually ship anything, you have to purchase goods as well (unless you dropship). By default, many facets of logistics are not handled by Magento. These will be briefly discussed later. The main goal of this is to give you an idea of what things should be arranged either outside of Magento or through Magento extensions. The reason Magento does not include functionality for the following aspects of logistics is because most of them are highly company-specific and as such difficult to include in a general e-commerce system like Magento. The fact that Magento has blind spots is not bad per se. Magento is an excellent marketing tool, product catalog, and transaction processor, and was built with the reasoning that more detailed business processes are better suited to be handled by other information systems that were built to support those processes specifically.

Purchasing

In the beginning phases of a new store, managing purchases to replenish stock is usually relatively easy. Volumes are still low and a large part of knowledge about what's available is often monitored by the people responsible for purchasing. Magento offers a low stock notification feed under **Catalog | Manage Products**, which can also be used to get an idea of which products to purchase.

However, Magento does not have a supplier management or purchasing component. When your purchasing processes get bigger, you will desire to know about each of your suppliers: about the purchases you've made, if they have been delivered, how good or bad each supplier is (what the open issues are), and also what the contractual agreements with each of them are. A proper purchasing support system also automatically monitors sale trends and matches those with delivery times of your suppliers, ensuring that the products are always reordered just in time. The biggest stores even have multiple suppliers for individual products and their purchasing systems advise which supplier to use for a product based on real-time prices and quality ratings.

Of course, not all of these functionalities are interesting for a starting shop immediately. If the need arises for detailed purchasing management, an outside business process support system should be sought.

Warehousing

Magento does not include functionality to manage your warehouse in much detail. For each product, a stock level can be set, and that's it. Some stores add product attributes that can help them find products in their storage facilities, for instance by adding an attribute called "Pick location", which indicates the shelf a product is placed on.

That was all about Magento regarding the warehouse management. If you need things such as managing stock on multiple stock locations (multiple warehouses), insights on what products are picked from stock, packed after picking, and offered to a shipper for sending to your customers, you will need customizations or an integration with another system.

Returns processing

Managing returns, when customers receive undesired or faulty goods, is something almost every store deals with. Magento Enterprise Edition actually has a returns management component included, but Magento Community Edition does not. As your volumes increase, managing returns becomes very hard if you try to do it through e-mail. It will become difficult to know which products still have to be inspected, what your most faulty products are, which customers still need a reply, and what is the total amount of money lost through refunds. Because proper returns management is such a vital part of online stores and because it's something that lends itself to be built as a standardized component, several Magento extension vendors have built commercial returns management extensions for Magento Community Edition. The one you decide to use is based on your demands of course; some of those available are:

```
http://ecommerce.aheadworks.com/magento-extensions/rma.html
```

```
http://www.magesolutions.com/#!__rma-module
```

```
http://mageconsult.net/rma-177.html.
```

Cheaper is not necessarily better and using a well-known supplier such as aheadWorks is usually safest.

Summary

Magento offers a range of default shipping methods that allow you to either set Flat Rate shipping, Free Shipping rates, or shipping rates based on a combination of factors. These factors can be weight versus destination, number of items versus destination, and order value versus destination. Although this helps most stores with their basic shipping pricing and in their checkout processes, additional wishes are also common. When these occur, suppliers such as Webshop Apps are a good place to go to find shipping solutions. Besides shipment method pricing, Magento does not offer many functionalities related to the logistics process. To get proper ways of dealing with product purchasing, warehouse management, and handling returns, third-party systems or modules are needed.

In the next chapter, Magento's frontend will be discussed. Pointers will be given on how to change your homepage and how to go about getting a top notch frontend theme.

9

Customizing Your Store's Appearance

The appearance of your store is a big factor in getting your visitor's trust and helping them find the right information. The way your site looks also determines for a large part how easy or hard it is to actually purchase something. Because of that it is no surprise that many store owners want complete control over their store's look and feel. This chapter shows the first steps in getting acquainted with changing things in your store's design.

Magento themes

A Magento theme is a collection of files that determines the look and feel of your Magento store. Instead of the word "theme" people who work with Magento often use the word "template", although strictly speaking this is not the proper terminology. Compared to other software packages the way Magento handles themes is pretty elaborate. Because of this your store's appearance can be changed very flexibly, but the downside is that working with themes in Magento has a steeper learning curve.

In this chapter, we shall cover:

- ◆ Editing your home page and other CMS pages
- ◆ Changing transactional e-mails
- ◆ Dealing with the many premade themes you can find online
- ◆ What to watch out for when you let a freelancer or agency make your theme
- ◆ Making some minor changes in your theme.

Your home page, CMS pages, and static blocks

As a store owner, your first focus point regarding the design of your site is often your home page. A home page in Magento is a part of Magento's **content management system (CMS)** by default. Magento's CMS allows you to add pages and static blocks. A **page** is, as expected, a web page that can be accessed on your store. A **static block** is a piece of content that can be used anywhere *on* pages within your store, such as the list of links in your site's footer.

The CMS of Magento can be accessed directly from the main menu in the admin. To edit the home page, open **CMS | Pages**. You'll see several pages, including an **About Us** page that is included by default. An example overview of CMS pages, as they are found in a default installation with sample data, is shown in the following screenshot:

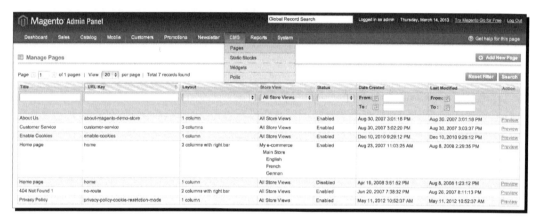

Click on the page titled **Home page**. Now an edit screen opens with several input fields visible immediately. The URL key merits special attention; the value you enter here is the part of the URL that will be placed after your domain name to access the page. For instance, the home page has **home** as the URL key. Because it's the home page, this means that this page can be accessed from `http://www.yourdomain.com/` as well as `http://www.yourdomain.com/home/`. In the next screenshot you can see what the CMS page edit screen looks like:

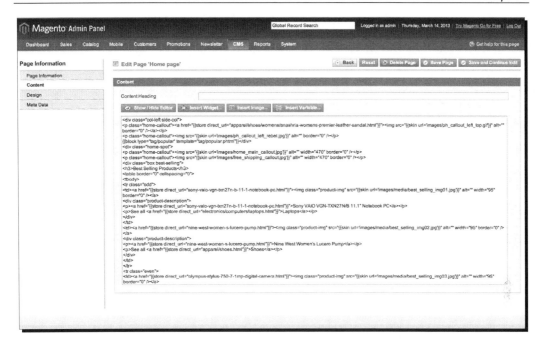

Editing the content of the home page can be done by clicking on the **Content** tab in the menu on the left of the screen. When the editor, which can be switched between WYSIWYG (what you see is what you get) and HTML mode, opens you will find the following screen:

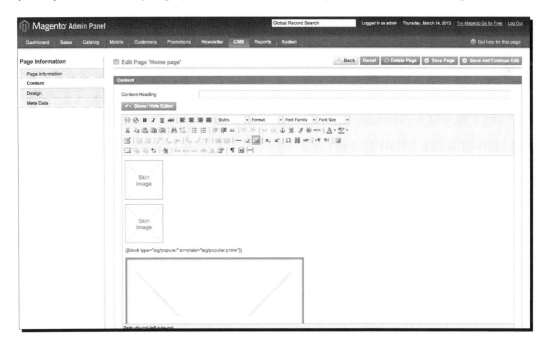

The preceding screenshot is what HTML mode looks like, while the WYSIWYG mode is displayed as follows:

In our current example, the left column is part of the home CMS page. The standard home page with Magento's sample data shows an image of women's shoes as you can see in the following screenshot:

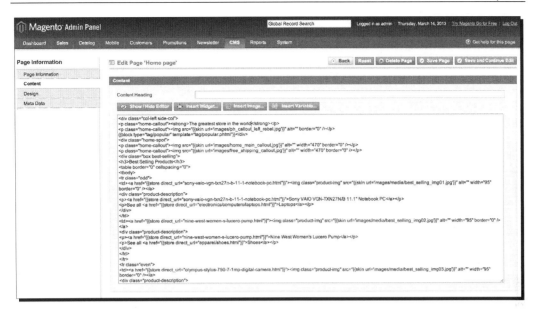

After removing the top image from that column and replacing it with the text `The greatest store in the world`, the change is visible immediately after saving:

Making changes in HTML mode allows for more precise edits but requires HTML knowledge.

After making the change the above the CMS edit screen is displayed, while the following screenshot shows what your front page looks like after making the edit:

Editing static blocks follows a similar method. For instance, footer links are displayed as follows. As previously mentioned, the footer links are an example of a static block:

You can edit the footer links by going to **CMS | Static Blocks** as displayed in the following screenshot and opening the block with title **Footer links**.

After clicking on the **Footer links** block, a familiar edit page opens:

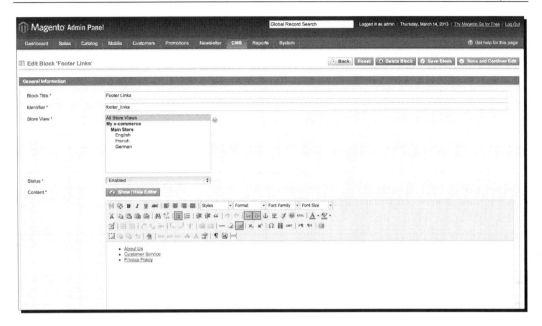

In our example, we've changed the first link to say **About our awesome store**, which is reflected on all pages. In a Magento installation without sample data, **Footer links** is the only static block that is present by default. Adding and displaying additional static blocks in your store requires Magento theming knowledge that is outside of the scope of this book:

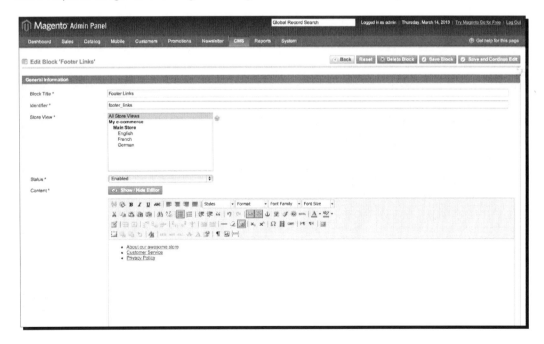

In the following screenshot you can see the change reflected in the frontend of the store:

Changing transactional e-mails

Transactional e-mails are informational e-mails sent by Magento. They are used, for instance, to let your visitors know about their placed orders, send password reminder e-mails, and to send product recommendations. Besides informing customers, they are also used to send store administrators updates such as low stock notifications. In this section we will only focus on the e-mails intended for customers.

In general, there are three things store owners want to change in transactional e-mails:

♦ The logo used in the e-mails

♦ The text inside the e-mails

♦ The layout of the e-mails

The first and second should always be done as otherwise your store will be sending e-mails to your customers with Magento's logo and default texts. However, you can skip the third (recommended) as Magento's default layout for the transactional mails is usually fine to start with. If you do want to change the layout of the transactional mails, we suggest contacting somebody who has experience with styling e-mails and have them perform the work. Creating proper e-mail layouts that work well in different kinds of e-mail programs is different from creating layouts that work inside web browsers, so you should check for the proper expertise if you want to have e-mail layouts made. We will discuss changing the logo and text inside transactional e-mails in the following section. As an example, in the following screenshot a default order confirmation e-mail can be seen:

Have a go hero – changing the logo used in transactional e-mails

As previously mentioned and shown, a Magento logo is shown by default in transactional e-mails. You can change the logo used in transactional e-mails by going to **System | Configuration | Design** in the Magento admin. There, open the section called **Transactional Emails**. In the following screenshot you can see what this section looks like:

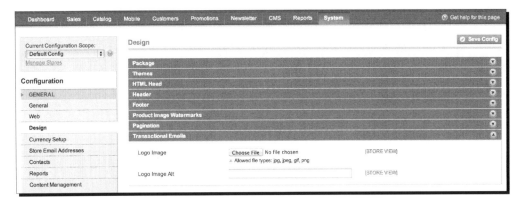

In the **Transactional Emails** section, click on the **Choose File** button. Now a dialog from your operating system (usually Windows or Mac OS) will open. Select the proper e-mail logo image file you want from the dialog and submit it. This means that the logo you want to use should be present on your computer somewhere, of course. After you have chosen the proper file, click on the **Save Config** button.

> Refresh Magento's caches after saving configuration settings. *Chapter 11, Maintaining and Administrating Your Store*, provides more information on Magento's cache management.

Time for action – changing the text inside transactional e-mails

To change the text inside a transactional e-mail, you will have to make a new e-mail template inside the Magento admin. In the following steps we will show how to do that, with the new order e-mail for guests as an example. What this e-mail looks like by default can be seen in the screenshot shown earlier. As a simple example, we will be changing the text "Thank you again for your business" to "Hope to see you again soon".

1. Open Magento's transactional e-mail management and add a new template.

Transactional e-mails can be added by going to **System | Transactional Emails** in Magento's admin. Once there, click on the **Add New Template** button, which is found in the top-right corner of the screen, as can be seen in the following screenshot:

2. Choose the proper default settings to load.

A fairly big, empty form should be shown now. Luckily, you do not have to input all the required settings for the new order e-mail manually. In the drop-down menu called **Template**, select the **New Order for Guest** option and click on the **Load Template** button, as shown in the following screenshot:

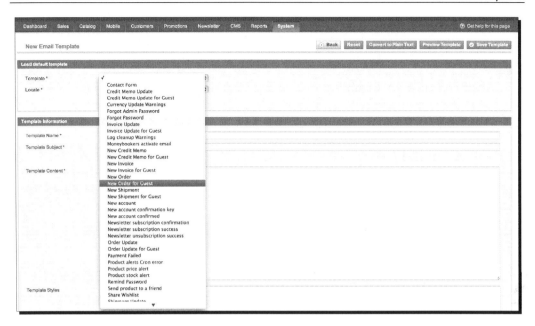

Now the form will be filled with the default settings for the new order e-mail that is sent to customers who are not logged in when they order.

3. Make the desired changes and save.

The **Template Name** field reflects the name you want to give this template to use internally inside the Magento admin. Your customers will not see this name; the name you give the template here is purely to make it easy for you to find. We recommend something like `Store Name - Language - Type of email`. In our current example, we have used `Demo Store - English - New Order for Guests`.

The **Template Subject** field is the subject line the e-mail will have. Inside this input field, you will see strange characters such as **{{** and **}}**. For the purposes of this book, we recommend not touching anything that starts with **{{** and ends with **}}**. These are bits of content that will be replaced by Magento when the e-mail is actually sent, and are called **variables**. For example, **{{var order.increment_id}}** will be replaced by Magento with the unique order code for a customer's specific order. Just leaving them as they are is a good idea; editing everything else in the subject line is safe.

The **Template Content** input area is what we are currently interested in. In this area, you will see a mix of HTML, regular text, and variables. We recommend to leave everything that is enclosed between **<** and **>**, or **{{** and **}}** intact. The former are HTML tags and the latter are Magento's variables.

For the current example, scroll down inside the **Template Content** field until you see the text "Thank you again for your business" and replace it with "Hope to see you again soon", as shown in the following screenshot. After that, click on the **Save Template** button:

4. Configure Magento to use the e-mail template.

Just making the transactional e-mail inside the **Transactional Emails** section in **System** does not actually have any effect yet. In order for Magento to actually use the template, we have to tell Magento to use it through the configuration section, and specifically the configuration of sales order e-mails.

Go to **System | Configuration | Sales Emails**, found in the left-hand menu of the configuration section of the Magento admin. There, open the **Order** section. In the **New Order Confirmation Template for Guest** drop-down menu, select the template we just made, as shown in the following screenshot:

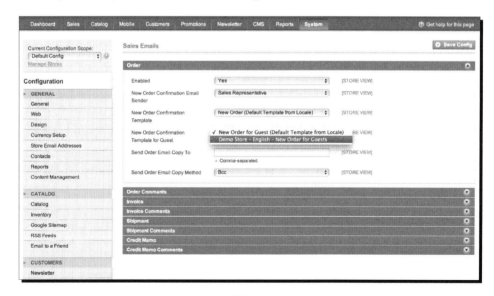

After selecting our own template (note that you will see the template name you entered earlier inside the drop-down menu in this configuration section), click on the **Save Config** button.

You are now done! You may need to refresh Magento's caches; refer to *Chapter 11, Maintaining and Administrating Your Store*, for more information about that.

What just happened?

Changing the contents, or layout if you are confident enough, of transactional e-mails always involves two steps: creating the transactional e-mail in **System | Transactional Emails** and after that configuring Magento to actually use the newly-made transactional e-mail. In *Chapter 6, Customer Relationships*, we already showed where most configuration settings relating to customer account e-mails can be found. In the preceding discussion, we mentioned going to **System | Configuration | Sales Emails**, where you will find the configuration settings for the various order-related e-mails Magento sends out. Other often used configuration sections for transactional e-mails are **System | Configuration | Contacts, System | Configuration | Newsletter**, and **System | Configuration | Wishlist**. A practical way of tackling transactional mails is simply testing your shop thoroughly. Note every e-mail that is not to your liking and determine which template you should add to the **Emails** section to solve that.

It is very important to understand the difference between a guest order and an order by a registered customer. Please refer back to *Chapter 6, Customer Relationships*, for more information about this difference if necessary. Magento sends out different order, invoice, and shipment e-mails to guests and logged in customers!

Choosing between a pre-made and a custom-made theme

The first important choice regarding your store's theme is whether to use a premade theme or to have a theme custom-made for you. In the following table you will find the advantages and disadvantages of both. These are rules of thumb and greatly depend on the suppliers you pick:

	Premade	Custom-made
Price	++ (possibly free)	-
Technical quality	+	++
Graphical quality	-	++
Match with your vision	+/-	++
Uniqueness	--	++
Time before you can go live	++	--

As you can see, you can assume it will be cheaper with a premade theme but the quality and uniqueness of the theme will be less. Because you can start selling quicker and the price is lower, a downloadable premade theme can still be a very attractive option to start with. Also remember it's possible to start with a premade theme and to have a custom-made theme built at a later time, when you have the time and money for that. A common way to work is to start with a premade theme and to make minor customizations to it to suit your needs.

What to watch out for with premade themes

The important aspect of everything you buy, is determine who is supplying it to you. This holds true for your downloadable theme as well. If you buy a theme from a well-known theme builder, the risk of a failure is much smaller. Later on in this chapter we have provided a list of several good suppliers of premade Magento themes.

When choosing your downloadable theme, you should at least watch out for the following:

- Does the theme have enough room for your logo?

- Do the colors of the theme match the products you will be selling?

- Is the home page of the theme suitable for your store? Big pictures look nice for instance, but remember that you will have to arrange for your own big pictures then, and that you are spending a lot of important screen real estate that could have also been used to promote several individual products.

- Are the theme's product lists suitable for your products? If you are selling products that need to be experienced visually, for instance – jewelry, bigger images in your product list are very important. When you're selling things such as electronics, however, it is equally important to be able to show some extra product specifications such as hard drive space, and so on. Think of what your products need presentation-wise and look for a theme that matches this.

- Is the product detail page structured well? Information on this page should be presented clearly. Most important is the grouping of information related to a purchase near the **Buy** button. Make sure that the **Buy** button is very noticeable, and that pricing information is close to the button. The product page is one of the most important pages of your store together with the shopping cart and checkout process! Unfortunately, many store owners spend more time on their home page than on the product detail page. Remember that a large portion of your visitors will enter your store on a product page and generally many visitors gloss over a home page quickly.

Technical aspects to watch our for are as follows:

- The theme should be compatible with your version of Magento.

- Check if the theme comes with additional Magento extensions. Some themes do not work without custom extensions. These kinds of themes are not preferable.

◆ Ask how many changes to the standard layout (page structure) of Magento were made. If you want to use some presentational modules such as slideshows, it greatly helps if the theme builder stuck close to the standard layout of Magento. It is also easier to follow tutorials and tricks that can be found online when you have a theme that is close to a default theme.

◆ Check if the theme uses the standard Magento JavaScript library—Prototype. Some themes come with the JavaScript library jQuery. Those themes cause the loading time of a first visit to increase as the visitor will need to download both Prototype and jQuery when they access your store. On fast connections this effect is not a big problem, but if you have visitors on slow connections this can pose a problem. Another issue with using Prototype and jQuery in the frontend is that bugs may arise because the two libraries can interfere with each other.

Do not base your choice for a premade theme on just some screenshots of the theme. Most stores that sell Magento themes also offer the possibility to view the theme in the live mode, so try before you buy.

What to watch out for with custom-made themes

By having a Magento theme custom-made for your store, you can get many advantages. The most important one is that you will get much more freedom in arranging the way visitors can find and navigate the information in your store. Often you will only get the necessary insights for this after you have been running your store for a while, and have had interactions with your customers. This again emphasizes that starting out with a premade theme is fine as is switching to a custom-made one later on when you're ready.

Immediately starting with a custom theme offers some other advantages though. Your store will usually look more professional (where your image "fits"). How important that is can only be decided by you. If establishing your brand is very important, a custom theme might be best for you. Starting online stores often overestimate the importance of branding, but if you already have an existing store or brand, this is of course something to give you more weight.

Another less obvious advantage of a custom theme is that you will get a development partner who knows your theme through and through and as such can perform adjustments relatively quickly.

A combination

As mentioned earlier, if you like a particular premade theme but need some improvements, and you cannot tackle it yourself. You can think about having only those changes custom-made for you after you purchase the theme.

Suppliers for premade themes

There are many places to find themes; the list that follows is not exhaustive. A Google search for "Magento theme" will reveal more suppliers. The following list is ordered by number of themes available; the first in the list has the most themes.

- **Templatemonster** (`http://www.templatemonster.com/magento-themes.php`): Here you will find a wide range of wildly differing themes. Unfortunately the quality of the themes can differ widely too, so make sure to at least use the live preview function.

- **Themeforest** (`http://themeforest.net/category/ecommerce/magento`): This site has a good system in place that allows you to recognize the good themes (based on number of downloads and ratings), and themes are priced relatively cheaply.

- **AheadWorks** (`https://ecommerce.aheadworks.com/magento-themes-and-templates.html`): This site is a quality extension builder that also sells some decent Magento themes.

- **Polarthemes** (`http://www.polarthemes.com`): Here, only a couple of themes are available, but their work is high on quality. Their templates are also highly suitable for further enhancements by you.

Partners for Magento themes

On Magento's website a list of Magento partners sorted by country can be found. These are divided between Gold, Silver, and Bronze partners. These designations currently do not say a lot. Magento partners have sufficient Magento project experience, but the Gold, Silver, and Bronze designations have been mostly decided by how much money a Magento partner is willing to pay to get the partnership certificate.

Magento is planning to make the demands for the different partnership programs depend on, for instance, the number of Enterprise projects delivered and the number of certified developers employed by the partner.

This does not take away the fact that you can find experienced Magento partners in Magento's partner list. You can find the list at the following link:

`http://www.magentocommerce.com/partners/find/solution-partners/`

Of course there are many companies who are not on Magento's partner list, but are still perfectly able to perform Magneto work for you. A Google search for "Magento project" or "Magento store" will yield ads and search results for multiple suppliers.

Another possibility is hiring a freelancer. The advantage of a freelancer is that you will be talking directly to the person building the theme. Finding a good freelancer is considerably harder than finding an Internet agency that can make a Magento theme though.

If you commission a freelancer or agency to develop for you, we recommend that you ask for references and check up on them.

Installing a theme

Getting a theme to work has two steps: installing the theme and configuring the theme. These will be discussed for premade and custom-made themes respectively.

Have a go hero – installing a free premade theme

Free themes can sometimes be installed through MagentoConnect. This works in the same way as installing an extension: retrieve the extension key and enter it in the MagentoConnect Manager. An example of retrieving an extension key and using it can be found in *Chapter 7, Accepting Payments*, about the MailChimp extension integration. After you have installed the theme, the theme will be present among the files in your Magento installation. What the file structure of the theme looks like can be found in the *Have a go hero – configuring a theme*. It will also be discussed in more detail in *Making changes to your theme*. Usually, some installation and configuration information is also provided with the theme. If your free theme is delivered as a downloadable package rather than through MagentoConnect, please read the following section.

Have a go hero – installing a paid theme

A theme is usually delivered as a ZIP package (a small file that contains all required files). The contents of the ZIP package need to be copied inside Magento's file structure according to the instructions from your supplier. You can also ask your supplier to install the theme for you. Often there is a surcharge for that. An example file structure of such a package is displayed in the following screenshot (the Magik Gifts theme that can be found at http://www.magikcommerce.com/magik-gifts-pro-magento-theme):

Name	Date Modified	Size	Kind
▼ 📁 app	Today 15:52	--	Folder
▶ 📁 code	16 Jun 2011 16:56	--	Folder
▼ 📁 design	Today 15:52	--	Folder
▼ 📁 frontend	Today 15:52	--	Folder
▼ 📁 default	Today 15:52	--	Folder
▼ 📁 magik_gifts	20 Jan 2012 11:04	--	Folder
▶ 📁 etc	20 Jan 2012 11:04	--	Folder
▶ 📁 layout	6 Feb 2012 15:31	--	Folder
▶ 📁 template	20 Jan 2012 11:04	--	Folder
▶ 📁 etc	16 Jun 2011 17:00	--	Folder
📄 magik_gifts_psd.zip	14 Feb 2012 14:47	10.1 MB	ZIP archive
📄 magik_gifts.pdf	1 Feb 2013 14:15	573 KB	Portab...(PDF)
📄 readme.txt	7 Feb 2012 15:12	1 KB	Plain...cument
▼ 📁 skin	Today 15:52	--	Folder
▼ 📁 frontend	Today 15:52	--	Folder
▼ 📁 default	Today 15:52	--	Folder
▶ 📁 magik_gifts	20 Jan 2012 11:05	--	Folder

This is a free theme that is available as a download, which is similar to how paid themes are distributed. The files displayed should then be copied over to your website's Magento file structure in order to make the theme work.

Have a go hero – configuring a theme

After you have installed your theme through any of the aforementioned means, you still have to configure it. Magento will not know how to show your theme otherwise. To configure your theme, go to **System | Configuration | Design**. There are several input sections, as usual. The most important ones are "package" and "themes". In the package section, the input field will show **default** in a standard Magento installation. The themes section will have **default** listed as well next to the input field that is also named **default**.

The package and theme name you can enter will correspond to the location of your theme in Magento's filesystem. Most themes that you download, especially the paid for ones, contain an installation manual. The manual includes what you should enter under the package and themes sections to get the theme to work. It is useful to know what the terms mean. A theme with a package called **beginner** and theme called **guide** means that the HTML files of the theme can be found at the file location `app/design/frontend/beginner/guide`, and the images and styling at `skin/frontend/beginner/guide/`.

If your theme does not include clear installation instructions, you can always check the `app/design/frontend` folder to check where the theme is located and what package and theme configurations you have to use. In the previous section we showed what the file structure of the Magik Gifts theme looks like: the theme is located at `app/design/frontend/default/magik_gifts`. This means that you would input **default** as the package and **magik_gifts** as the theme, at **System | Configuration | Design**.

It is possible that your theme does not supply all the files that are theoretically possible in a Magento theme. If you only see a couple of files listed in your downloaded theme, while Magento's standard theme folders show many more files, there does not have to be a problem. Magento has a fallback system where ultimately files from the `app/design/frontend/base/default` folder are used when your package or theme does not include them. A downloaded theme that does not include all of Magento's files often means the maker of the theme understands Magento well!

Making changes to your theme

In this section we will take a look at how to configure your theme and also look at what kinds of changes can be made.

Kinds of changes

When making changes to your theme, it's important to know what you are working on and where to look. Magento themes are complex for beginners: if you open a theme folder, it will not be immediately clear where to search. It is not recommended that you make many changes to your theme as a beginner.

To paint a picture: it can take an experienced web developer several weeks to really get a grip on Magento's theming system. Because of this, it is a good idea to consult an expert for middle to large adjustments.

 Magento beginners are advised to not try making many changes to their own theme unless expertise in PHP, HTML, XML, and CSS is present.

In the following sections we provide some examples of what we consider small, medium, and large changes. This is only as an illustration, based on what we've encountered.

Small changes

In general this is changing colors and/or wordings, and simple layout adjustments. For example:

- Changing a heading to normal text
- Removing some links from the store
- Making words or headings bold or italic
- Removing a block from the right column (for example, the Recently Viewed block)

Medium changes

These include changes to the layout of your store and more complex HTML and XML work. For example:

- Hiding a column from product information in your shopping cart because it's not relevant for your store
- Using a different zoom method for your product images
- Correctly displaying new Magento extensions
- Moving the search form from the top of your site to the right column

Big changes

Big changes are those where parts of your theme need to be (re)built. Often this requires programming (PHP) logic. For example:

- Changing the way the drop-down menus of your categories are structured.
- Showing your checkout process on the same page as your shopping cart.
- Showing different kinds of product information at different locations on the product detail page, depending on the type of product. For instance, showing a color selector for your products as a list of clickable color images instead of a drop-down menu containing color names.

Here, we will discuss a way to perform some of the smaller changes previously mentioned, to give you a feel of how to approach similar problems. If you want to read more, it's best to go to `http://www.magentocommerce.com/design_guide/articles/working-with-magento-themes`, where you will find a manual for people working on Magento themes, written by Magento themselves.

The changes we will use as an example are: removing a block from the right column, changing the color of certain headings, and changing certain headings to normal text.

As previously discussed, you can find the files of your theme in the `app/design/frontend/` and `skin/frontend/` folders. We'll assume a package called `beginner` and a theme called `guide`. Of course, replace these names with your package and theme names wherever necessary. Looking inside the `app/design/frontend/beginner/guide/` folder, we see a couple of folders. For changing the look of your theme, the `layout` and `template` folders are important. The `layout` folder contains XML files that tell Magento where the blocks of information in your store should be positioned. The `template` folder contains PHTML files as per the Magento component that display the information of the information blocks defined in the `layout` folder. A PHTML file contains PHP code (programming) and HTML code (markup).

All of the discussion in the following sections assumes your theme is structured exactly like the package/theme of a standard Magento theme.

Before you change any code, it's useful to turn off Magento's cache. Otherwise, often your changes will not show. The process to disable the cache can be found in *Chapter 11, Maintaining and Administrating Your Store*.

Time for action – changing a heading to normal text

In this example, we shall change the display of the product's name on a product detail page from a heading to normal text.

1. Turn on **Template Path Hints**. The heading that we'll use in this example is a product title on the product details page. In a default Magento installation, the product title will look as follows:

We will now display the text "Nokia 2610 Phone" as normal text instead of as a heading.

To achieve that, we have to find the file in the `template` folder of our theme that retrieves product titles and displays them.

Which file to open is easiest to determine when you turn on the so-called **Template Path Hints** that Magento has. You will find these in the Magento admin in **System | Configuration | Developer**. Before you get the option to turn on **Template Path Hints**, you have to choose a website in the store drop-down menu in the top-left of the configuration section:

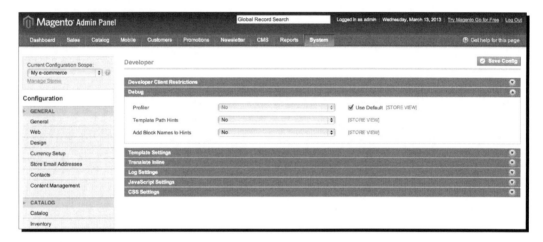

Enable the template path hints and head back to the product detail page.

2. Find Magento's hint for the location of the PHTML file.

You will now see rectangles made by red lines, which indicate several sections within your product page. In the top-left corner of the rectangles are designations such as **catalog\product\view.phtml**, as shown in the following screenshot. These designations are the template files you should look in to make changes:

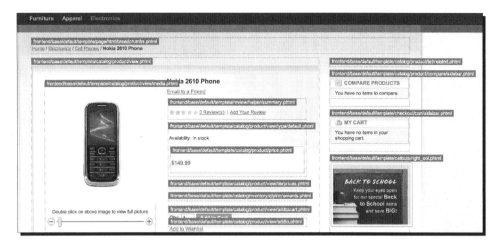

 Don't do this in a live store! You can specify some allowed IP addresses in **System | Configuration | Developer**, so only people who have one of those IP addresses can view the red rectangles. That way you can ensure that only you can see the template path hints, but a mistake is quickly made and to avoid the risk of all your visitors getting the path hints it's better to have a safe testing environment for this kind of thing.

3. Follow Magento's hint. Now open the `template` folder at location `app/design/frontend/beginner/guide/`.

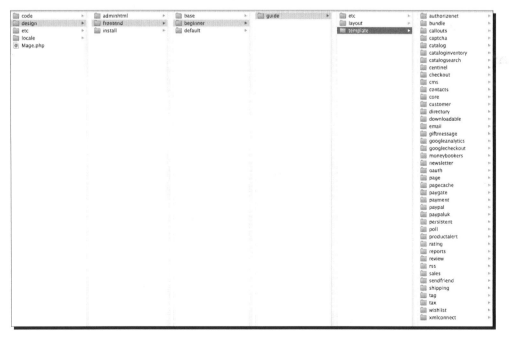

This will result in a list of folders that matches the different components of Magento. For example, the `checkout` folder, which contains all PHTML files that are connected to the shopping cart and checkout process, and the `customer` folder, which contains the PHTML files that arrange for the display of customer accounts. In our example, we need the `catalog` folder, which contains files relating to the display of categories and products. Open the `app/design/frontend/beginner/guide/template/catalog/` folder.

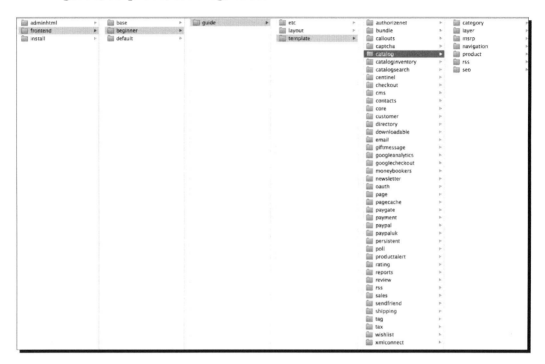

The file we need is not present yet. We do see a folder called `product`. Open that. This makes our current location `app/design/frontend/beginner/guide/template/catalog/product/`:

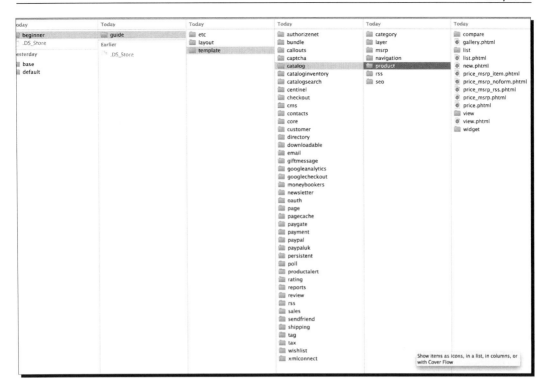

The `view.phtml` file is, as we saw earlier, the file in which we need to make the desired change.

4. Open the PHTML file with a text editor:

5. Change the code. The file contains a lot of HTML and some programming (PHP code). The relevant part for us is as shown in the following code snippet:

```
<h1><?php echo $_helper->productAttribute($_product, $_product-
>getName(), 'name') ?></h1>
```

The `<h1>` and `</h1>` pieces (called tags) cause the product title to be displayed as a heading. If we remove these and do nothing else, the line will become as follows:

```
<?php echo $_helper->productAttribute($_product, $_product-
>getName(), 'name') ?>
```

Do not change anything between the `<?php` and `?>` bits unless you know exactly what you are doing. After changing the H1 tags your product detail page will look as follows (we turned **Template Path Hints** off before taking this screenshot.) By making this change, we're telling browsers and search engines that the product's name is not a heading for our product detail pages. It should be clear that this is an example only as your product's name is usually a fine heading for product detail pages! Making the change outlined would be logical if you would be adding the H1 tag back somewhere else on the page:

Time for action – changing the color of a heading

Follow these steps to change the color of a heading:

1. **Using a browser CSS styling inspector**: When changing colors, the folder to be in is not `app/design/frontend` but rather `skin/frontend`. Because of that, template path hints are of no use now. What does help is using a browser that supports viewing styling information (CSS). One of the most used browsers for that is Firefox with the plugin Firebug installed. You can install Firefox by browsing to `http://www.firefox.com` and following the instructions to download and install there.

After you have installed Firefox, open Firefox and click on the menu option **Extra | Add-ons**. In the next screen, click on **Get Add-ons** and in the search field enter "firebug":

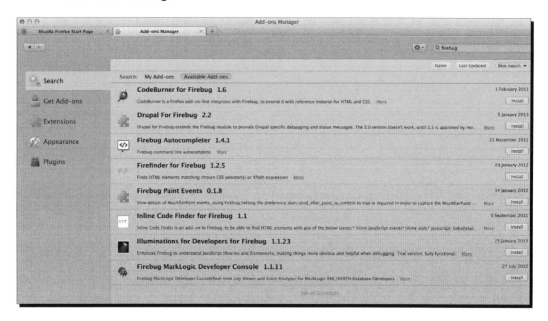

In the resulting list, click on **See all results** (the way this is displayed differs based on your version of Firefox and if you use an Apple computer or not) . Now you will see a page where the first result is **Firebug**. Click on the green **Add to Firefox** button, and your tools to attack page styling are installed. As an example for changing the color of a heading, we shall use the same text as in the previous paragraph. If we want to change the product title to display in red, we first have to know where the the styling of product titles is arranged. To find this out, Firebug allows you to inspect elements of web pages.

2. **Inspecting the page element you want to change**: Go to the product title, press the mouse button and then select **Inspect Element**. In the bottom-right of the screen you will now see styling information as shown:

3. Changing the styling: In the current example you can see that the relevant place to make the adjustment is `skin/frontend/beginner/guide/css/styles.css`, line 1112 (if you do not have your own theme, the default location to look at is `skin/frontend/base/default/css/styles.css`). If we change this style definition to make product titles red, the style definition will look as follows:

```
1104   .send-friend .form-list textarea { width:294px; }
1105   .send-friend .form-list li.wide .input-box { width:612px; }
1106   .send-friend .form-list li.wide textarea { width:609px; }
1107   .send-friend .buttons-set .limit { float:right; margin:0 7px 0 0; font-size:11px; line-height:21px; }
1108   /* ============================================================================== */
1109
1110
1111   /* Content Styles ============================================================== */
1112   .product-name { margin:0; font-size:1em; font-weight:normal; color: red; }
1113   .product-name a { color:#1e7ec8; }
1114
1115   /* Product Tags */
1116   .tags-list { display:block; font-size:13px; border:1px solid #c1c4bc; background:#f8f7f5; padding:10px; }
1117   .tags-list li { display:inline !important; margin:0 4px 0 0; }
```

    The `color:red;` bit is added by us. To make these kinds of changes, knowledge of CSS is necessary. For an overview of CSS rules, you can visit `http://reference.sitepoint.com/css`.

4. **Refreshing the product page**: The end result of the change we just made is visible after we refresh the product page. Because this is a change in CSS and CSS information is often not fully refreshed when a browser reloads a page, it is usually required to press *Ctrl + F5* on your PC or *command + R* to refresh the page properly. Using these keyboard shortcuts ensures the browser will reload the page fully.

If you are following along, results will only be visible if you also removed the H1 tags as shown in the previous section!

After making the changes and refreshing the page properly the end result looks like this:

Time for action – removing a block from the right column

Most of Magento's pages have either two or three columns, with the right column containing information such as the shopping cart contents and a product comparison block. We will be removing one of these; the technique shown can be used for removing most unwanted blocks from the frontend of your store.

1. **Turning on Template Path Hints and block names**: As mentioned we'll pick removing the "product compare" block from the right column of Magento for our example:

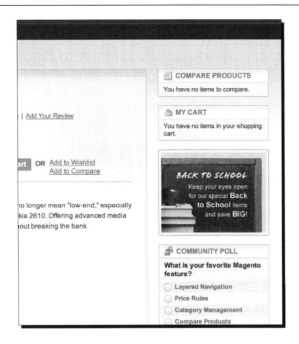

To find out where to look we have to know what kind of block we are dealing with.
Template Path Hints can be turned on for that purpose, with the additional option
to display "block names". In the following screenshot you can see how the frontend
of your store will look after activating these:

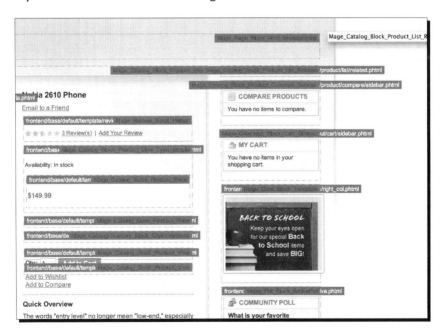

2. **Finding the block and layout update file to edit**: As you can see in the screenshot, the compare block is of type `catalog/product_compare_sidebar`. The first bit, `catalog`, is what we are interested in.

3. **Finding the section for the compare block inside the layout update** file: In the `layout` folder we can now open the `catalog.xml` file.

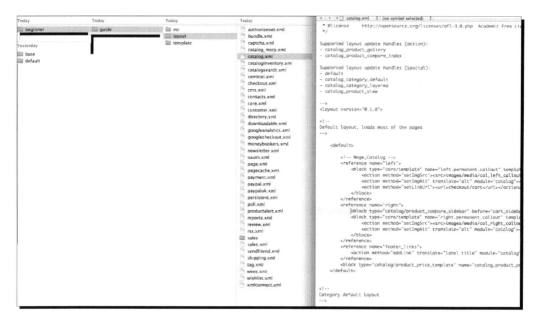

In this file we can see a section called `default`, which contains a section that says `<reference name=right>`. In this `<reference name=right>` part are all the blocks that should be displayed in the right column according to `catalog.xml`. It's possible that other layout update files also add blocks to the right column by referencing the right column! For example, the `checkout.xml` file also uses `<reference name=right>` to add the shopping cart sidebar to the right column.

4. **Removing the compare block from the layout file**: After this search, removing the product compare block is easy. Remove the line that starts with `<block type="catalog/product_compare_sidebar"` and save the file. The result should look like the following screenshot:

```
41  <!--
42  Default layout, loads most of the pages
43  -->
44
45  <default>
46
47      <!-- Mage_Catalog -->
48      <reference name="top.menu">
49          <block type="catalog/navigation" name="catalog.topnav" template="catalog/navigation/top.phtml"/>
50      </reference>
51      <reference name="left">
52          <block type="core/template" name="left.permanent.callout" template="callouts/left_col.phtml">
53              <action method="setImgSrc"><src>images/media/col_left_callout.jpg</src></action>
54              <action method="setImgAlt" translate="alt" module="catalog"><alt>Our customer service is available 24/7. Call us at (555) 555-0123.
55              <action method="setLinkUrl"><url>checkout/cart</url></action>
56          </block>
57      </reference>
58      <reference name="right">
59          <block type="core/template" name="right.permanent.callout" template="callouts/right_col.phtml">
60              <action method="setImgSrc"><src>images/media/col_right_callout.jpg</src></action>
61              <action method="setImgAlt" translate="alt" module="catalog"><alt>Keep your eyes open for our special Back to School items and save
62          </block>
63      </reference>
64      <reference name="footer_links">
65          <action method="addLink" translate="label title" module="catalog" ifconfig="catalog/seo/site_map"><label>Site Map</label><url helper="c
66      </reference>
67      <block type="catalog/product_price_template" name="catalog_product_price_template" />
68  </default>
69
70
71  <!--
72  Category default layout
```

The product compare block will now be gone when you click on through your store!

Magento uses a method of quickly remembering some of your settings called **caching**. After you have made changes to the design configuration or layout update files, it may be necessary to go to **System | Cache Management** and clear all the caches. You do this by selecting all the checkboxes (clicking on **Select All** also works), then selecting **Refresh** from the drop-down menu in the top-right and clicking on the **Submit** button. When you are working on your store, it is often handy to choose **Disable** from the drop-down menu instead, so you don't have to refresh the caches after every change. Remember to re-enable caches when you are done!

It should have become apparent by now that making adjustments to Magento themes should not be underestimated. We advise you to make a careful consideration between spending your time on your store's content or on messing with themes. Often calling in the services of an expert helps free your time for all the other essential e-commerce activities.

What just happened?

The `app/design/frontend/beginner/guide/layout` folder shown in the following screenshot contains XML files that tell Magento what information to show where. All the XML files define blocks, and the frontend of your store is always constructed by composing multiple small blocks together into one big page. The blocks to load for a certain section of the website are defined in the XML files. In other words, which HTML files Magento should show is determined in those files. Explaining all the intricacies of the XML structure is outside of the scope of this book. For that we point to Magento's theming guide, which was previously mentioned.

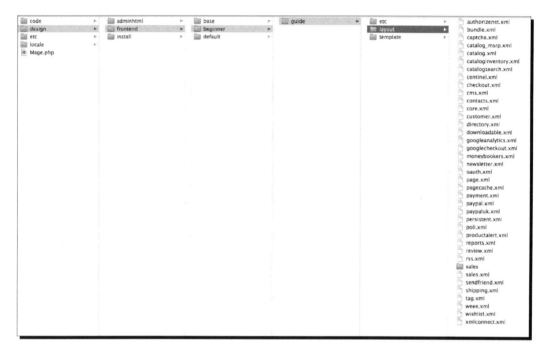

In the `layout` folder shown in the preceding screenshot, you'll see that the XML files are named according to Magento components such as `customer`, `catalog`, and `checkout`. Every frontend component in Magento has its own logic and you can often use that to find the relevant XML file quickly as well. For instance, if you want to edit the shopping cart sidebar block that is shown in the right column of the store, the `checkout.xml` file is a logical place to look even without having to turn on **Template Path Hints** and accompanying block names!

Summary

After discussing how you can edit CMS pages and specifically Magento's home page, we discussed how you can go about getting a solid Magento theme. The most basic choice is whether to use a premade theme or a custom theme, with picking a good supplier being crucial for each one. Practical guidelines were given for editing the frontend of your store yourself, although making use of Magento experts remains highly recommended. In the next chapter we will see how to handle the order handling process, from the moment the order is received, to invoicing and shipping.

10
Fulfilling Orders

Now that we have products, configured e-mails, payments, and shipping and had a closer look at our store's appearance, it's time to start doing some real sales! But what happens once we do? How do we keep track of our orders, deliveries, and invoices after that? This chapter describes exactly those processes.

In this chapter, you will learn:

- Working with Sales Orders in the Magento frontend to test drive your sales process
- Working with sales orders, invoices, and shipments
- Creating a sales order directly in the Magento backend
- What Magento can and cannot do when you have to handle returns and credit memos
- What you need to do if you need integration with other software solutions

Sales orders on the frontend

So far in the previous chapters we've spent lots and lots of time in the Magento backend. Except for the chapter about themes, you've hardly spent any time in looking at what your customers will see in the frontend. And that isn't good, because the end result of your work is of course why you're taking all the steps from the earlier chapters.

Since we have already taken a lot of steps to prepare ourselves it's time to have a closer look at what your customers will see when they are visiting your store. Of course the look and feel of your web shop highly depends on the theme you've chosen. To keep everything as standardized as possible, we'll be using the default Magento theme throughout this chapter. And we're using the sample data available to decently fill the store. Let's do some sales orders!

◆ We're assuming here that this won't be your first time ever in buying something from an online store. So you'll know what such a process generally looks like. Even though a lot of the steps we'll take here will be pretty obvious for you, we'll still show them just to make you aware of all the Magento-specific things that will be visible. It's good to have a closer look at this process and be aware of what is happening exactly. Remember that everything that we did so far in the Magento backend will have its consequences in the frontend for your customers.

Time for action – creating a first sales order

Let's start with creating a first sales order, just to have a closer look at what your customers will see in your store:

1. From our demo store home page, just select a product, or first click on a category in the main menu and select a single product from there:

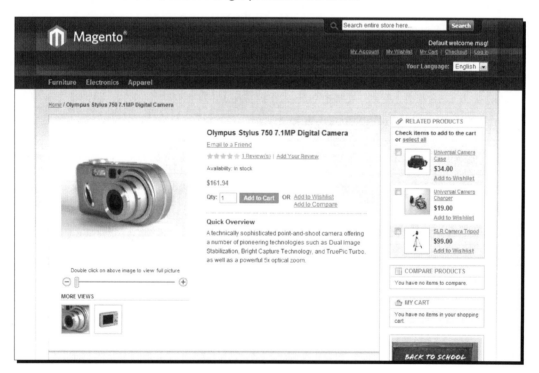

2. On your product detail page, take a closer look at all the items that are being shown. Remember that by playing with Magento's settings it's possible to influence what is and isn't visible here. Anyway, add the item to your cart.

3. Next, your cart is shown. In here pay attention to items such as the shipping calculator (see *Chapter 8*, *Configuring Shipping*), the products on the right (*Chapter 4*, *Simple Products*), and the possibility to check out using multiple shipping addresses:

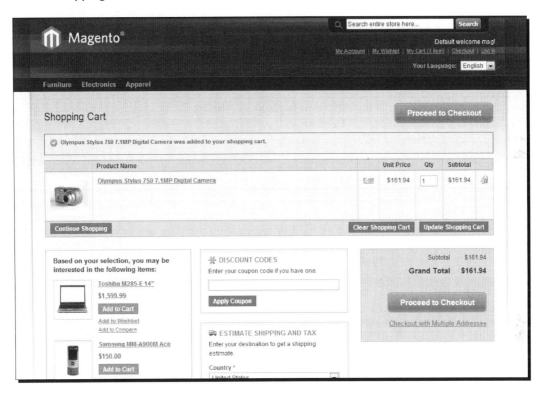

4. When we're continuing our sales process in the checkout, the first step a customer has to take is to login, create an account, or to checkout as a guest. This last option can be enabled or disabled. It's up to you whether or not you want to allow Guest Checkout. Just be aware that in a consumer-oriented website enabling the Guest Checkout can really increase your sales. Navigate to **System | Configuration | Sales | Checkout | Checkout Options**:

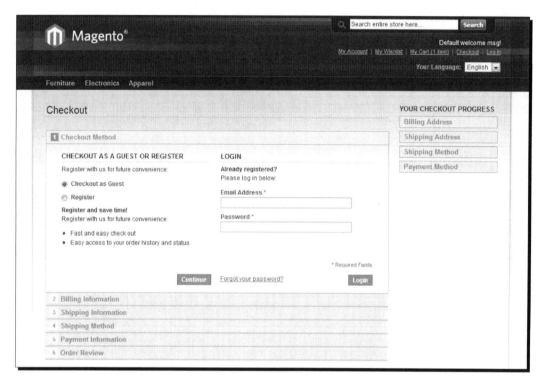

5. If you take a closer look, you will notice that the Magento Checkout procedure requires six steps for the customer to take. This might seem overwhelming, but in fact you're staying on the same page all the time. It isn't bad at all, but some store owners just want a simpler method and less steps to take or even a "One Step Checkout". If you want to change the default steps of Magento you'll need an extension to help you out. More on this topic can be found in the next chapter. For now, just continue taking all the necessary steps and start with entering your personal details, as shown in the following screenshot:

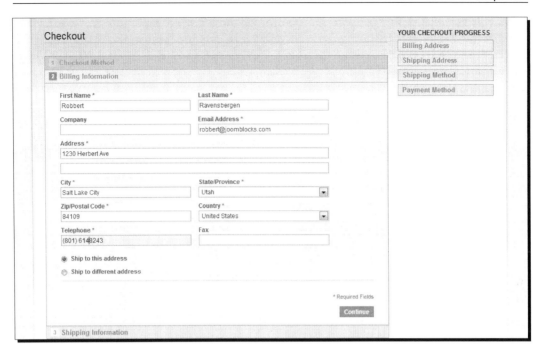

6. Note that the customer can decide to use the same address as a shipping address or enter a different one. If you keep the default, step 3 of the checkout process will be skipped.

7. Next, choose the shipping method. In our example, we just used one fixed rate for all items. More on configuring shipping methods has been discussed in the previous chapter:

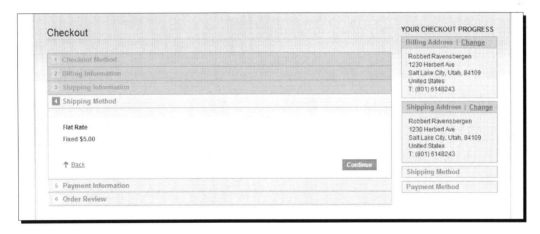

8. In step 5 of the checkout form, you can select the payment method you'd like to use. The contents of this part, of course, completely depend on the configuration of your payment methods, which we've discussed during *Chapter 7, Accepting Payments*. In the following example, we simply enter our credit card information, using a test account:

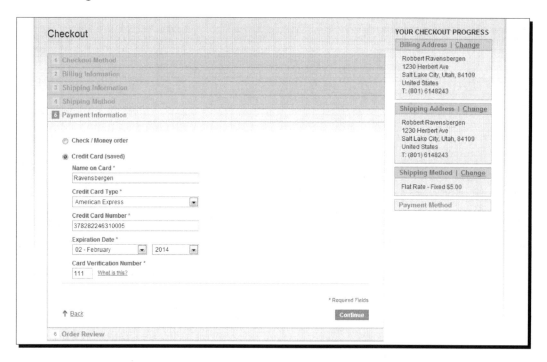

9. Finally, check your order once more for all the details in an overview. Confirm it by clicking on **Place Order**. Note that in this example, there's no additional sales tax applied! More on using tax for your orders was discussed during *Chapter 2, General Configuration*:

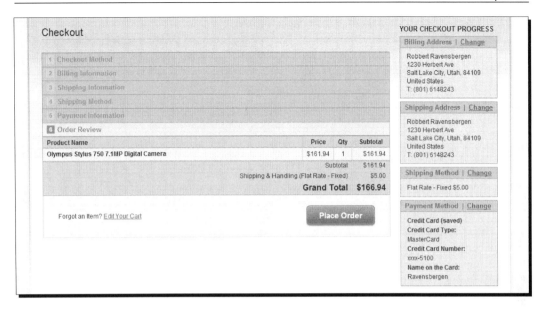

10. Once confirmed, your customer will receive an order confirmation by e-mail and will be redirected to the **Thank you** page. As a store owner, you might want to receive these confirmation e-mails as well. You can enter your e-mail address to do so in the backend. Navigate to **System | Configuration | Sales | Sales Emails**, if you want to receive a copy of all sales orders:

The confirmation page may have additional information. For instance, when ordering a downloadable product, Magento will show a link to your account, where you'll be able to download your item. Because of this, it is always required to create an account in Magento when you're ordering downloadable products. Therefore, a guest checkout isn't possible in this case:

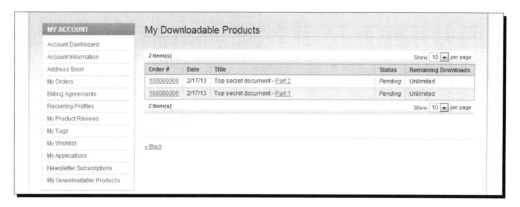

Managing sales orders on the backend

Once a customer goes through the checkout in your online store a sales order will be created. It doesn't matter if the order was paid for or not. As soon as the customer confirms the order in Magento, it has been created.

Navigate in the top menu to **Sales | Orders**:

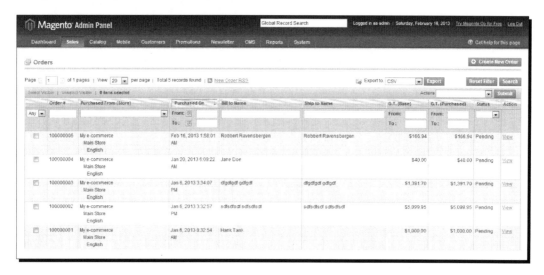

This page shows all the sales orders that have been received in your Magento installation with the newest one on top. Strangely though, there's no possibility here to filter on website or storefront scope.

From here you have several possibilities:

- Create a new sales order directly in the Magento backend. This could come in handy if you're also taking orders by telephone and want to register them all in Magento.

- Change the status of an existing sales order.

- Print a document for the received sales order.

- Add a filter on the shown sales orders by using the label fields on top of the order grid.

- Export orders to a CSV file format. This default export function won't be very useful in practice though. Yes, it's possible to export your orders to Excel using the CSV export, but often you'll need something that is tailor-made for your situation.

- Open an existing order to look at the details and perform further actions.

Just as in every grid page in Magento, there are several ways to browse through your sales orders using the pagination on top, or use the filters to search for specific sales orders. Please note that when using filters, only those orders that meet all criteria will be visible. It's always possible to delete all filters and show all orders again by clicking on the **Reset Filters** button:

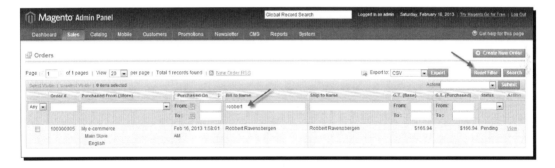

Besides that you have several options to select and deselect orders and use the same action for all selected orders. Be careful though, as it's easy to accidentally cancel orders, even canceling multiple orders at the same time!

Order numbering

Magento uses default number ranges for orders, invoices, shipments, and credit notes. If you're running only one website and store front these will all start with number 10000001, 9 numeric digits, going up from this number. However, if you are running multiple store fronts, Magento will automatically assign 200000001 to your second store front and so on. Sometimes it is necessary to change the way Magento handles these number ranges and you could even use a smaller or longer number to fit your needs. Unfortunately, there's no immediate setting available that you can use to change its behavior. You need to go into the `eav_entity_store` table to make changes. If you need to do this, we recommend that you consult a Magento specialist to help you out.

Looking at our Sales Orders grid, there are several fields immediately available that you can use to make sure you identified and are working on the correct Sales Order. One of the fields that needs a better explanation is the **Sales Order Status** field.

Depending on where your order is in the sales process, the status of your order will differ. Some of the following statuses may not even occur, depending on your settings and the payment methods you use:

◆ **Canceled**: This speaks for itself. A canceled order can get this status because the payment was canceled by the customer, or if you manually canceled the order in the Magento backend.

◆ **Closed**: A closed order is generally an order that was partly delivered, but where it wasn't possible to deliver the remaining items anymore. You close the order to mark it as "done", being aware that it was never fulfilled completely. You should be in contact with your customer when closing an order.

◆ **Complete**: An order that has been delivered to the customer completely is marked as complete. Note that the order receives this status as soon as all items have been shipped (this doesn't mean that the customer also received the items!).

◆ **Suspect Fraud**: This is used for orders paid with the PayPal gateway only, where the PayPal service is expecting a possible problem with the transaction. Normally you will receive an e-mail message from PayPal as well, describing the problem and the steps you need to take. This status might be used by third-party extensions for other payment methods as well.

◆ **On Hold**: If there's any reason why you temporarily need to wait before delivering an order to your customer, you have the possibility to put it on hold manually in the Magento backend.

◆ **Payment Review**: This status means that the external payment gateway is still verifying the transaction. Do not yet deliver your items without checking if the order has really been paid for. This status is closely related to **Pending Payment** and actually it is uncertain what the exact difference between those two is.

◆ **Pending**: This is the first status an order receives when it has been placed. A pending order means that the order was created, but hasn't been paid for yet.

◆ **Pending Payment**: The order receives this status as soon as the customer is in the payment process, but hasn't completed that yet.

◆ **Pending PayPal**: This is the same as **Pending Payment**, but this one's specific for the PayPal payment method. All other payment methods would receive **Pending Payment**.

◆ **Processing**: As soon as an order has been paid for and invoiced, the status changes to **Processing**. This means that from here you can continue with the delivery of your order. An order with the status processing could have been shipped or invoiced, but not both! Note that invoicing a pending order will also change its status to processing. Be careful, because you might think that it has been paid for, which doesn't necessarily have to be the case!

Your sales orders will receive most of the statuses described above automatically, depending on the actual status of your order. You can control some of them manually as well, like putting an order **On Hold** or setting it to **Canceled**.

It's also possible to define additional Order Statuses yourself. You may do so by navigating to **System | Order Statuses**.

Time for action – opening and processing an order

This is how we open and process an order:

1. Search for your order by using the filters and just click on it as soon as you've found the order you want to process. In our example, we're going to process the order of the camera that we bought ourselves earlier in this chapter. Clicking your order will open it. Note that our sales order has the **Pending** status, which means that it has not been paid for yet. Why not, we entered our credit card information, right? Yes, that's true, but our Magento system isn't connected to a payment provider that will actually check if the card is valid and is able to do the transaction. If your payment is validated and accepted online, the order status will automatically change to **Processing**.

2. From here, you have several possibilities to process your order. On the top-right corner there are several buttons available that you can use:

- **Edit**: Actually you will not edit this particular order. The current one will be canceled and a new one will be created.

- **Cancel**: This really cancels the current order and reverses any stock transactions that have already been made.

- **Send Email**: This sends the order confirmation to the customer once more.

- **Hold:** This changes the status of the order to **On Hold**, just in case there's any reason for you to not to process this order yet.

- **Invoice**: This will bring you to a new page to create a sales invoice for this order.

- **Ship**: This will also take you to a new page, where you can confirm the shipment for this order or a part of it.

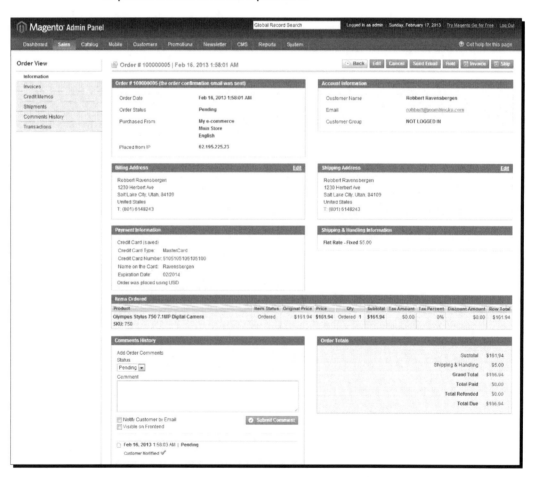

3. The menu items on the top left of this page will let you navigate through various documents that could exist for this order, such as the invoice and shipping documents. Note that in this case, where this sales order was just created, those sections will all be empty.

4. At the bottom left of the page you have the possibility to add a comment to this order and if you want, you can send this comment along with a copy of the order confirmation to your customer again. This comes in handy, for instance when there's any reason why the order cannot be delivered immediately. Note that the drop-down box holding the order status cannot be changed! The order status will change once you create an invoice for your order.

5. The next step in handling your order is to create an invoice for it. Click on the **Invoice** button on the top, to create an invoice as shown in the following screenshot:

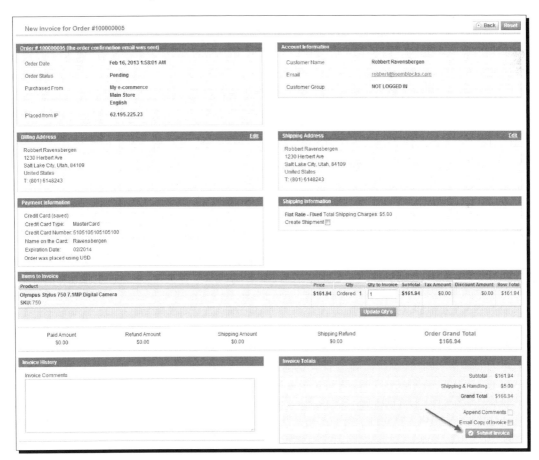

Normally it isn't necessary to make any changes to the invoice, although it is possible to change (decrease) the quantities of your item and add a comment to the invoice. You can only lower the quantities to split your order into two or more different parts. It isn't possible to invoice more than originally ordered. If you want to send the invoice to your customer by e-mail and include your comments in it, you have to click on the appropriate checkboxes. Next just click on the **Submit Invoice** button at the bottom. Since we have now invoiced the order, its status will automatically change to **Processing**.

6. Once your invoice has been created, the **Invoice** button disappears from the row at the top of your screen. It is now possible to create a credit memo, in case you need to credit the created invoice. Note that although your invoice has been created, you did not automatically receive a print of it. If you need one, click on the **Invoice** menu on the left, open your invoice, and click on the **Print** button. A PDF file will be generated like seen in the following screenshot, which you can open and print using Acrobat Reader or any other tool that is able to open PDF files:

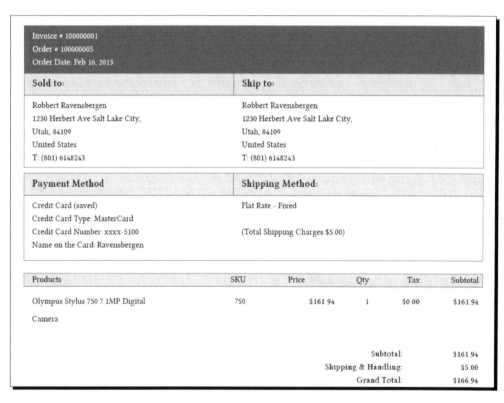

Invoice # 100000001
Order # 100000005
Order Date: Feb 16, 2013

Sold to:	Ship to:
Robbert Ravensbergen	Robbert Ravensbergen
1230 Herbert Ave Salt Lake City,	1230 Herbert Ave Salt Lake City,
Utah, 84109	Utah, 84109
United States	United States
T: (801) 6148243	T: (801) 6148243

Payment Method	Shipping Method:
Credit Card (saved)	Flat Rate - Fixed
Credit Card Type: MasterCard	
Credit Card Number: xxxx-5100	(Total Shipping Charges $5.00)
Name on the Card: Ravensbergen	

Products	SKU	Price	Qty	Tax	Subtotal
Olympus Stylus 750 7.1MP Digital Camera	750	$161.94	1	$0.00	$161.94

				Subtotal:	$161.94
				Shipping & Handling:	$5.00
				Grand Total:	$166.94

Your customer is also able to open the same PDF invoice, in the **My Account** section of the frontend website, but only if the customer decides to create an account before finalizing the order.

Document layout

Magento uses a default layout for all documents that will be generated, such as Invoices, Credit notes, and Packing Slips. Although they are generally OK with changes, they do not appreciate other documents that will be used throughout your company. You may add your own logo, but that's about it. There's no good solution available within Magento yet to change the look and feel of these documents. Some information is available here at: `http://www.magentocommerce.com/wiki/5_-_modules_and_ development/orders/editing_an_invoice_pdf`.

But the problem is that programming skills for Magento will be required to really make some progress in this area. Another possibility would be to use an extension to help you. One of the offered extensions to do this task can be found here at: `http://www.magentocommerce.com/ magento-connect/pdf-invoice-shipment-credit-memo- documents-5843.html`.

7. Next, we are going to ship our sales order. From the Sales Order page, click on the **Ship** button on the top-right corner of the screen. It is similar to creating an invoice, as this will open a page that will let you enter the quantities that we will ship. As when creating an invoice, it's possible to lower the quantities that we will ship.

On this page it's also possible to add a tracking number from your carrier, so that your customer can track where the package is. If you choose to send your customer an e-mail about the shipment from this page, the tracking number will be included in the message.

Once ready, just click on the **Submit Shipment** button at the bottom of the page:

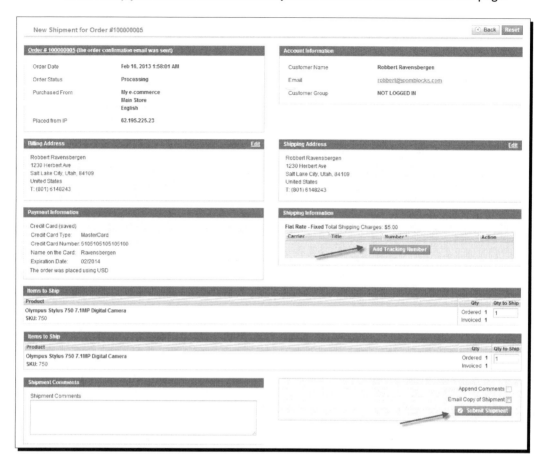

Carrier integration

As there are lots and lots of carriers worldwide that you could be using, we are showing the manual process here. However, it will make life easier for you that some of them have integrated extensions for Magento. One of the examples is ShipRush for FedEx: `http://fedex.shiprush.com/magento/index.shtml`.

What just happened?

If you shipped all items, the status of your order has now changed to **Completed**. Congratulations, you just processed your first order! Now, repeat this process multiple times and learn as much as possible about the status an order can get. Use different scenarios for combinations of payment and shipment methods you are using in your store. You cannot practice and verify your process enough!

Some tips to handle your orders more efficiently

When your store grows, performing all these tasks, and keeping track of what's happening in your backend may become a problem. There are a number of things that you can do to increase the efficiency in this area that we would like to share with you:

1. Automatic invoicing. If you're working with a payment service provider to handle your payments, it's often possible to change the order status after a successful transaction to processed automatically. The invoice will be created and there's no need to do this manually anymore for the majority of your orders.

2. As an alternative you could use an extension to bulk invoice and/or ship your orders. One of the offered extensions can be found at: `http://www.xtento.com/magento-extensions/simplify-bulk-order-processing.html`.

3. There are a percentage of customers that click on the **BUY** button, go through checkout, and reach the payment service provider, but after that do nothing or just close their browser. For some shops, this percentage can amount to 5-10 percent of the total orders. In Magento, these kinds of orders would stay in pending status indefinitely until the shop owner cancels them manually. If your store gets a fair number of these orders, having a developer create a small piece of software that cancels these orders for you can help greatly. The extension mentioned above could probably solve this problem as well.

Creating sales orders on the backend

Sometimes it's necessary to create orders directly in the Magento backend yourself. This is a situation that occurs regularly in a Business to Business (B2B) environment, where customers are still used to picking up the phone and ordering what they need. Luckily Magento offers functionality to support this process. First go to **Sales | Orders** using the menu.

Time for action – creating a manual Sales Order

In here, you'll be adding a Sales Order directly in the Magento backend.

1. Click on the **Create New Order** button on top of the screen:

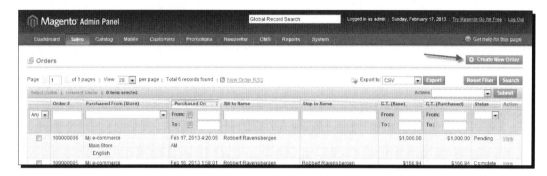

2. Next, select a customer from the existing customer list using the filters or create a completely new customer. It isn't possible to do a guest checkout here and create an order for a customer without a customer record in the database:

3. Next, you might need to select a store front for your order. This question will appear only if you have more than one store front available in your Magento installation:

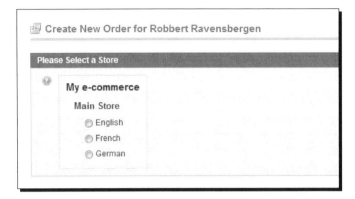

4. In the next screen, you will start filling all details for your order. Start with selecting an invoice and shipping address for your customer. The default address will already be preselected. You can choose a different one or create a new address on the fly.

5. Next, start adding products to your order. There are several ways to do this. For example, you can use the search function by clicking on the **Add Products** button on top of the page, but there are more options. The left part of the screen shows various areas holding products that this customer has on his/her wishlist, recently viewed and compared products, and products that the customer has bought before. Note that functionality like this will only work if the customer always starts with logging into your store when visiting your website. Unfortunately, this is not always the case. If there are items available on the left part of the screen, you can simply add them by clicking on the checkbox and by clicking on the arrow at the top of every area.

6. Once you add your products, you must select a payment method and calculate the shipping costs for your order. Without these, it will not be possible to finalize your order and save it. Note that it's only possible to select payment methods that are available "offline". If normally your customers go through a payment solution provider to make the payment, you cannot do that automatically here. So a manual order requires a manual payment process!

7. The final step is clicking on the **Submit Order** button. This will create your order with a **Pending** status. By default, Magento will e-mail the **Order** confirmation to your customer. From here on this order can be handled like any other regular sales order:

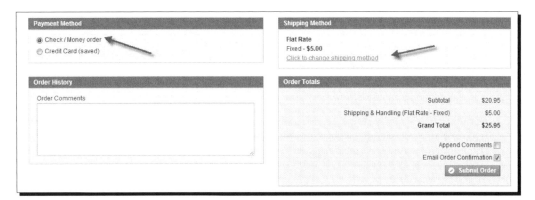

Returns and Credit Memos

Every online store owner will have to deal with returns. And your return percentage could even be very high if you're selling clothes, shoes, or any other product that needs to 'fit'. Returns of 30 percent or more are quite common for a certain product types! This is something you have to take into account, not only from the financial side, but also from the operational point of view. How are you going to take care of returns? How do you keep track of them? The community version of Magento isn't very helpful in this area. The only thing that you can actually do is create a Credit Memo (also called a Credit Note) for your customer. The Credit Memo is a record of a refund, without meaning that the paid amount was actually returned to the customer. We will take a closer look at the return process later on, but first let's have a look of what can be done in Magento.

Time for action – creating a Credit Memo

Follow these steps to create a Credit Memo:

1. Creating a Credit Memo in Magento is a very easy and straightforward process. You can only create a Credit Memo for an order that has been invoiced. To do so, search for your sales order via **Sales | Orders**. Note that there's also a direct shortcut to Invoices using **Sales | Invoices**, but from there you won't be able to create a Credit Memo! Once your order is open click on the **Credit Memo** button in the top-right corner:

2. A new page will open, giving you the possibility to make changes to the Credit Memo, if needed. Just as we've seen earlier during the sales order process, it isn't possible to credit more than originally invoiced. You can only lower the quantity field.

3. Note that there's a field available for every line of your Credit Memo, giving you the possibility to add your item back to your stock again. By default it is switched off, so no stock level change will be applied! This is important to know when you are using the Credit Memo during your return process.

4. Once done, there are a couple of fields left at the bottom of your Credit Memo, that you may use to adjust the totals:

- **Refund Shipping**: Do you want to refund the shipping costs as well? By default, this field shows the original shipping amount, assuming that you'll refund it.

- **Adjustment Refund**: If there's any reason to give an additional refund besides the total of the products and shipping, enter it here. It's not possible to refund more money than originally paid though.

□ **Adjustment Fee**: This is the opposite of **Adjustment Refund**. An amount entered here will be subtracted from the total amount that will be refunded to your customer.

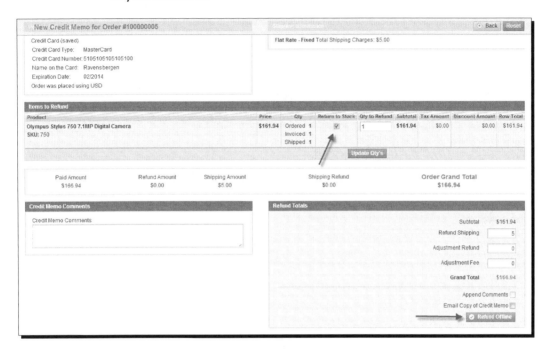

5. Click on the **Refund Offline** button to finalize the Credit Memo. The name of this button has been chosen because creating a Credit Memo doesn't mean that the customer actually received back the paid amount. That's normally something you'll have to do manually, depending on the way the customer paid you.

Google Checkout

There is an exception to this rule though. If you're offering Google Checkout as the payment method, you'll be able to refund the amount automatically. In that particular case, the button will be named as **Refund** instead of **Refund Offline**. More information about Google Checkout integration can be found here: http://www.magentocommerce.com/wiki/welcome_to_ the_magento_user_s_guide/chapter_4#google_checkout.

Note that now your Credit Memo is final, the status of the sales order is changed to **Complete**.

But what about my return process?

That's a really good question. Magento offers no functionality besides the Credit Memo in the Community version. Sometimes it would be handy to register what your received, or to ask your customers to enter an **RMA (Return Merchandise Authorization)** before sending anything back. In the Magento Enterprise version, there is some functionality available to better support this process now. Community users should look for extensions if they want to have more features than available by default. There are multiple possibilities here; AheadWorks, one of the largest Magento extension providers, offers a good one at a reasonable price at: `http://ecommerce.aheadworks.com/magento-extensions/ rma.html`.

What if I need to handle these processes out of Magento?

For a lot of companies the functionality that Magento offers will not be enough to run all their processes. For instance, bookkeeping; this is something that Magento obviously doesn't offer. Magento is an e-commerce solution and not more than that. If you feel the need to integrate Magento with other software solutions then don't worry. First of all there are basic export possibilities available in Magento itself. You can find them in the menu by navigating to **System | Import/Export**. This offers already a lot of functionality that you can use to export data from Magento to third-party solutions and vice versa. You can do a lot with these functions, but unfortunately exporting orders or invoices isn't one of the offered functions. It can only be used for customers and products.

So, if you need to interface orders and/or invoices with other software solutions you'll need to use extensions or sometimes even custom software development. There are often extensions available for widely used standard solutions. Even if your bookkeeping software is developed by a local company there are still chances that someone has already developed an integration tool for it. However, even if an extension is available for your situation, we still recommend that you discuss this topic with a Magento partner or an experienced developer. Integrating different pieces of software is always more difficult and time consuming than you would think. And you cannot afford to miss orders or create errors in your bookkeeping software because the integration isn't working completely correct! Looking for a Magento partner to help you? Search for one using the search engines in your area or start here: `http://www.magentocommerce.com/partners/`.

Do not forget to ask for references and really check them! Preferably check references of companies that are close to your own business. In case of integration projects ask for a proven track record. Experience in this area has proven to be really important.

Summary

In this chapter you've seen how a customer sees your sales process. Test, test, and test it again! Further on, you've worked with Sales Orders, Invoices, Shipments, and Credit Memos in the Magento backend. This is enough to get you started for selling, but it is also important to take a closer look at all different scenarios that might occur in your situation.

Magento isn't an "all-in-one" solution and sometimes you'll need extensions to manage your processes in a more efficient way. That brings us to our next and final chapter where you'll learn how to work with extensions and how to maintain your store.

11
Maintaining and Administrating Your Store

Finally, the big moment is there: your site goes live! It took a lot of preparations, but you're there. Before you flip the switch, it's a good idea to make sure your affairs are really sorted. You should have an overview of any and all modifications to your website, and you should know all the login credentials to the systems you use. It's also essential to properly test and maintain your store. These subjects will be discussed in this chapter.

Managing your store

Maintaining a store is a very different process from getting it live. After the initial development efforts are done, exhaustive testing should be done to make sure the store functions as expected. After you're live, you are not dealing with a completely clean slate anymore and you won't have to go through the prelaunch checklists again. However, you then have to carefully consider if the things you want to do really add to your store's success, and in which way you are going to add functionalities to your site. In this chapter, the following will be discussed:

- Collecting all relevant information about your Magento store
- A launch checklist as well as a collection of common gotchas
- Managing your ever-growing list of wishes and requirements for your online store
- Working with development partners
- Dealing with Magento upgrades

Overview of your Magento installation

Before you can go live, a lot of work will go into setting everything up. The process can take a while and because of that it's possible to forget about things that were arranged during the start of the entire process, such as logins to your payment service provider, all of the different modules you installed, and so on. Because of that, it's useful to make an overview containing all general system information regarding your store. Should problems arise in your final tests, solving them will be a lot quicker when you have an idea of where to search for the cause. At least the following should be known and documented prior to launching:

◆ **Modifications to Magento**: For examples, what theme you are using, where that theme is located, which e-mails you translated and which still need translating, and which extensions you have installed. Check that you are really using each extension present in your store. If you are not using a custom extension, it's better to remove it. Any superfluous extensions inside your Magento installation will increase the chance of problems later on, as custom extensions can conflict with each other and have problems when you upgrade Magento.

◆ **Login credentials for Magento**: Where is the Magento admin located, and what is your admin username and password? The Magento admin can be found by placing `/admin/` behind your domain name by default. It is a good idea to set it to another location through **System | Configuration | Admin** (this menu option is all the way to the bottom of the menu in the left column in the configuration). Open the section called **Admin Base URL** and set the **Use Custom Admin Path** drop-down menu to **Yes**. After that, fill in the desired admin path in the **Custom Admin Path** input field.

◆ **FTP information**: How do you get into your FTP server, and in which directory is Magento located? If your hosting provider offers SFTP access this is preferred. SFTP is similar to FTP but more secure.

◆ **Login credentials to your payment systems**: For each different payment processor you are using, note the URL to log in as well as the required username and password.

◆ **Login credentials to other systems**: Note where and how to log in to other systems such as your fulfillment software, bookkeeping software, Google Analytics, Google AdWords, and so on.

◆ **E-mail addresses**: The addresses that you use in your store as well as how to retrieve and send e-mails using them. Check which e-mail addresses you are communicating to your customers and be completely sure that you are receiving e-mails for them in your e-mail software. The fastest way of getting a bad reputation is not answering customer queries.

In the following screenshot, you can see the configuration section for the admin base URL path:

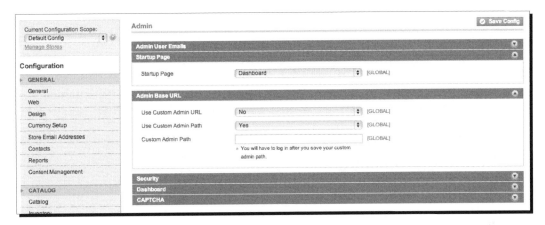

The only way to be sure you are launching a store without major problems is to test your shop thoroughly before you go live. Make sure to test all important parts of your store and give extra attention to places where you are using custom modifications (the overview we discussed in the previous paragraph is handy for determining which places to emphasize).

During the construction of your shop, you should be testing thoroughly as well; the earlier you find a problem the easier and faster it is to fix. Special emphasis should be given to testing several real payment transactions and all the processing actions associated with them (such as fulfillment). Make sure to make live payments using each of your payment methods and test for the amounts of 0.01, 1, 1.51, and 5.02 at the least, so that you know different possible values are supported. If you are expecting order values above $100 or $1000, it's useful to test those too. You don't want to find out from real customers that your payment gateway has capped your transactions at $1000 if you're selling kitchens for $15000, for instance! You should be able to refund any transaction costs you're making during testing by yourself, through your payment processor.

Remember to check your secure connections in your storefront and disable the inline translation tool and any other activated developer settings (which can be found under **System | Configuration | Developer**). Often the actual products that are going to be sold are only placed inside the store just prior to the launch. It's much better to have at least some of your actual products inside your Magento installation, with the actual images you are going to use, because only then do you get a good impression of how your shop will be experienced by your customers!

An example of the development configuration settings can be seen in the following screenshot:

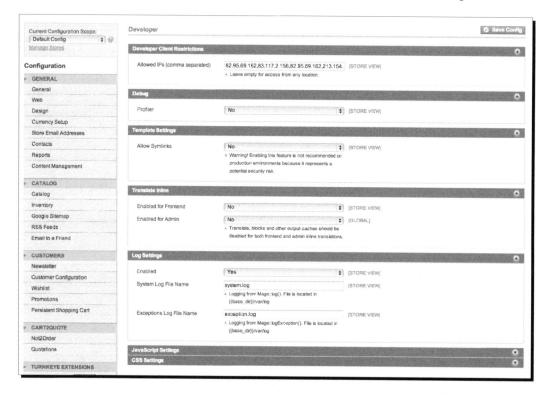

Have a go hero – testing your store

A **checklist** can be used to test your store in a structured fashion. Because it is not possible for us to predict how your shop will function exactly, the example list we provide contains only standard sections of Magento. Do not forget to include any additions and modifications in your own testing table!

Going through such a list is not the most exciting job, but ensures that you can be more confident when launching and that you have a better overview of any areas that may need improvement (in our example, this is the **My orders** view in the customer account). If necessary you can add or remove columns as desired of course. A tool such as Microsoft Excel or a Google Docs spreadsheet is handy as they support working with columns easily. The most important thing to remember is to test your store in a structured manner, and to give anything relating to the purchase process special attention. This means emphasizing on these aspects of your store:

 ◆ **Navigation and catalog**: Can your products be easily found? And is the information presented clearly? Are your add-to-cart buttons easy to find?

- **Shopping cart and checkout process**: Are the totals and taxes right? Are all the forms working properly?
- **Payment**: Can a live payment be made properly? Is the redirect to the payment processor quick enough?
- **Shipments**: Are the amounts shown for the shipping options correct? Are the correct shipping options appearing at all?
- **Follow-up information to a placed order**: Do your order statuses properly reflect paid and unpaid orders? Are customers receiving the right e-mails?

Anything not working right in these aspects of your shop should be considered a showstopper. In other sections of your store you may wish to be a little less strict and elect to fix those later.

When you've determined that your site looks and functions as expected, it's wise to have somebody proofread (parts of) your site. It's important to know you're communicating clearly, as visitors have very little patience for finding information. Check your store for "Coming Soon" and "Under Construction" pages and consider disabling those, as they may give the impression that you are still building your website and launching in the indefinite future, instead of actively selling right now.

In the following table we've provided a sample table that can be used to test your shop:

Section of store	Functionality	Passed?	Remark
Product list – list view	Add to compare	Yes	
	Add to wishlist		
	Add to cart		
Product list – grid view	Add to compare	Yes	
	Add to wishlist		
	Add to cart		
Product page	Add to cart	Yes	Make warnings for Add to cart problems to be clearer
Note: Test the product pages for simple, configurable, bundle, virtual and downloadable products.	Price notifications		
	Stock notifications		
	Add to compare		
	Add to wishlist		
Shopping cart	Change quantity	Yes	
	Remove product from cart		
	Add product to wishlist		
	Continue to checkout		

Section of store	Functionality	Passed?	Remark
Checkout process	Log in	Yes	
Note: Test all your payment and shipping methods in separate orders!	Register		
	Billing address form		
	Shipping address form		
	Payment methods		
	Shipping methods		
	Review information		
	Secure page (https)		
Customer account	Log in	Yes	My orders overview is messy
	Register		
	Log out		
	My orders overview		
	My wishlist		
	Secure page (HTTPS)		
	Mijn verlanglijst		

Go-live checklist configuration settings

In this section we will briefly go through a number of Magento settings that were discussed earlier in this book. Besides the aforementioned functional checks, making sure that your configuration is set properly is another essential factor in the store behaving as you expect it to.

General settings

Check if all settings in **System** | **Configuration** | **General** are right. Your time zone and language are evidently important, and the **Default Country** field determines which country is selected in your checkout by default for your customers. An example of the **General** settings section can be seen in the following screenshot:

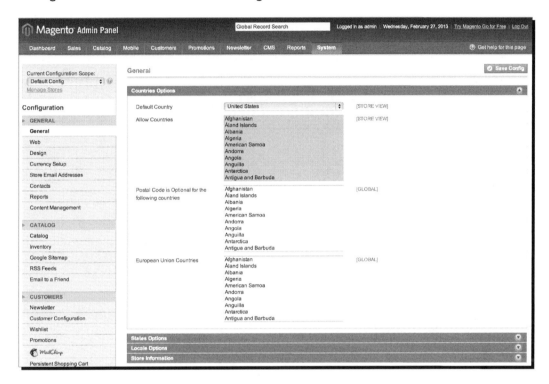

Web settings

In **System** | **Configuration** | **Web** there are many essential settings. Under **Search Engines Optimization**, it's important to have the **Use Web Server Rewrites** setting set to **Yes**, to make your site rank better in search engines and to have cleaner URLs to present to your visitors.

Without setting this to **Yes**, a product URL will look like `http://www.example.com/index.php/product.html`. If the rewrites are enabled, the same product's URL will look like `http://www.example.com/product.html`. All hosting companies that say they are able to host Magento should support the web server rewrites. It's always a good idea to check with your potential web host before you enter into an agreement.

What you set as the base URL in the **Unsecure** and **Secure** sections is very important. Usually, the secure base URL would be a domain that starts with `https://` and the unsecure base URL starts with `http://`. However, you can only set the secure base URL to your HTTPS domain if you have arranged for an SSL certificate with your hosting provider! Check the other settings in the **Web** configuration thoroughly as well. The **Web** configuration section looks like the following screenshot:

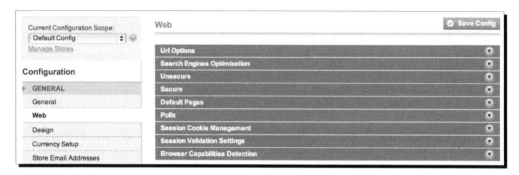

HTML Head

In **System | Configuration | Design | HTML Head**, you will find information about your website that is set to some text about Magento by default. The different settings you find here are very important for search engines, so make sure to change all of them to something specific for your store.

Placeholder images

When a product in your store does not have an image set, Magento will show a gray Magento logo by default. You can change this by going to **System | Configuration | Catalog | Product Image Placeholder**. Of course, it's best to prevent placeholder images from appearing at all. Having good images in your store is essential to selling most products. The gray Magento placeholder logo can be seen in the following screenshot as the second product's image:

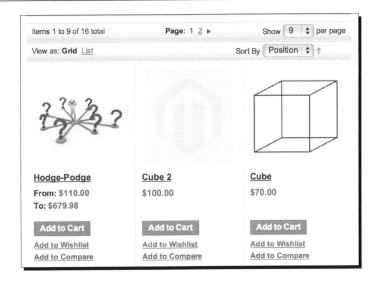

Contact information and e-mail addresses

Check the contact information that was set up in **System | Configuration | General** and **System | Configuration | Store e-mail addresses** to be sure customers can reach you.

Tax rates

Not having your tax rates set up properly from the beginning can cause a nightmare when you're filing your tax returns and can potentially cause direct losses as well, so make sure to place some test orders to test different taxation scenarios in your store.

Payment methods and shipping methods

In **System | Configuration | Payment Methods** and **System | Configuration | Shipping Methods**, check if your payment- and shipping-related settings are correct. By performing some test orders you will find problems quickly. Remember to check for each scenario. For instance, if you have shipping methods that apply for different weight classes, place a test order for each weight class. It's better to spend 30 minutes extra in testing them than to miss revenue.

Currency

Check if the settings in **System | Configuration | Currency Setup** are correct for the allowed and default currency in your store.

Transactional e-mails – password text

All e-mails dealing with the purchase process should be set properly. The customer registration e-mail warrants special attention: as soon as a customer registers in your store, Magento sends the customer's password through an e-mail. This is unsecure. We recommend removing the customer's password from the standard registration e-mail. To do that, remove the following from Magento's transactional e-mail for customer registrations:

```
<strong>Password</strong>: {{htmlescape var=$customer.password}}
```

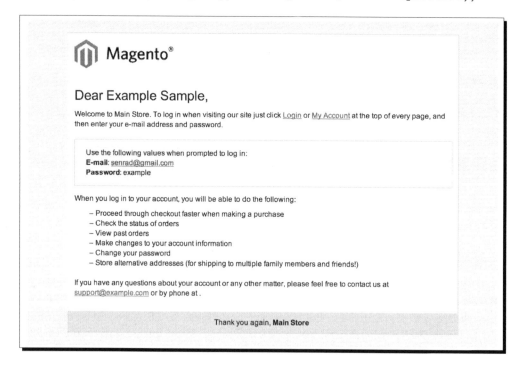

Admin URL

As mentioned earlier in this chapter, you can change the admin URL in **System | Configuration | Admin**. This makes breaking into your admin a little harder.

404 (page not found)

The standard 404 (page not found) page that Magento shows is not tailored to your store. To edit it, go to **CMS | Manage Pages** and edit the page that has the URL key **no-route**. It is a good practice to have an upbeat text here instead of a scary "not found" message, and to show your visitors some of your main categories so they can resume their search easier.

Stock

You can check if all of your products have stock and have stock management turned on if applicable.

Google Analytics

Once your shop is up and running, analytics about the usage of your store are an important steering mechanism to base decisions on. You can register an analytics account for free on `http://analytics.google.com` and set up the tracking through **System | Configuration | Google API**.

Caching

During the development of your store, your store's cache management was probably turned off. A cache greatly improves the speed of your store, so turn it back on by going to **System | Cache Management**, selecting all the checkboxes, choosing **Enable** from the drop-down menu in the top-right corner, and submitting.

Index Management

Go to **System | Index Management** and refresh all the store's indexes, by clicking on **Select All** and clicking on the **Submit** button.

Licenses

Magento modules made by third parties, especially the paid for ones, are sometimes tied to domain names. Check if you have a valid license for each of your modules, and if you have set up the license in the configuration section properly.

Daily tasks / cron jobs

Some of Magento's behind-the-scenes maintenance routines require running daily. You can arrange for these automatic scripts through a so-called **cron job**. Ask your hosting provider to set up a cron job for the file `cron.php` in your Magento folder's root.

Log cleaning

Magento keeps records inside its database of every visit to your site. Your database can grow quickly if you do not empty these regularly. In **System | Configuration | System**, you can find a section called **Log cleaning** where you can set how often Magento should empty the log tables. We recommend a daily purge.

 This requires the cron job as previously mentioned.

Database backups

Check with your hosting provider how often backups are made and in what way you can access them. It is also a good idea to assess how quickly you can retrieve a backup and get it online. Should a calamity strike your database, the worst things that can happen are not having backups and not being able to restore your backups.

Product meta information

The product edit screen in Magento also has a section called **Meta Information**. The fields in this section are important for search engines, and properly filling them can help you achieve good rankings quickly.

Default images in columns

By default Magento has some images placed in the left and right columns of a template, such as the chalk board in the right column. When developing your store, it is easy to start ignoring them and forgetting to remove them. That's why it's good to check your store for default Magento images. In the following example, the infamous Magento dog and blackboard can be seen. Visiting some newly-minted Magento sites by searching for them in Google is bound to get some results that still have these inside their categories! For a method to remove blocks such as the dog from the following screenshot from one of the columns in your frontend, please refer to *Chapter 9, Customizing Your Store's Appearance*.

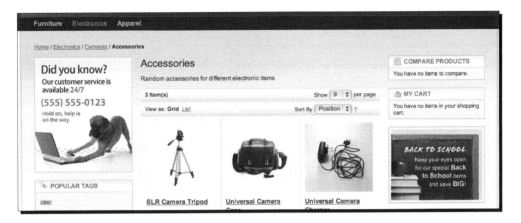

Escalations

If anything happens that causes your store to experience problems, you should know who to contact. Considering your Magento installation, at least these two scenarios should be considered:

◆ Who can you reach when you experience critical bugs? When can you reach them? And how quickly can they help you should you have a critical problem?

◆ What can you do when you have hosting problems? How quickly can you get in touch with the right people at your hosting provider? And how quickly can they take action?

What kinds of guarantees does your hosting provider give and what can you do if they are not met? Downtime for a regular website is a hassle, but downtime for an e-commerce site is immediate loss of revenue. Of course, the impact of downtime and the kind of guarantees you should arrange with your hosting provider are highly dependent on your size. A hosting provider will charge a lot more if they have to guarantee you near-perfect uptime.

Further development of your website

If you're starting with a relatively small budget, Magento offers the huge advantage that you can launch quickly with a minimum feature set. You can always improve and change your website at a later time, because it is open source software. Launching quickly means getting indexed by search engines quicker, and being able to test how to get customers quicker. The work on your store is never done. Trying to emulate the giants, such as Amazon, when you launch is impossible, so try not doing everything under the sun before you have even had one order. This goes for all aspects of your shop: marketing, sales, purchasing, customer support, and so on. You will only find out what's really important after you go live.

That said, your store should at least look reliable and work properly. Do not give your customers the impression you threw it online in a weekend. There are a number of ways to achieve this: good content, a nice logo, a well-picked theme, and more. A useful rule of thumb to remember when you start with limited means is to start with the absolute bare minimum of features on your site, and to start getting some order flow going as soon as possible. Only when you have real paying customers can you judge what you really need to grow revenues and profits.

If you already have an existing store or if you are going online with an already popular offline brand, the game changes. In this situation you have a prior reputation to uphold. This means you should perform a lot more analysis up front, primarily to match your existing business processes. As a result, your project will probably be longer in this case. However, the same rule of thumb applies: try to launch with the bare minimum of features.

Time for action – planning for the future

E-commerce is never done. During the construction of your new store and while running it as well, many new ideas will pop up. If you don't prioritize and log those, your store may suffer as things get forgotten and less important tasks get executed before urgent ones. That's why planning for the future is important.

1. **Creating a living document**: You will probably not have everything you want in your store when you go live. That's why it's a good idea to have a plan for further developments on your website. The easiest way to do that is by simply keeping a list of any desired modifications to your store. This only works if you keep a living document! This means that if you encounter new wishes, these should be added to the document, and if anything in the list becomes redundant, it should be removed.

2. **Deciding on what factors to keep track of**: An example list will be provided in a later step. We will keep track of five aspects:
   - **Functionality**: The feature or modification that is desired.
   - **Department**: This specifies which area of your business will improve because of the functionality.
   - **Benefit**: The benefit you expect from this feature, indicated by plus signs. A benefit can either be in efficiency or in revenue earned. In our example, features giving a moderate benefit get a plus one, and features with a high expected benefit get two pluses.
   - **Risk**: The risk of developing and implementing the new feature, also indicated by plus signs. More pluses means more the risk. Some things can be risky because of reasons such as them having a lot of impact in your current business processes, or because they mean you have to venture into new market territory.
   - **Delivery time**: The expected time needed to fully develop the feature.

Keeping track of the department that benefits from the feature is useful when your list grows and your company does as well. For example, if you notice your customer service is getting swamped, you can filter the wishlist for all features that benefit the customer service department, so that you can quickly decide what to implement to lessen the burden there.

If you want to keep track of the category a feature belongs to, we recommend that you keep *broad* categories to help you choose. For instance, a feature such as "image zoom upon hover over product images" might be placed in a category called "design improvements" instead of something like "product page design improvements". By keeping categories broad, you ensure that your list remains manageable and you do not lose too much time deciding in which category a feature belongs.

3. **Creating the list**: An example list based on the factors we listed in step 2 can be found in the following table:

Functionality	Needed for	Benefit	Risk	Delivery time
Integration with financial software	Financial administration	+	+	2 weeks
Different logo for Christmas season	Marketing	-	--	2 hours
Integration with warehouse management software	Conversion on site (faster deliveries), everybody dealing with order fulfillment	++	++	2 weeks
Landing page for new product	Marketing	+	--	2 days

Of course you can always expand the list with more columns if needed. However, in our experience having many columns does make maintaining the list take a long time, and as a result the list will quickly collect dust. If nothing else, it's better to remove any columns you don't need. Microsoft Excel or a Google Docs spreadsheet are good ways to create the list.

4. **Deciding on which functionality to give priority**: Based on the example list we provided, we can conclude that building a landing page for a new product has good expected benefits, low risk, and a quick delivery time. As such, it would be one of the first things to tackle. Every time some collection of features for your store is finished and pushed to live, take a look at the list again and determine what to build next. Always keep adding feature wishes and remove wishes that are either done or irrelevant.

Have a go hero – constructing a list based on your current ideas

Without any doubt, you already have multiple ideas for your store. Start by writing them out in a simple list, and then decide how to prioritize them. Try to give an honest appraisal about the effort required to implement each idea as well!

Working with partners

It is common to work with a development partner when setting up your shop. This can either be a freelancer or an agency. In this section we give some pointers to get the best result when working with such a partner. We will not go into details about project management or communication as that is a huge subject outside of the scope of this book, and also highly dependent on how involved you want to be in the development of your shop.

In this section we will discuss two possible tasks:

- Creating a design and theme
- Creating a functional enhancement

When you're working with a development partner, you will generally have both of these tasks for them as they probably will be building a theme and some functionalities.

A Magento theme

This is the situation where you are not using a premade theme, but rather a custom-built one. When you're doing this, a good theme developer will go through the following steps with you:

1. **Making a wireframe of your website**: This is a schematic view of the layout of your site's most important pages. The amount of detail in a wireframe depends on the amount of analysis work that is agreed upon. Even a rudimentary sketch of your home page, category page, and product detail page is highly useful to quickly agree on what information is to be shown and where.

    Ensure that any parts of the site that are important are present in the wireframe, such as customer account links, layered navigation, buy buttons, and so on. A proper wireframe ensures the graphic designer understands what he/she is designing. Magento is a big software package and most graphical designers do not know every detail about how Magento functions. An example wireframe can be found in the following diagram:

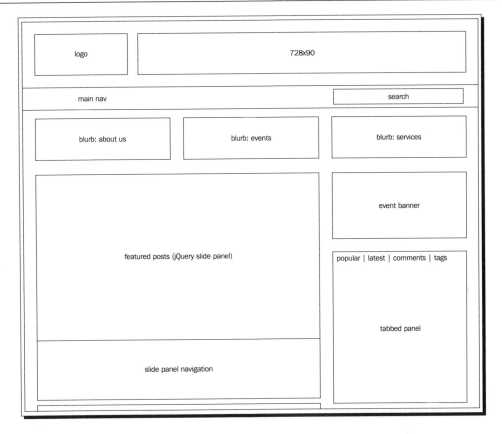

2. **Making the graphical design**: Based on your preferences for the look and feel of your store and the wireframes from step 1, a design is made. Often a sketch of the home page is made first, feedback is collected and processed, and after that subsequent pages are designed.

3. **Making the Magento theme**: The graphical design is cut up into logical blocks, and based on that the different parts of the theme (layout XML, HTML, and CSS) are made. Usually this step takes most of the time. The delivery time (and costs) of this step can be lessened by having your wireframe stick close to the default Magento theme.

4. **Installing and refining the theme**: In this step, the theme is copied into your Magento installation and activated. Now your store will not look like a default Magento store anymore! Usually in this stage minor design tweaks have to be made to fit your product catalog perfectly.

Have a go hero – wireframe your ideal product detail page

Your product detail page is one of the most important pages of your store, as it is usually the place where your visitor decides to buy your product. Think about what you want your product page to look like. Visit other e-commerce sites you admire and try to determine the similarities between the ways they display information on their product pages. Also, try to think about whether the kind of product you will be selling should be displayed differently or not! After you have determined the ideal product page layout, make a simple wireframe or sketch that indicates the positions of the various page elements.

 Coming up with a good layout can be hard. If you are in doubt about the layout of a particular segment of your site, it's a good idea to stick to something that resembles the biggest stores in your niche. In general, it's a good idea to have your store look and function as normal as possible, as familiarity breeds trust.

Functionality

Working with a development partner works out great in most cases, but it can also be cumbersome. It helps to have some structure to prevent bad experiences.

Time for action – structuring development partnerships

When you let a development partner build modifications, in general, this is a good way to work:

1. **Document all that exactly needs to be built and communicated**: This does not need to be an enormous document, rather it should describe the goals and how they will be reached as succinctly as possible. Usually your development partner will construct this document, and you will provide feedback on it. This step is a great way to ensure you have something to fall back on should discussions arise.

    For each feature that is being built, it should indicate what the goal is, how that goal will be reached, what a user's interaction with that feature will be like, and how much time and money it will cost. It's also important to agree upon how often you will get progress reports and how much communication is required, and who to contact with questions.

    Regarding the code quality, it's a good idea to at least agree that the Magento code inside the app/code/core folder is not allowed to be changed, and all changes to core functionality will be made through a Magento extension in either the app/code/local/ or app/code/community/ folder.

2. **Let the functionalities be built**: You may not be able to see much during the time it takes to build some functionalities, because it is difficult to present Magento extensions that are in development. However, it is recommended that you request a preview environment and at least have weekly updates on that environment, where all code that is able to be previewed is pushed to the preview site. At the very least, your partner should be able to report to you through e-mail of the progress that has been made, at fixed intervals.

3. **Test the functionalities**: In this step you will have access to a testing system and you can collect feedback. It is important to test as thoroughly as possible and to let your partner know in as much detail as possible what is going wrong. Making screenshots and providing step-by-step reports to reproduce errors helps greatly with that. Screenshots can be easily made with a tool such as **SnagIt** (`http://www.techsmith.com/snagit.html`). Many such tools exist. On an Apple computer, pressing *command* + *shift* + *3* makes a screenshot that is saved to your desktop immediately.

4. **Integrate the functionalities in your store**: It is a good practice to have a copy of your live site and to test the functionalities in the copy first before integrating them in your production environment. Sometimes, a Magento extension developed by a partner can work in step 3, but still cause problems in your store because of the other modifications present in your site. It's best to agree with your partner on what to do in that scenario beforehand.

Pop quiz – handling partner relations

Q1. A common occurrence when working with development partners is that the end product does not match the buyer's expectations. Which of the following are good ways to manage that risk?

1. Choosing a partner that shows they understand what you are trying to achieve.

2. Agreeing on communication schedules and having a single point of contact for both parties, who respond quickly when questions arise.

3. Having timely previews of and updates on progress of the development and letting your partner know when things are going the wrong way as early as possible.

4. Choosing the cheapest partner because the costs of a failed end product will be less.

5. Choosing the most expensive partner because the most expensive partner is always the most professional.

6. All of the above.

General guidelines

In general, the better you know what you want, the better is the chance that the end result will match your expectations. Because of that, it pays to research the theme or function you want to have developed and to form a clear idea about it. Try to document what the end result of custom work should be before a developer starts. This can prevent a lot of discussions.

A final note: do not let a development partner convince you that you absolutely need some feature. Most Magento developers have no experience with running a store themselves (though there are exceptions of course), and they do not know your plans and market. Often a technical partner prioritizes technical fanciness above possibly simple revenue-increasing features. That said, good suggestions can always, and should, be placed on your desired features list.

Modifying Magento

If you want to modify Magento yourself, there are three things to watch out for:

- Try to limit the amount of technical work you will be doing in your store to a bare minimum. Often, even the time it takes to develop simple things is underestimated.

- With any change you make, ensure you can go back to a state *before* you made the change. Concretely this means copying all files you will be changing, and backing up the database as well if you are changing anything in that as well. Always have a way back.

- *Never* develop and test changes live. Always have a copy of your site present where you can mess things up without consequences. Once you are completely sure everything works in your development copy, you can perform the changes live. Even then, backup your live site just to be sure!

Cache

When you're making changes to Magento, it's necessary to disable the **Magento cache**. The cache is a tool Magento uses to quickly remember how your store is structured through a condensed summary of all the settings in your store. Anytime changes are made, this summary needs to be rebuilt. That's why it is easier to disable the cache until all changes are done. You can disable the Magento cache by going to **System | Cache Management**. There, click on **Select All** and click on **Disable** in the top-right corner of the screen. Finally, click on **Submit** and the cache is disabled. Another way of cleaning Magento's cache is by logging into your FTP server, and clearing the contents of the var/cache folder. The cache management section of Magento's admin is shown in the following screenshot:

Upgrading Magento

About twice every year Magento releases a new version. You are notified of this through a message that pops up after you log in to the Magento admin. New Magento versions contain bugfixes, security updates, and new features. When there is an upgrade, you can update your Magento installation through the MagentoConnect Manager. This way, you will get the new Magento files on your server easily. There is a big risk while doing that though: your store might not work with the updated Magento files. That's why a Magento upgrade should be handled like any other technical change in your store. Never upgrade live before you've tested the upgrade extensively in a copy of your live site. Go through all checklists in this chapter, even the items which you think haven't changed in the upgrade.

When following the guidelines of this chapter and the advice in this book, you should be able to launch a store within budget with a minimum required feature set, and have a solid roadmap for future developments driven by real-world experience!

Summary

This chapter showed you how to manage the go-live of your store and the developments after that. We advised you to use a general checklist, which can be used as an assurance that everything works correctly, and provided indications of things that are often missed in newly launched Magento stores. After that, working with Magento partners both for custom themes and custom software development was discussed, again re-iterating the point that selection of a good partner is critical. We showed some techniques such as wireframes that help communication with development partners. Finally, we discussed upgrades of Magento, recommending never to perform them live. You should now be ready to experience Magento's potential to establish a quickly growing online store!

Pop Quiz Answers

Chapter 6, Customer Relationship

Pop quiz – default address

Q1	2

Chapter 7, Accepting Payments

Pop quiz – the bare minimum for PayPal Payments Standard

Q1	1

Chapter 8, Configuring Shipping

Pop quiz – vital conditions for Table Rates

Q1	1. Yes
	2. No
	3. Yes
	4. Yes

Chapter 11, Maintaining and Administrating Your Store

Pop quiz – handling partner relations

Q1	1, 2, and 3

Index

Thank you for buying
Magento Beginner's Guide Second Edition

About Packt Publishing

Packt, pronounced 'packed', published its first book "*Mastering phpMyAdmin for Effective MySQL Management*" in April 2004 and subsequently continued to specialize in publishing highly focused books on specific technologies and solutions.

Our books and publications share the experiences of your fellow IT professionals in adapting and customizing today's systems, applications, and frameworks. Our solution based books give you the knowledge and power to customize the software and technologies you're using to get the job done. Packt books are more specific and less general than the IT books you have seen in the past. Our unique business model allows us to bring you more focused information, giving you more of what you need to know, and less of what you don't.

Packt is a modern, yet unique publishing company, which focuses on producing quality, cutting-edge books for communities of developers, administrators, and newbies alike. For more information, please visit our website: www.packtpub.com.

About Packt Open Source

In 2010, Packt launched two new brands, Packt Open Source and Packt Enterprise, in order to continue its focus on specialization. This book is part of the Packt Open Source brand, home to books published on software built around Open Source licences, and offering information to anybody from advanced developers to budding web designers. The Open Source brand also runs Packt's Open Source Royalty Scheme, by which Packt gives a royalty to each Open Source project about whose software a book is sold.

Writing for Packt

We welcome all inquiries from people who are interested in authoring. Book proposals should be sent to author@packtpub.com. If your book idea is still at an early stage and you would like to discuss it first before writing a formal book proposal, contact us; one of our commissioning editors will get in touch with you.

We're not just looking for published authors; if you have strong technical skills but no writing experience, our experienced editors can help you develop a writing career, or simply get some additional reward for your expertise.

Linux Shell Scripting Cookbook

ISBN: 978-1-84951-376-0   Paperback: 360 pages

Solve real-world shell scripting problems with over 110 simple but incredibly effective recipes

1. Master the art of crafting one-liner command sequence to perform tasks such as text processing, digging data from files, and lot more

2. Practical problem solving techniques adherent to the latest Linux platform

3. Packed with easy-to-follow examples to exercise all the features of the Linux shell scripting language

Moodle Administration

ISBN: 978-1-847195-62-3   Paperback: 376 pages

An administrator's guide to configuring, securing, customizing, and extending Moodle

1. A complete guide for planning, installing, optimizing, customizing, and configuring Moodle

2. Secure, back up, and restore your VLE

3. Extending and networking Moodle

4. Detailed walkthroughs and expert advice on best practices

Please check **www.PacktPub.com** for information on our titles

9563127R00177

Printed in Great Britain
by Amazon.co.uk, Ltd.,
Marston Gate.